German Essays
on Music

The German Library: Volume 43
Volkmar Sander, General Editor

GERMAN ESSAYS ON MUSIC

Edited by Jost Hermand
and Michael Gilbert

CONTINUUM · NEW YORK

1994
The Continuum Publishing Company
370 Lexington Avenue, New York, NY 10017

The German Library
is published in cooperation with Deutsches Haus,
New York University.
This volume has been supported by Inter Nationes, and
a grant from Robert Bosch Jubiläumsstiftung.

Printed in the United States of America

Library of Congress Cataloging-in-Publication Data

German essays on music / edited by Jost Hermand and Michael Gilbert.
        p.   cm. — (The German library ; v. 43)
                        In English.
    ISBN 0-8264-0720-X. — ISBN 0-8264-0720-X (hardcover : acid free).
                — ISBN 0-8264-0721-8 (pbk. : acid-free)
        1. Music—History and criticism—Translations into English.
    2. German essays—Translations into English.   I. Hermand, Jost, 1930–
        II. Gilbert, Michael. 1953–   .   III. Series.
                        ML55.G44   1994
780—dc20   93-37888
                                                               CIP
                                                               MN

Acknowledgments will be found on page 309,
which constitutes an extension of the copyright page.

Contents

Introduction

U p until the end of the nineteenth century, the Germans (or at least their cultural elites) largely perceived themselves as "the nation of poets and philosophers." Lessing, Goethe, and Schiller as well as Kant, Hegel, and Schopenhauer: these were the cultural idols who established their national identity, not some painters, architects, or composers. It was not until the early years of the twentieth century—following the Bach renaissance, the elevation of Beethoven to a titanic cult figure, the rising popularity of Schubert, and the enormous impact of Wagner's music dramas—that this changed. Suddenly composers, too, came to be accorded greater prominence in theories of national identity. Indeed, they gradually began to displace the leading writers in their central role as shining examples of the German spirit. One of the most famous representatives of this development was Thomas Mann, who in these years did his utmost to enshrine Romantic music as the nation's greatest cultural achievement, an effort that met with widespread approval among the educated middle classes.

But this process was by no means limited to Germany. During the late nineteenth century, other countries as well—prompted by the popularity of national-psychological typologies—began to equate the "essentially German" ever more strongly with music per se. After all, this country had not only brought forth Schütz, Bach, and Händel (the most important Protestant Church composers of Europe), not only Haydn, Mozart, and Beethoven (the best-known representatives of the so-called classical period), but had also produced Schubert, Schumann, Mendelssohn-Bartholdy, Wagner, Brahms, and Bruckner (the chief exponents of that type of music understood as specifically Romantic). By 1900, their works already enjoyed a virtually unsurpassable level of popularity in the concert halls of that entire portion of the world deemed "civilized."

And so, while the saying about Germany being "a nation of poets and philosophers" continued in usage for a time (for such formulaic slogans are not done away with all that easily), it was increasingly hollowed out. Especially abroad, awareness grew that the most important German contributions to world culture were less in the realm of literature than in the areas of theorizing and composing, in other words, philosophy and music. And following in the footsteps of Schopenhauer and Nietzsche, both of whom had seen in music the highest incarnation of the artistic, many people also began to reflect with considerable acumen about the whys and wherefores of this combination. This group included not only such writers as Thomas Mann, whose novel *Doktor Faustus* (1947) still exalted the composer as the quintessence of all that is specifically German in both its best and worst variants, but also philosophers and social theoreticians such as Theodor W. Adorno and Ernst Bloch, who invariably cited the musical achievements of the nation when speaking of the highest aspirations of the German soul.

Why the relationship of philosophy and music was considered so especially close by thinkers who—like Nietzsche and Adorno—composed as well as philosophized, can be dealt with here only in the form of a brief historical sketch. Certainly the most widely accepted thesis in this regard was long the notion that the German bourgeoisie and the artists allied with it had a deficient relationship to sociopolitical reality. We read time and again that, in contrast to both England and France, where middle-class artists had begun emancipating themselves from the cultural norms of feudalism in the eighteenth century and devoted themselves to the creation of "realistic" arts and letters (in the liberal sense of the term), German artists—because of the economic, political, and social backwardness of this country's middle classes—had retreated instead into the abstract realms of philosophy and music. Thus one hears repeatedly that whereas genre painting and the social novel had become the leading artistic genres in France and England during this era, the Enlightenment had unfolded in Germany largely in the realm of self-isolated genius and intellectual introversion. And the necessary outcome of this "inner emigration" was those philosophically revolutionary but nevertheless abstract systems of thought advanced by such figures as Kant and Hegel as well as those intensely felt, indeed soulful and pathos-laden, but equally abstract works of instrumental music by such composers as Haydn, Mozart, and Beethoven: works interpreted as early as the mid-nineteenth century as the expression of an aesthetic escape from "plain misery" into "overwrought misery."

This thesis may be somewhat unrefined, but in contains a grain of truth. After all, even in the nineteenth century, as a consequence of the delayed development of bourgeois liberalism, the German cultural elite brought forth neither realistic novelists of the caliber of a Balzac, Dickens, Flaubert, and Thackeray, nor realistic painters comparable with Constable, Turner, Delacroix, Courbet, and Degas. Thus, when German literature and art are discussed outside of Germany, works of the nineteenth century (apart from Heine's) are hardly mentioned, whereas many of the foremost German thinkers and composers of this era are world-famous. In fact, the same is true even with regard to the late eighteenth century, often termed the Age of Kant in the history of philosophy and likewise dominated by Germany in terms of music. There are quite a few musically literate people in France, England, and America who can readily distinguish between Carl Philipp Emanuel Bach and Johann Christian Bach, while at the same time they have never heard of Friedrich Gottlieb Klopstock, Christoph Martin Wieland, or Johann Gottfried Herder, all literary stars of the first order of magnitude from the German perspective.

A series of books calling itself The German Library must therefore devote due attention to German philosophy and music in addition to German literature. In the field of philosophy this is relatively simple, since the thought of figures such as Kant, Hegel, Schopenhauer, Marx, Nietzsche, Freud, and others is recorded in an abundance of significant writings easily condensed in a work edition or anthology. This sort of undertaking is far more difficult in the area of music and most challenging in the case of the composers themselves (as documented in volume 51 of this series, entitled *Writings of German Composers*). To be sure, a multitude of German composers—Weber, Wagner, Schumann, Hugo Wolf, Schönberg, Pfitzner, Hindemith, Eisler, Henze, and others—were also quite active in the area of music theory. At the same time, however, any number of other, equally significant composers—including Bach, Haydn, Mozart, Schubert, Beethoven, Brahms, Bruckner, and others—hardly ever made theoretical statements. Their views on music can only be gathered (if at all) from their letters or the testimony of third parties.

If there is a dearth of writings by composers, we suffer from an embarrassment of riches in the case of the present volume. Here, the quantity of material is virtually limitless. German scholars, theorists, and essayists have produced such a wealth of academic-historical and critical-theoretical publications on music that even the most diligent reader can scarcely gain an overview. To avoid getting stuck in the narrow realm of academic scholarship, we have selected for inclusion in this volume not just writings by musicologists in the strict sense of the term, but also texts by writers, philosophers, social historians, music critics, singers, and conductors, insofar as these figures have exerted a decisive influence on the development of German musical culture. Apart from the question of influence, some of the essays and statements included here were selected for their elegant language and richness of ideas, since any anthology of purely academic musical essays and treatises would be certain to have a lethally boring impact on non-musicologists.

This breadth of inclusion is especially necessary for the early stages of music criticism in Germany, when almost all important commentaries of enduring interest were penned by philosophers and essayists, whereas the academic music criticism of this period was marred by a decidedly technical, even pedantic character. And there are important reasons for that. While eighteenth-century audiences were keenly interested in questions of literature and art— and Gotthold Ephraim Lessing could create a furor with his *Laokoon,* in which he expounded at length on the contrast between the transitoriness of literature and the intransitoriness of the pictorial arts—they paid far less attention to theoretical writings on music. Since the performance of music was largely confined to aristocratic and ecclesiastical settings until well into the eighteenth century, this art was not regarded as culturally, let alone sociopolitically relevant by the middle classes in their strivings to emancipate themselves. Be it the cantata, the passion, the opera, the instrumental concerto, or the symphony, almost all of the sophisticated musical genres required performance conditions that existed only in the courts and churches. Consequently, between 1750 and 1800, only the song *(Lied)* as well as smaller forms of chamber music such as the sonata or trio were viewed as middle-class music.

But bourgeois critics regarded even these forms of music as unworthy of theoretical investigation.

Thus, for the aestheticians of the Enlightenment, music played at best a decidedly subordinate role. Their greatest prejudice was against operas, above all the Neapolitan variety that prevailed until the mid-eighteenth century. These compositions were assailed as an unforgivable offense against naturalness and credibility, particularly by the representatives of the strictly rationalistic Gottsched school, including Christian Gottlieb Ludwig. But purely instrumental music was likewise considered "useless" by many Enlightenment thinkers because of its presumed lack of content *(Inhaltslosigkeit)*. Accordingly, such luminaries as Lessing and Kant conceded to it only a subordinate position in the hierarchy of the arts. Their dismissal of instrumental music was based not on philistinism but on the Enlightenment notion that art as well as philosophy had to contribute something to the advancement of mankind. Because of its seemingly nonconceptual and purely sensual character, they found instrumental music lacking in progressive ideas and concepts.

Positive perspectives on music are therefore relatively rare in the second half of the eighteenth century. The few who did look favorably upon music came either from the Christian camp, where noble *Frau Musica* was assigned the role of serving religion by heightening the content of confessional texts, or from the courtly domain of the aristocracy, where music provided a festive or at least tasteful background for absolutistic ritual. Overall, Enlightenment thinkers maintained a rather reserved attitude toward music as late as the 1780s, largely because of their antipathy toward the circumstances of musical performance. The first signs of a middle-class reevaluation of music finally emerged in connection with the rationalistic theory of affects. Repudiating counterpoint, which was perceived to be "baroque," this school of thought called for greater clarity, simplicity, and naturalness in melodic structure; furthermore, it granted even "useless" instrumental music a rhetorical or illustrative function perceived as realistic.

This longing for the natural gained force in theories of music influenced by Rousseau. Especially during the era of so-called sentimentality *(Empfindsamkeit)*, critics placed ever greater emphasis on the intensity of feeling and associated tendencies toward subjectivizing and psychologizing. Since not only language, but melody as well was supposed to follow the "voice of the heart," this type of theorizing led directly into the movement referred to in literary and (more recently) music histories as Sturm und Drang. Among the key representatives of this trend were Johann Gottfried Herder and Christian Friedrich Daniel Schubart, who not only repudiated the prevailing doctrine of normative affects in favor of true subjectivity, but also elevated music to the status of a personal avowal, an expression of freedom beyond all rules and restrictions, by emphasizing its passionate expressive qualities. However, since this new, impassioned outlook was not backed up by revolutionary stirrings as it was in France, it remained abstract, inward, subjective. On the other hand, it opened the way for an expressive aesthetics, which ultimately, with the music of Beethoven, burst the fetters of the old courtly and ecclesiastical order and sought to realize in music the aspirations of all humankind.

In spite of the enormous, positive reevaluation of music inspired by the Sturm und Drang movement and further stimulated by the hopes awakened by the French Revolution, culminating in works such as Mozart's *Marriage of Figaro* and *The Magic Flute* as well as Beethoven's Eroica Symphony and *Fidelio,* German music praxis in the last two decades of the eighteenth century remained tied to aristocratic performance conditions due to the underdevelopment of middle-class concert and operatic life. Consequently, this music did not reach the masses in the manner of the music performed at the great festivals of the French Revolution. Rather, it continued to be a manifestation of privilege. Indeed, as the surge of revolutionary fervor subsided after 1800, it was precisely the abstract, non-textbound, purely instrumental form of music which became an oft-cited and favored refuge for inwardness, as Germany underwent the aforementioned shift from a plain to an overwrought form of misery.

This process is generally subsumed under the name of *Romanticism*. But such a label is misleading in more than one respect. After all, in dealing with the concept of Romanticism, we are faced with a notion that is highly contradictory or, at the very least, multifaceted in nature. On the one hand, what has traditionally been understood by Romanticism—in the wake of the dissolution of the Holy Roman Empire and the conquest of Germany by Napoleon—is a striking nationalization of German cultural life, including music, as documented (for example) in the musicological writings of Johann

Nikolaus Forkel. On the other hand, the term Romanticism designates an emotional intensification of musical expression dating
back as far as the era of *Empfindsamkeit* and the aesthetic genius-
cult of the Sturm und Drang, a process that was reinforced by the
profound disappointment over the lost hopes bound up with the
French Revolution and an associated, compensatory inclination toward increased subjectivity in music, making it the highest form of
expression for the isolated artist. The latter is prominently manifested in the writings of Novalis, Ludwig Tieck, Friedrich Schlegel,
Wilhelm Heinrich Wackenroder, and Ernst Theodor Amadeus
Hoffmann—and ultimately in Arthur Schopenhauer's voluminous
The World as Will and Representation (1819), in which music,
specifically textless, merely suggestive instrumental music, is elevated and beatified as the very essence of an artistic soul yearning
for the absolute and the purely poetic, providing urgently needed
spiritual release from all tribulations suffered in the ugly world of
social reality.

With this, the foundation was laid for a heightened appreciation
of instrumental music, which in the course of the nineteenth century assumed ever more importance in Germany because of its
continuing political fragmentation, social inequality, intellectual
frustration, and consequent tendencies toward inwardness. Ultimately, this trend led to a theoretically grounded musical formalism
that largely dispensed with content, as manifested most prominently in the writings of the Viennese critic Eduard Hanslick, who
promoted Brahms and his followers (whose chief domain was the
symphony and instrumental chamber music).

In this period, the only theories of music oriented toward social
and political concepts were those inspired by the writings of Richard Wagner and his music dramas. These works initially had an
extremely progressive tone, that is, were allied with the ideals of the
March Revolution of 1848. Subsequently, however, in the phase of
the so-called post-March era between 1848 and 1871, such
rebellious notions increasingly yielded to an otherworldly neo-
Romanticism à la Schopenhauer. From a fusing of these two lines
of development arose Wagner's Bayreuth idea, which is characterized by a deep contradiction between a powerful ideological program and a simultaneous disavowal of its realization in political
practice. As is well known, its most passionate defender was
the young Friedrich Nietzsche; ultimately, however, he became

Wagner's most passionate enemy when he recognized the paradoxical contradiction in Wagner's efforts. Nietzsche therefore finally imputed Christian-reactionary tendencies to the elderly Wagner, above all on account of *Parsifal.* This is clearly demonstrated in writings such as *The Case of Wagner, The Twilight of the Idols,* and *Ecce homo,* in which Nietzsche expressed an extreme love–hate relationship with Wagner.

What followed in the last two decades of the nineteenth century in the area of music criticism was mostly associated with the controversies stimulated by Wagner. Not until the turn of the century did new theoretical perspectives gradually emerge, which once again were marked by strong tendencies toward philosophical abstraction and a consequent favoring of instrumental music. The prelude to these developments was provided by the writings of Friedrich von Hausegger, who attempted as early as the 1890s to create a new aesthetic of musical expression based upon psychomotoric concepts. Not long thereafter, similar attention was given to the theoretical views of Theodor Lipps, Johannes Volkelt, Hugo Riemann, and Hermann Kretzschmar. To a greater or lesser extent, all these critics declared allegiance to an aesthetics of empathy based largely upon individual forms of psychological perception (that is, emotion–and imagination-based responses) while viewing literary, so-called extramusical interpretations of music with extreme skepticism. Whereas these theorists at least treated subjective emotions as a concrete, reality-based substrate of music, other critics such as August Halm and Heinrich Schenker increasingly elevated music to the status of the "absolute." Halm emphasized the formal imperatives of music as reflected in the fugue and sonata, while Schenker was preoccupied with musical laws that corresponded "organically" to certain primal rhythms of life and the cosmos.

Not until the founding of the Weimar Republic in 1919 did German music criticism gain a footing on substantially new ground. In contrast to Thomas Mann, who was still under the spell of the Wagner–Nietzsche controversy and in these years even broadened it into the intellectual–historical realm of *Geistesgeschichte,* other critics more attuned to the contemporary situation gave increasing attention to changing economic, social, and industrial developments. The primary focal point of this new body of criticism in the 1920s was the mass impact of music first made possible by its technical reproducibility via the invention of radio and sound recording, making it accessible to wider and wider audiences and thus changing the entire outlook on music in general. Probably the most significant reflections of this transformation can be found in the works of Max Weber and Arnold Schering, who analyzed the complex interrelations of music and its social functioning. Other writers concerned with more practical aspects of musical life, such as Peter Suhrkamp and Bertolt Brecht, repeatedly took up the question of the possibilities of music in terms of its role in schools and theaters. The polar extremes of musical criticism in this period are undoubtedly represented by Hans Breuer and H. H. Stuckenschmidt. While Breuer propagated a renewed cultivation of folk song in conjunction with the *Wandervogel* movement, as a means of counteracting the trend toward leveling of specifically national musical traditions, Stuckenschmidt supported a thoroughgoing mechanization of existing musical institutions as a way of purging bourgeois-sentimental subjectivism once and for all, in keeping with the goals of the broader movement of New Objectivity *(Neue Sachlichkeit)*.

All of these deliberations and debates, which reflected the enormous fragmentation of traditional musical life into a spectrum of highly varied subcultures, came to an abrupt end in 1933. Once power was handed over to Adolf Hitler and his party, a relatively rapid process of *Gleichschaltung* (establishing uniformity) ensued, which, while not eliminating the qualitative differences within musical life, nevertheless attempted to relate everything to concepts such as the "German," "Aryan," or "Nordic." In keeping with the Nazis' propagandistic proclamation of a new *Volksgemeinschaft* (folk community), only that which served the common will of the nation was deemed positive, while all fragmenting, aestheticizing, solipsistic, modernistic, cosmopolitan, or Jewish works and tendencies were abjured as decadent or alien to the people. This applies above all to the writings of National Socialist music critics, such as Friedrich Blume, Wolfgang Boetticher, Fritz Bose, Rudolf Gerber, Werner Danckert, Robert Lach, Alfred Lorenz, and Hans-Joachim Moser, who in the years from 1933 to 1945 raved on relentlessly about the German racial type in folk song, the harmful influences of Americanism, the supposedly perverse character of Jewish compositions, or the truly Nordic German music. Most of the arguments propounded in these writings were so predictable and dogmatic that it is not worth including any of them, even for illustrative purposes, in an anthology such as this.

Following the military defeat of German fascism in May 1945 and the subsequent division of Germany, music criticism also split into two rather clearly demarcated camps. A unified Marxist-oriented approach based on the theory of mimetic reflection came to the fore in the German Democratic Republic to the East. Its most important representatives were Georg Knepler and Günter Mayer. At the same time, a methodological pluralism was developing in the Federal Republic to the West; for all its diverse perspectives, however, it also displayed some unifying elements. Here the major trend was modernism, which, drawing upon the work of Theodor W. Adorno and Carl Dahlhaus, sought to downplay mimetic elements in music in order to avoid any suspicion of being content-oriented. Consequently, West Germany witnessed in the 1950s a conspicuous renaissance of those formalistic concepts that had already culminated in the idea of an "absolute music" in the late nineteenth century. Even the emergence of a leftist-oriented music criticism in the wake of the so-called '68 movement, of which Hans Werner Henze appointed himself chief spokesperson, was unable to challenge the dominating concepts of autonomy carried over from the 1950s. And thus, well into the 1980s, West German academic critics continued to devote most of their energy to arguments over formal characteristics of the various trends of so-called New Music, debating whether they should be labeled serial or aleatoric (and therefore "modern") or eclectic (and therefore "postmodern").

For the better part of this century, however, such debates have avoided the issue at the very center of their concerns, namely, the highly tenuous status of serious music, mistakenly taken for granted and even fetishized by academic music theorists. Overshadowed by the commercially driven expansion of pop, rock, and folk music, serious music has long since lost the kind of cultural status still ascribed to it in culturally elite circles. Yet it is precisely for this reason that present debates about the survival of a noncommercialized, difficult, demanding type of music—be it avant-garde, modern, or postmodern—take on added urgency. After all, what is at stake is not only the survival of an endangered species of music, one increasingly suffering from neglect and at risk of extinction, but also the broader problematic of the general cultural situation at present. Even more crucially than current discussions concerning the prospects for higher forms of contemporary literature or painting, the debates about serious music need to address the question whether so-called high art in general must yield to the strict laws of supply and demand in democratized and simultaneously commercialized societies. If so, this would inevitably lead to a marginalization of works of the cultural heritage as well as those produced by modern movements, a process that could only be stopped if the state continues to intervene in the market by subsidizing serious art in order to maintain a certain level of sophisticated cultural activity alongside the commercialized sphere.

It is well known that the German state performs this function to a greater degree than most other democracies that are organized around a market economy. For that reason, the debates concerning these issues are still of considerable cultural-political relevance. Thus, music criticism continues to be an arena of lively controversies, despite the marginality of its subject matter. It is only to be hoped that this process will not succumb to the growing trend toward cultural leveling now evident worldwide, and that critics concerned with serious music and its role in modern life will not be silenced.

J. H.

Christian Gottlieb Ludwig

From *An Attempt to Prove That a Musical Play or Opera Cannot Be Good* (1734)

Before I had the opportunity to see the public performance of an opera, I thought this would be something of exceptional beauty; indeed, out of ignorance, I preferred it over tragedies and comedies. When I was finally fortunate enough to see the opera *Cleofide,* staged a few years ago in Dresden, I thought I would abide by this judgment since at first a masterpiece, and nothing imperfect, was presented to me. The stage decorations were magnificent; the music complete and quite decent; the characters adept at acting; in a word: it was everything one could want from an opera. Many spectators also showed particular delight at this piece, although the least among them understood the Italian, the poetry, or the music, and were therefore able to judge neither the art of the composer nor that of the libretto writer. But in my imagination I had deceived myself.

I became quite disconcerted about this. I was well aware that many things had seemed unnatural to me, and yet I didn't want to let go of my predisposition in favor of opera, which I had based on the praises expressed by so many others. Soon thereafter I had the opportunity to see several musical plays in the course of my travels. I discovered the difference between the French variety and the Italianate *[Welschen].* I had certain aspects of the opera clarified to me by various musical experts, and made an effort to settle my judgment of the musical plays, so that I didn't have to torment myself any longer with others' prejudices.

I almost do not know what to say: whether it is the poetry that enlivens the music, or whether it is the latter that lends true emphasis to the former. A pleasant combination of tones is like a body without a soul, because, while the ears are tickled, one's faculty of reason has little—which is not to say nothing at all—to do. A good poem is rendered just as beautiful by pleasing pronunciation as it is through appropriate instrumental accompaniment. These are experiences that anyone who does not allow himself to be governed by prevailing biases must admit. To be sure, the combination of the arts of poetry and music is of no mean strength, unless the composer, through badly inserted tones, weakens the passion at that point where its strength should be most evident. Thus I would act foolishly were I to dismiss all poetry suitable for singing. If a poet has used words that can heat up, quiet, or sustain the emotions; and if a skilled hand knows how to use tones in such a way that their combination strengthens the poet's intent: then the results are without a doubt something incomparable. But this mustn't be all too long; otherwise the patience of the listeners is taxed, and through frequent repetitions one awakens mere disgust. For the attainment of restrained beauty, the so-called cantatas are therefore the very best. Through the intense emotion it stimulates, one single aria is often capable of giving us more pleasure than ten others sung along with it, which only weaken the emotion because they try to sustain it too long.

This is not without foundation. Composers have something they call a theme, which, like the plot in the dramatic fable, is the soul of the entire aria. Multiple plots confuse the spectator of a theatrical piece in the same way that many themes confound someone listening to music.

Thus, when I praise the music linked with poetry, then I am allowing only those pieces that are short; those that in a quarter hour sustain and heighten the emotion, in the same way that the progression of the plot customarily does in a theatrical piece.

This I can accept. But then it is precisely on account of their duration, far too long, that the musical plays utterly fail. The question is whether the continuation of this treatise will provide even stronger reasons to dismiss them.

If entertainment were the sole purpose of theatrical performances, then I would be the first to admit that the opera is the masterpiece of the stage. I am speaking here only about sensual pleasures, for which the opera initially offers us precisely the same opportunity we can expect of the tragedies and comedies. Beyond this, however, it has the advantage of the most pleasing harmony of musical instruments that by itself is in a position to delight the ears.

If, however, we wish to listen to the Roman poet Horace: he calls not only for delight, but also for the edification of the listener.

Omne tulit punctum qui miscuit utile dulci
Lectorem delectando pariterque monendo.

In Gottsched's translation: "He will be perfect, who is in part instructive in nature, who in part sings of something lovely through his verses, who in part is useful to the reader, and in part brings him delight." And Guenther states that the poets, "through wisdom in their images and solely with the desire to do good, must pull mankind forward, whose eyes flee from naked truth."

Indeed, it would be a disgrace to literature, if such important works as those for the theater should merely amuse and fail to reform people at the same time. Otherwise, a worthless puppeteer, a buffoon on a marketplace stage, and the colorful obscene jokers would in the end all dare to call themselves the sons of Phoebus as the poets do.

Turning now to an investigation of the means by which theatrical pieces should instruct: in accordance with the teachings of Aristotle, Horace, and many latter-day critical experts, I find that it should not happen through a good moral idea inserted here and there, but rather, through the context of the fable that presents the action to us as either a good or evil one. The former are but a small means to be used here and there by the poet to hold the attention of the people; but the latter is the true basis of theatrical edification. The former must be observed by a poet in even the smallest poem; but he can only bring in the latter in a well-devised connection with the imitated action.

I do not doubt that a more skilled pen than my own could for this reason demonstrate quite a few special rules that, out of ignorance, are considered ridiculous by those who despise thoroughness. But at least this much is certain: the hitherto existing and as yet very much prevailing bad taste in theatrical pieces could be completely defeated if the spectators were to seek in them as much instruction as diversion.

However, I must show that an opera cannot instruct. The philosophers quite properly maintain that the all-too-frequent sensual images hinder the operation of the mind's capacity to reason. For if reasoning represents a power of the soul to imagine something clearly: then we mustn't paint before it an unceasing series of unclear, indeed, even obscure images. Clear concepts teach us; unclear or obscure ones are capable, if combined with clear ones, of ruining even them.

A well-made tragedy shows me no more than one primary moral. It teaches me to love a virtue or hate a vice: all other things are nothing more than means by which to achieve this end. The decoration of the stage, the differences between the characters, become familiar with the initial, for the most part, rather frosty speeches of the actors. The incidental music is nothing more than an intermediate space that merely permits me to catch my breath, to reflect on what has happened, and to await impatiently that which is to come. The conclusion then finally allows me to gather together the fruits of my considerable efforts. I realize what it is that I should love or hate, what I should seek or flee. The same process can easily be demonstrated for comedies.

Someone might object that I am talking about something that is supposed to happen, but that in reality does not happen. It is not necessary to take up this objection here. However, I can give assurances that there already are spectators out there who are not merely seeking amusement, but rather an instructive, edifying form of delight. Without a doubt, the reforming of the plays will gradually lead to a reforming of the spectators themselves.

If, on the other hand, I look at the operas or musical plays: oh, what a marvelous transformation captivates the senses of the spectators! They are not capable of giving their faculty of reason something to do; indeed, even if they wanted to escape this, they would be more likely to think about the future construction of the stage devices than the moral of the fable. Even if one were to present operas in as orderly and regular a fashion as the tragedies and comedies; even if one were to reject all scenic transformations and the stage machinery: then it would be solely the music, the essential part of the work, that would hinder the ultimate instructional purpose.

Were one to ask a person whether he is able to understand the singing characters, he would answer no and simply appeal to the printed libretto. If this is able to instruct him, then he can already achieve the ultimate purpose before he sees the curtain rise. If one says that the live performance is to do the most, then I ask again whether the spectator will have many orderly thoughts if he intends to consider the characters, the libretto, and the music at the same time.

If the music wishes to demonstrate its strength properly, then this must happen more in arias than in recitatives. Recitatives are still rather natural. If I now concede that their spoken elocution may be rhymed, I would think of allowing this to be done solely while *singing* recitative, whether or not the former is any more excusable than the latter.

But what am I supposed to do with the arias? When the recitative is concluded: one can guess without great difficulty what one wishes to state in the aria. I just do not see why one should allow something to be presented for some ten minutes merely on account of newly concocted words and expressions, since this hinders for so long the appreciation of the truth one seeks.

The so multifarious repetition of the syllables, words, and thoughts in the arias also creates disgust. The presentation should be clear, and the faculty of reason is certainly capable of grasping the matter the first time. The superfluous only causes annoyance. In this regard, I have noticed that the French operas are more pleasing than the Italian ones, even if the music does not so readily fall into one's ear; for seldom do the French repeat something more than once, just as their execution is more recitative-like than the Italian.

In this context I cannot refrain from referring to the thoughts of a great connoisseur of music and poetry that he disclosed to me. One must not imagine, he said, that the Italians are the great masters of music the way most Germans think. Among them prevails a corrupted taste, just as in their poetry. To be sure, their music is easy to listen to and appears to be excellent: but we are biased and go by the prejudices of the masters. If we were to examine the matter properly, were we to inquire about the naturally beautiful: I think we would find it rather austere. Earlier many Germans attempted to imitate the Italians in poetry; now that has for the most part gone out of fashion. And perhaps a skilled master of music will soon relieve us of the bombastic and lead us toward the natural in his art. But I must stop here and return to what I had intended to say.

I have only been able to demonstrate that the operas hinder the ultimate instructive purpose, because I myself raised the objection that an opera, apart from the music, can in all respects be done as a regular tragedy or comedy. But the fewest among the friends of opera will desire this. They would declare its enchanting changes of scenery, its flying deities, the incredible, wondrous deeds of its heroes, and other such things to be essential parts of an opera. If I now wanted to show how this would be contrary to the instructive purpose emphasized above: I would be able to fill many pages and nevertheless say nothing that others have not long since pointed out. People do indeed like to see such things, but they also come running when horses and dogs do their business and consider it something extraordinary.

But I am straying too far from the point. Now I must also show that the operas or musical plays cannot cleanse the passions. It is understood that tragedies or comedies are supposed to do this, as well as being able to. However, I want to prove the opposite of operas, taking only the music into consideration: because I once again assume that the others could all certainly be improved. I said above, that an expert composer can heighten the emotion stimulated by the poet through an appropriate use of tones; and therefore I appear to be contradicting myself. But I wish to explain myself briefly.

In a tragedy, the poet needs different emotions: he allows one or the other to prevail alternately, but always in such a way that the primary emotion is ultimately ignited most. In this context what the philosophers say about the engendering of the emotions fits in beautifully: how one emotion can and must arise from the other; what someone does, in order to move a person who is in one emotional state into a more intense one, and so forth. But does this also apply to the opera? Initially, it appears to do so quite well. For example, one wishes to have a character brought to despair: oh! One awakens a feeling of shame in an aria. One continues and creates the character so cleverly that he feels regret about the misdeed he committed; a special aria, as in the following instance, can always accomplish this. Finally, one creates hope that the matter will pass and will not amount to much. But an incident arises that creates terror and disturbs the character's satisfaction. If differing emotions are presented one after the other, the anger and despair can reach the highest level.

However, the question arises whether the dissimilar presentation in arias and recitatives constitutes yet another hindrance. At least that has been my experience. An aria has often stimulated in me the emotion that it was supposed to. But as soon as the voices stopped and the next recitative began, my emotion subsided. Granted, the singer was taking a rest from the hard work he had done in the aria, buy my passion dissipated, and even if the following aria was supposed to strengthen the same emotion, a good beginning was no longer to be found. One can put up with this for a while; one rises and falls in one's emotions, as the performance intends for us to do, but one also grows tired of this fairly quickly and perhaps might even fall ill due to the vehemently stimulated but then quickly subsiding emotions, unless one relaxes and pays more attention to the change of scenery than the action itself.

I have already discussed the repetitions above, and now I actually want to talk only about the so-called da capo. This is utterly contrary to the stimulation of the emotions and I almost think that one couldn't present a single one that would be good. The stimulation of an individual emotion takes place in just the same way that one arises from the other. A thought arising from another makes the feeling somewhat stronger or weaker. If I now start to induce the emotion in the first part of the aria, heighten it in the second, and fall back again onto the first: an attentive listener thinks I just want to seduce him, and the emotion that is supposed to be awakened often dies away due to the continuing singing. And that is only the beginning of it. Is not the da capo in the music in and of itself a mistake? Contemporary music experts have rejected the ritornello: and what was this other than a repetition of the first section that occurred immediately? Is it not then a matter of being ritornello-ized if I repeat the first section of the aria after the second? The distinction is of little importance; it appears that one error was dismissed in order to commit the second.

How often it happens that ill-conceived beauties of music are responsible for the fact that the passions are not aroused. An infuriated hero wants to consume the whole world, and a trill, placed in his mouth by the composer, holds back his rage for a minute. The listener is made to laugh, and the beauty is spoiled. But this

isn't a flaw of opera itself, but rather of the composer. I recall
something else in the musical plays that always struck me as being
ridiculous. The aria begins and the musicians take up a good three
minutes with their instruments before the singer is allowed to sing
something. Finally, he begins to show anger and sings a few words,
but after that he must be silent again for a while. Is this not absurd?
I am talking with a good friend, and when I have expressed to him
half of my thoughts I let him wait awhile; after that I repeat them
again, and finally I say what it is that I want. A sick person with
a high fever could be excused for this, but I would consider a
reasonable person foolish if he behaved this way.

From all of this I conclude that certain arts in this world by
themselves possess a beauty that they lose when combined with
others. If a painter invents a splendid historical or otherwise fabu-
lous painting the viewers come in great numbers, admire it, and
try to discover what he meant by this or that. And this effort brings
them great pleasure. But as soon as a poet comes and says to them:
this thin man resting on his sacks of gold represents greed and so
forth—the viewer goes away and finds no more pleasure than if he
had heard a stout balladeer prophesying pestilence, hunger, and
war from an ominous interpretation of the northern lights.

With music it is the same way. I demonstrated above how pleasing it is when combined with poetry, and thereafter I feel I showed
that in the opera it is contrary to the ultimate purpose of theatrical
texts, namely, moral instruction and cleansing of the emotions.
Should one then create such expense on account of mere amusement? Even worse, should one waste so much time? In this respect,
the tragedies and comedies will always retain the advantage no
matter how many people are against them. And is that such a pity?
The music nevertheless remains a splendid thing, even if an opera
is useless.

Were I to be mindful of matters of secondary importance, I
would have much to recall and also much to refute. Great kings
and princes love the operas! Perhaps operas were performed as
well in Roman times! Perhaps the Biblical Jubal [the Hebrew Bible
inventor of the lyre and flute] was the first *operiste!* And so on.
One is often accustomed to fighting with pretexts.

With this I close, and feel that I have sufficiently demonstrated
that the opera is neither natural, nor reasonable, nor useful. Even

musical experts themselves will grant me this, if they don't let themselves be dominated by biases. And since I changed my opinion of operas through painstaking observation and investigation, perhaps others can have the same experience in the future. My thoughts on this will not be altered further. For as long as opera remains what in reality it now is: I will believe what I now believe.

Translated by Michael Gilbert

Karl Wilhelm Ramler

In Defense of the Operas
(1756)

Operas are being criticized by some because they have been criticized by distinguished persons; many have passed judgment on things they did not see or did not see well. Our protective writ could be the general acclaim that will always fill the largest opera house with as many spectators as it will hold. However, we do not wish to satisfy ourselves with the dictum: *vulgus interdum recte videt* (sometimes the crowd sees correctly) but rather to help liberate the musical play *[Singespiel]* from the reproach of improbability without palliating it via the tragedies of Corneille and the English—which, in spite of all their flaws, are pleasing—when in the main the work has been pleasingly made. We want to speak about an opera that is full of well-drawn characters and great emotion; whose plot is suitable and limited to a brief time and confined place; whose knots of dramatic intrigue are tied in a timely way and unraveled late; whose action fills and enlivens the theater; where dry moralizing talk and prosaic speeches are both carefully avoided. But we also want to leave the arias, the instruments, decorations, mechanical devices, and dances undisturbed. We want very much to see them and must wish to see them gladly in a play that has been invented so that the poetry should have the most powerful impact, like an arrow when it is feathered, and like a beautiful woman when she is dressed to her best advantage. The fine arts all offer their hand, they are all imitators of nature, and it is the opera in which they should all appear together.

People are aggravated by the fact that this tragedy is sung and that they find such a lack of verisimilitude in it that they are more inclined to laugh than to cry. But if one can find the well-done imitation in an engraving beautiful, and can forget human color in admiring a beautiful marble statue, one will also be able to overlook the dissimilarity when human actions are imitated in sung tones, to which the instruments merely add an after-effect, as it were. Can't one imagine that one is in another world where people talk and act more slowly? However, people easily forgive opera for its recitatives, because they are the most similar to speech and because the ancients already set their declamation to music in order to make it perfectly correct. Many people speak daily in a songlike manner when they lament something, show anger, express flattery, or read an ode. But how are people to endure the fact that such recitatives finally break out into a real aria, in which the lines and music are often repeated. For we never, ever speak in this manner? Yes, in our moments of great emotion we speak precisely this way, repeating what touches us most deeply:

> I, most unhappy one! I have strangled you! Oh, I, most unhappy one! have strangled my Procris! Oh, look at me in my despair! Oh, where do you hasten to? Oh, Procris, where do you hasten to? Oh, Procris, come back, and look at me, most unhappy murderer, in my despair!

In such moments of great emotion the name of the beloved, the deed done, the self-condemnation are often repeated. Thus the aria is not wrong when it repeats things, and moreover it expresses whining and crying in its accentuations and thus more strongly affects the heart of the listener. How can the aria miss its mark if a composer who understands affections makes use of all its frequent repetitions to portray in tones all the expressions of the heart that he has experienced in human life? How can the aria fail to reach our hearts when a singer knows how to express his language well and how to accompany it with all kinds of gestures! To be sure, it takes a great actor to repeat an aria often. But if, for example, Iphigenia had already stirred the heart once through her voice and action, she then reinforced the action the second time, bringing tears to the eyes, and the third time one had to conceal one's eyes from others, she intensified the action again, and people thought they were succumbing to the pain. Real proof that in the opera one can see beyond the inauthentic and deceive oneself for one's own enjoyment. In order to perfect the opera, one could specify that the arias should not occur until it becomes probable that the actor really wanted to sing a song. For example, when someone greets a victorious hero, or a lonely princess sings a song to Venus. But one does not let the aria come until the emotion of the speaking person has climbed high enough; this demands the very best music. To refine things further would mean wanting to make the speech of the animals in Aesop's fables sound probable. The frogs would then be the ancient frogs of Latona, and Balaam's ass. But the speaking of the animals is already overlooked, and one asks nothing more than that the lion speak in a lionlike manner, that the fox be clever, and that the ape be droll. Likewise, the singing is already altogether forgiven, and one asks nothing more than that the rules of music be followed all the better and that not every simile or cold moral be sung, for these are not important enough to the heart that they be frequently repeated.

As far as the scenery is concerned, it imitates nature quite nicely and through this gives us new delight; only the mixing of real nature with its imitation would be a mistake—for example, if one created the forest out of real trees, or brought in a large water container upon which to float a small ship. Just as it is no sign of a great intellect if a person looks about everywhere in the tragedy for the inauthentic—inauthenticity in speaking in verse, talking in another language (as do Mithridates and Agamemnon), in the lamps, the helmet, the creased coat—it is just as little a sign of a sublime intellect if a person is so cold-minded that in the opera he contemplates that the sea is a linen screen, a lighting man turns it around, the trees are pushed away, and the statues of idols are made of pasteboard, at a time when he should be paying attention to the acting persons and the all-powerful music. Is it a greater art to let one's heart be deceived for a short while, or is it more important to discover quickly the great truth that everything is deceptive? The decorations do not hinder the person who directs his attention to the action and the stirring music, and he does not regret the glance he casts at them, for there he discovers nature well represented in the palaces, forests, and gardens.

Observing verisimilitude in the decorations seems beneficial, as does changing the splendid scenes for each act—but not in the middle of the act and in so doing introducing only the nearby places and not those far away. It is even worse if one is at a distance one moment, close by the next, and then at a distance again. At the very least, the progression of scene changes should be carefully considered, approximately in the following manner: the stage is a marketplace, in the distance stands a great temple, on the other side a palace; farther back a park can be seen, and on the distant horizon the sea. Then, in the next set of scenery I can present the temple closer up, and let the action take place therein; the spectator can easily help himself be deceived here. In the third set, I can open up the palace, show the forest behind the town in the fourth, and in the fifth have the shore of the sea before me; only one should not then come back to the capitol or the marketplace. But, concerning the first point, changing the scenery only once per act might be too little for the splendor of opera, since it typically has only three acts because of the slower pace of speech. At the same time, however, in no well-made opera does one see the house being built around the hero; the characters have already left the stage, and, contrary to the rules of tragedy, have left the place empty in order to follow another rule that helps make the set seem more probable.

To the splendor of the opera belong as well triumphal horse-drawn wagons, floating admiral's ships, goddesses in the clouds, Furies with the distinguishing marks of hell, and other such things, which reverse the rule of Horace that dictates that one should bring nothing onto the stage that may have happened in a more probable manner off the stage. Except here, where one is enchanted by the instrumental symphony and the most pleasing voices, captivated by the splendid costumes and processions, and bewildered by the labyrinth of the dances, it does not take much effort to suppose a few divine apparitions on this magic isle, the same way we do when reading the epic poems. And human imaginings all find a place easily in these spectacles, in which painting, music, and poetry should rival each other.

A word remains to be said about the dances that conclude each act. These would be quite well received if they were connected with the preceding material, as the choruses were at one time connected with the tragedies. But such a precise connection is not necessary; rather, it is sufficient that one can discern that the dancers have some reason to dance and that they belong to the performing party, more distantly or more closely. The dances must always be meaningful and in themselves perfected if they are to please. Because they are tied to the action, the opera suffers from no such interruption or empty space as is present in our orderly tragedies, where we have to amuse ourselves with our own violin no less than four times. Here, we are delighted by a new imitation of nature, without being drawn away from the main action.

In their tragedies, the Greeks, our masters in the fine arts, already had choruses and dances, declamations set to music, mechanical devices, and instruments. The more significant the talents required for it, the greater the glory that comes from having made a good opera. Here the poet must be concise and has no expansive field for development as in the regular tragedy. He must bring passions into his poetry, which the music expresses well, and must vary them often so that there is no displeasing monotony in the music. He must choose words with good vowels, and beautiful types of verse in his arias would also be an aid to the music. He must not give any singer a role in which he would sing himself to death, but rather conceive them carefully in accordance with their individual ability. He has to work in the musical duets and tercets in a probable manner: a difficult task! He must also keep an eye on the dances and sets and tie these in with his plot, whereby he must show much skill and understanding. It would be worth writing a separate treatise on the perfect opera, from which the poet, the designer, the ballet master, and composer could all draw useful lessons. For its part, the music would have to perform its former miracles anew, calling forth terror and tears. *Scribe, & eris mihi magnus Apollo* (Write, and to me you will be great Apollo). If one has a great creative mind for the music, and great singers and actors; if one has an inventive designer, and great painters as assistants; if one has a creative dance master and skillful male and female dancers; and finally, if one has a good tragedy writer and song poet in the same person: shouldn't a piece then arise from this that is made to enchant? There are reasons why the opera falls short of delighting some: the rabble and the young men gape at the decorations and female dancers alone; the pedant who plays music listens only to the piano and violins; the pedant who writes only pays attention to the questions and answers. It is said that the person of good taste has a book in hand or else in memory, in order to comprehend and feel the tragedy being sung; he lends his entire ear to the singing and the accompanying music, his eye admires the beauty of the action and the place where it occurs, and the absolutely incredible dances. Such a person enjoys it all and enjoys it often, as no human mind is capable of perceiving so many beautiful things in their full strength at one time.

Translated by Michael Gilbert

Christian Friedrich Daniel Schubart

Concerning Musical Genius
(1784)

As certain as it is that every human being brings a musical seed into the world, it is just as certain that the organs of the ear and throat, the awkward structures of the hands, as well as one's upbringing prevent some from cultivating this seed. The musical genius has the *heart* for its foundation and receives its impressions through the ear. "He has no ear, no musical ear!" means, in musical terms, as much as, "He has no musical mind." Practical experience teaches that men come into the world without the feeling for rhythm and that they are oblivious and insusceptible to the beauties of music. On the other hand, the future virtuoso announces himself already in his youth. His *heart* is his principal chord and strung with such tender strings that they harmonize from every harmonic touch. All great musical geniuses are consequently self-taught [αὐτοϑίϑαχτοι], for the fire that inspires them charms them incessantly to seek their own path of flight. The *Bachs,* a *Galuppi, Jommelli, Gluck,* and *Mozart* distinguished themselves already in their childhood with the magnificent products of their genius. Musical euphony *[Wohlklang]* was in their soul, and they soon threw away the crutch of art. The characteristics of musical genius thus are undoubtedly as follows:

1. *Inspiration* or enthusiastic feeling of musical beauty and greatness.

2. An extremely tender *feeling in the heart* that sympathizes with all nobleness and beauty that the music brings forth. The *heart* is, as it were, the sounding board of great musicians: [without] this [he] is worthless, for he will never be able to produce anything great.

3. A highly refined *ear* that swallows each pleasing sound *[Wohllaut]* and reluctantly hears each discord. If a child without any instruction produces a chord on the harpsichord; if a girl or boy can improvise the accompaniment of a folk song; if the brow of the young listener wrinkles at dissonances and smooths at consonances; if the young throat already in its youth trills individual melodies—then musical genius is present.

4. Natural *feeling for the rhythm and measure.* If one puts a key in the hand of a child six or seven years old and then sings or plays a composition, and if the child beats the measure all by himself, then a musical mind is certainly there.

5. Irresistible *love and inclination for music,* which carries us away so powerfully that we prefer music to all other joys of life, is a very strong criterion for the presence of musical genius. Yet this distinguishing mark is sometimes deceiving for there are people who fiddle, strum, and play the lyre all day long and who themselves hardly rise above the mediocre.

In a word, the heavenly *flash of genius* is of such divine nature that it cannot be concealed. It presses, forces, pushes, and burns so long until it bursts forth as a flame and glorifies itself in its Olympian splendor. The mechanical musician lulls to sleep, but the musical genius awakes and rises heavenwards. Yet he has room enough also to carry up the listener on his cherubic wings.

However, the musical genius without culture and practice will always remain very imperfect. Art must complete and fill out what nature threw down raw. For if there were men who were born perfect in any art, application and effort would easily die away in the world.

The history of the great musicians proves it: how much sweat falls with their practice; how much oil their evening lamp consumes; how many imperfect attempts they let evaporate in the fireplace; how, deeply concealed in loneliness, they practiced finger, ear, and heart until they finally appeared and elicited a jubilant "bravo" from the world through their masterpieces.

The greatest strength of musical genius manifests itself in composition *[Tonsatz]* and in the wise leadership of great orchestra. A true Kapellmeister and music director must know all musical styles and know how to prove himself as a master in at least one of them. He must have studied counterpoint to the most intimate understanding; he must be rich in great and interesting melodic motion; he must have profoundly studied the heart of humanity in order to be able to play on the heart strings *[Cordialnerven]* just as surely as on his favorite instrument. Finally, he must be an acoustician and know how to lead, with breath and stroke, a hundred minds as if they were one so that thereby a great, all-effective whole is formed. If one would only study *Der vollkommene Kappellmeister* or a *Mattheson* or *Junker,* he would be amazed at the wide range of its theoretical and practical requirements.

Woe to you, pupil of music! If you already dream of being a Kapellmeister before you have the qualities of the good ripienist, or as *Handel* used to say, "It is like wanting to be an admiral without possessing the knowledge of a sailor." The half-developed musicians, the traveling artisans, who today blacken the musical world like a swarm of locusts, might frighten you off that you wear yourself out in your chamber; for you must practice melody, modulation, and harmony—and then, in the glory of a cultivated genius, you can appear among your contemporaries.

Translated by Richard W. Harpster

Concerning Musical Expression

Musical expression is the golden shaft around which the aesthetic of music turns. We understand by that the *appropriate performance* of each individual piece, even of each single thought. Generally, the musical expression consists of three points: *correctness, distinctness,* and *beauty.* Correctness consists in the precise reading and in the strongest observation of rhythm.

Reading is far more difficult than many imagine. Since every musical thought contains its appointed performance within itself, it depends on whether I penetrate into the *nature* of this thought and describe it characteristically. It is the case in music as in rhetoric: thorough, tuneful reading must precede beautiful declamation. Long, continuous practice is required for reading. One must thoroughly study the scores of great masters many times, the hand must practice by the performance of difficult passages and must also not neglect the simplest phrases, for there are often easy phrases that are more difficult to perform than the most complicated [ones]. This paradox resolves itself thereby if one knows that easy phrases require deep feeling of beauty, whereas the difficult ones require mostly only mechanics. I have heard great singers as well as accomplished clavierists who performed the most difficult arias and concertos with admirable dexterity and yet were not capable of singing or playing the plainest chorale or the simplest folk song. Through diligent solfège and practice of fingerings, the singer and instrumentalist can acquire that skill in reading.

The *second* quality of good musical performance is *distinctness*. What one does not understand does not affect the heart. One must, therefore, sharply contour every musical comma, even every single note; he must practice the shortness *[Abstossen]* of sounds, for nothing is more distinct than a staccato phrase; he must never murmur when he should speak; and he must apply himself, particularly in performance, to *rounding off* the phrase. Quite preferably, the singer has need of this distinctness, for, unfortunately, often the most beautiful poetry is lost among the lips and teeth of most singers. For that reason the effect is only simple, when it should have been doubled: that is, music and poetry should have worked together on the heart. That is the reason why so little attention prevails in our concerts. If one would only sing one good folk song distinctly and understandably, and see there! all eyes would widen, all ears would listen carefully, and all hearts would open. Every singer should, consequently, read through their texts very closely, discern the power of each word, give to every word its determined pronunciation, and be especially on guard against the detestable lengthening and stretching of vowels, whereby the performance becomes, for the most part, incomprehensible.

The third quality of musical performance is, finally, *beauty.*

Whoever has a feeling heart; whoever knows how to perceive according to the poet and composer with whom the flow of song even waltzes away; whoever clearly saw the heavenly beauty in the hours of dedication—he requires only a nod, for he will sing beautifully and will know how to perform each piece beautifully.

The *beautiful* consists of so many infinite, fine nuances, even in music, that it is impossible to define them all. A girl full of innocence and charm is beautiful often without knowing it herself; at least she does not know her temperament and how to separate each feature of her beauty from one another. However, very interesting observations concerning this can yet be made.

The blending of sounds; the light, pleasing portamento or gliding from one sound to the other; the swelling, rising, falling, [and] dying of sound; the naïveté with which one adds little ornaments; the beautiful contour with which one marks each phrase, the gentle vibrato, the breathing of singers; the lovely trill; the melting execution; and finally the beautiful position of the musician and the heartfelt expression in his face—all these together make up the beautiful musical performance. Since each thought has its own color [and] since many pleasing shades of color, from the fiery color of pathos on to the rosy color of tender joy, lie in between, it is, as already mentioned, impossible to mark all of these gradations as to indicate each nuance of coloring in the case of *Titian, Correggio,* or *Mengs.*

One who merely performs things that another has composed has to observe this and still other obligations. But infinitely more important is the musical expression by the composer himself, for he must know what poet and speaker should know and still combine with all of that the most illustrious knowledge of music.

For example, *sacred pathos* has simple, great, thoughtful, all-penetrating expression. Some of our chorales have already for centuries affected all human hearts. What is the reason for this long effect: simplicity, the sense of devotion, [and] greatness, which always and above all subdues all hearts and rises heavenward. To the expression of sacred style belongs, consequently, much warmth for religion, great sense, and the tenderest feeling of the heart that a musical language can lend to the simplest form of prayer.

Musical expression in the churches changes according to the subjects. For example, the *triumphant style* prevails on feast days, the flood of sound surges and rolls and carries its joyful feeling toward heaven. If someone wanted to bring the words *"Gott fährt auf mit Jauchzen und Frohlocken"* to music, the prevailing idea would be the triumphant ascension of Christ, just as *Klopstock* has portrayed it.

With the idea *"Gott,"* the composer would have to linger, invert more often, and, by a general pause, impress the heart of the hearer.

The idea *"fährt auf"* as the prevailing idea, one would have to project over the whole composition. All tones would have to rise little by little and at the same time elevate the hero to heaven. *"Mit Jauchzen und Frohlocken!"* are merely subsidiary ideas *[Nebenideen]*. Consequently, it would be foolishness if the musician could be misled into making them, through careful elaboration, the principal notion of his work. *Jauchzen* and *Frohlocken* might well brighten the composition, but the *auffahrende Gott* must shine far above the rejoicing tumult.

A *Requiem,* or death music, must be immersed wholly in the color of sadness. The words *"Requiem aeternam da nobis, Domine!"* seem to have, as it were, only *one* expression. In a strongly colored key, as in A major, E major, B major, etc., these words can hardly be set. C major and A minor are too light for this theme. There remains, therefore, only the keys marked with flats. These sway not only by their gentleness in sleep, but also point out the nature of death through its fading gloominess. Every musician must consequently choose E-flat major or C minor, A-flat major or F minor, but best of all B-flat major or G minor for this theme....

Translated by Ted Alan DuBois

Immanuel Kant

The Division of the Fine Arts
(1790)

From *Book 2, Analytic of the Sublime*

The art of the BEAUTIFUL PLAY OF SENSATIONS, (sensations that arise from external stimulation), which is a play of sensations that has nevertheless to permit of universal communication, can only be concerned with the proportion of the different degrees of tension in the sense to which the sensation belongs, i.e., with its tone. In this comprehensive sense of the word it may be divided into the artificial play of sensations of hearing and of sight, consequently into *music* and the *art of color*.—It is of note that these two senses, over and above such susceptibility for impressions as is required to obtain concepts of external objects by means of these impressions, also admit of a peculiar associated sensation of which we cannot well determine whether it is based on sense or reflection; and that this sensibility may at times be wanting, although the sense, in other respects, and in what concerns its employment for the cognition of objects, is by no means deficient but particularly keen. In other words, we cannot confidently assert whether a color or a tone (sound) is merely an agreeable sensation, or whether they are in themselves a beautiful play of sensations, and in being estimated aesthetically, convey, as such, a delight in their form. If we consider the velocity of the vibrations of light, or, in the second case, of the air, which in all probability far outstrips any capacity on our part for forming an immediate estimate in perception of the time interval between them, we should be led to believe that it is only the *effect* of those vibrating movements upon the elastic parts of our body, that can be evident to sense, but that the *time interval* between them is not noticed nor involved in our estimate, and that, consequently, all that enters into combination with colors and tones is agreeableness, and not beauty, of their composition. But, let us consider, on the other hand, *first*, the mathematical character both of the proportion of those vibrations in music, and of our judgment upon it, and, as is reasonable, form an estimate of color contrasts on the analogy of the latter. *Secondly*, let us consult the instances, albeit rare, of men who, with the best of sight, have failed to distinguish colors, and, with the sharpest hearing, to distinguish tones, while for men who have this ability the perception of an altered quality (not merely of the degree of the sensation) in the case of the different intensities in the scale of colors or tones is definite, as is also the number of those that may be *intelligibly* distinguished. Bearing all this in mind we may feel compelled to look upon the sensations afforded by both, not as mere sense impressions, but as the effect of an estimate of form in the play of a number of sensations. The difference that the one opinion or the other occasions in the estimate of the basis of music would, however, only give rise to this much change in its definition, that either it is to be interpreted, as we have done, as the *beautiful* play of sensations (through hearing), or else as one of *agreeable* sensations. According to the former interpretation, alone, music would be represented out and out as a *fine* art, whereas according to the latter it would be represented as (in part at least) an *agreeable* art.

Poetry (which owes its origin almost entirely to genius and is least willing to be led by precepts or example) holds first rank among all the arts. It expands the mind by giving freedom to the imagination and by offering, from among the boundless multiplicity of possible forms accordant with a given concept, to whose bounds it is restricted, that one that couples with the presentation of the concept of wealth of thought to which no verbal expression is completely adequate, and by thus rising aesthetically to ideas. It invigorates the mind by letting it feel its faculty—free, spontaneous, and independent of determination by nature—of regarding and estimating nature as phenomenon in the light of aspects that nature of itself does not afford us in experience, either for sense or understanding, and of employing it accordingly in behalf of, and as a sort of schema for, the supersensible. It plays with semblance, which it produces at will, but not as an instrument of deception; for its avowed pursuit is merely one of play, which, however, understanding may turn to good account and employ for its own purpose.

After poetry, *if we take charm and mental stimulation into account,* I would give the next place to that art that comes nearer to it than to any other art of speech, and admits of very natural union with it, namely, the art of *tone.* For though it speaks by means of mere sensations without concepts, and so does not, like poetry, leave behind it any food for reflection, still it moves the mind more diversely, and, although with transient, still with intenser effect. It is certainly, however, more a matter of enjoyment than of culture—the play of thought incidentally excited by it being merely the effect of a more or less mechanical association—and it possesses less worth in the eyes of reason than any other of the fine arts. Hence, like all enjoyment, it calls for constant change, and does not stand frequent repetition without inducing weariness. Its charm, which admits of such universal communication, appears to rest on the following facts. Every expression in language has an associated tone suited to its sense. This tone indicates, more or less, a mode in which the speaker is affected, and in turn evokes it in the hearer also, in whom conversely it then also excites the idea that in language is expressed with such a tone. Further, just as modulation is, as it were, a universal language of sensations intelligible to every man, so the art of tone wields the full force of this language wholly on its own account, namely, as a language of the affections, and in this way, according to the law of association, universally communicates the aesthetic ideas that are naturally combined therewith. But, further, inasmuch as those aesthetic ideas are not concepts or determinate thoughts, the form of the arrangement of these sensations (harmony and melody), taking the place of the form of a language, only serves the purpose of giving an expression to the aesthetic idea of an integral whole of an unutterable wealth of thought that fills the measure of a certain theme forming the dominant *affection* in the piece. This purpose is effectuated by means of a proportion in the accord of the sensations (an accord that may be brought mathematically under certain rules, since it rests, in the case of tones, upon the numerical relation of the vibrations of the air in the same time, so far as there is a combination of the tones simultaneously or in succession). Although this mathematical form is not represented by means of determinate concepts, to it alone belongs the delight that the mere reflection upon such a number of concomitant or consecutive sensations couples with this their play, as the universally valid condition of its beauty, and it is with reference to it alone that taste can lay claim to a right to anticipate the judgment of every man.

But mathematics, certainly, does not play the smallest part in the charm and movement of the mind produced by music. Rather it is only the indispensable condition of that proportion of the combining as well as changing impressions that makes it possible to grasp them all in one and prevent them from destroying one another, and to let them, rather, conspire toward the production of a continuous movement and quickening of the mind by affections that are in unison with it, and thus toward a serene self-enjoyment.

If, on the other hand, we estimate the worth of the fine arts by the culture they supply to the mind, and adopt for our standard the expansion of the faculties whose confluence, in judgment, is necessary for cognition, music, then, since it plays merely with sensations, has the lowest place among the fine arts—just as it has perhaps the highest among those valued at the same time for their agreeableness. Looked at in this light it is far excelled by the formative arts. For, in putting the imagination into a play that is at once free and adapted to the understanding, they all the while carry on a serious business, since they execute a product that serves the concepts of understanding as a vehicle, permanent and appealing to us on its own account, for effectuating their union with sensibility, and thus for promoting, as it were, the urbanity of the higher powers of cognition. The two kinds of art pursue completely different courses. Music advances from sensations to indefinite ideas: formative art from definite ideas to sensations. The latter gives a *lasting* impression, the former one that is only *fleeting*. The former sensations imagination can recall and agreeably entertain itself with, while the latter either vanish entirely, or else, if involuntarily repeated by the imagination, are more annoying to us than agreeable. Over and above all this, music has a certain lack of urbanity about it. For owing chiefly to the character of its instruments, it scatters its influence abroad to an uncalled-for extent (through the neighborhood), and thus, as it were, becomes obtrusive and deprives others, outside the musical circle, of their freedom. This is a thing that the arts that address themselves to the eye do not do, for if one is not disposed to give admittance to their impressions, one has only to look the other way. The case is almost on a par with the practice of regaling oneself with a perfume that exhales its odors far and wide. The man who pulls his perfumed handkerchief from his pocket gives a treat to all around whether they like it or not, and compels them, if they want to breathe at all, to be parties to the enjoyment, and so the habit has gone out of fashion.

Among the formative arts I would give the palm to *painting:* partly because it is the art of design and, as such, the groundwork of all the other formative arts; partly because it can penetrate much further into the region of ideas, and in conformity with them give a greater extension to the field of intuition than it is open to the others to do.

Translated by James Creed Meredith

Johann Georg Sulzer

Expression in Music
(1792–1794)

The principal, if not indeed the sole function of a perfect musical composition is the accurate expression of emotions and passions in all their varying and individual nuances. A composition that merely fills the imagination with a sequence of harmonious sounds, without touching the heart, is like a picture of a beautiful sky in the glow of the setting sun. The attractive kaleidoscope of colors pleases us; but the heart is not involved by the cloudscape. If, on the other hand, we are also aware of a melodic language whose perfectly shaped and uninterrupted flow of notes reveals the outpourings of a sensitive heart, our sense of hearing is pleasantly stimulated. Our soul is borne to rest, undisturbed, on a kind of couch of sound, and can abandon itself to every emotion that is aroused in it by the expressive melody. The attention is totally held by the play of harmony, and the ear is induced into a state of complete self-forgetfulness, so that it concentrates only on the refined emotions that take possession of the soul.

Expression is the soul of music; without it, music is just a pleasant toy; with it, music becomes an overwhelmingly powerful language that engulfs the heart. It compels us in turn to tenderness, resolution, and courage. It successively arouses our sympathy and our admiration. At times it enhances and exalts the soul; at others, it takes it captive so that it dissolves in languorous emotion. How, though does the composer acquire this miraculous skill to dominate our hearts so completely? The foundations of his power must have been laid in him by nature herself. His soul must be responsive to every emotion and passion, for he can only effectively express what he himself keenly feels. The extent to which personality affects art is illustrated in the work of two much-admired German composers — Graun and Hasse. Nature endowed Graun with a tender, gentle, complaisant soul; though he may have mastered all the skills of his craft, he was at home only in the gentle, the pleasant, and the charming emotions; and more than once he ran into problems when he had to express boldness, pride, or resolution. Nature endowed Hasse, on the other hand, with loftier courage, bolder emotions, and stronger desires, and he was most at home with the emotions that were consistent with his character rather than with those that were gentle and pleasant.

It is very important for the artist to know himself, and, if the decision lies with him, to undertake nothing that is inconsistent with his personality. Unfortunately, the decision does not always lie with him. The epic poet must be able to capture every emotion, and, indeed, conflicting emotions when he portrays a submissive, a daring, or even a cowardly character. The composer, too, will encounter similar situations, so he must be able to help himself by diligent practice whenever Nature affords him little support.

In such circumstances, the musician must closely study how each passion is expressed. This point has already been dealt with in the article on the problem of expression in the arts in general. He must see people only from this point of view. Each emotion has its special character, its musical formulation [Gedanke] and its vocal quality, pitch, relative tempo, and rhetorical accentuation. Those who have studied this closely will often be able to grasp the correct sense of a speech even if they do not understand the words. They will know whether the individual sounds express joy or sorrow; they may even, in fact, be able to identify intense and moderate pain, deep-rooted tenderness, overwhelming or restrained joy. The musician must pay the most scrupulous attention to a study of natural expression; speech invariably has something about it that melody can imitate, however much the two may differ. Joy is expressed in sonorous tones, unhurried tempi, and in limited gradations of pitch and dynamics. Sadness unburdens itself slowly, from the depths of the heart, and is of somber hue. Every emotion, then, has its own character, one that the composer must observe and get to know as intimately as he can. Only in this way will he achieve correctness of expression.

Next, he should make every effort to determine how the various emotions affect the personality itself, its sequence of thoughts and emotions. Every emotion involves a sequence of images [*Vorstellungen*] somewhat akin to motion; the very phrase "motions of the affections" already indicates as much. There are emotions in which the images flow evenly like a gentle stream; there are others in which the sequence of images resembles a raging and turbulent flood, swollen with heavy rain, a flood that sweeps every obstruction before it. At times, the images within us resemble a wild sea that dashes violently against the shore, and then falls back, only to surge forward again with renewed force.

Music is ideally suited to the portrayal of all such movements. If the composer is sufficiently aware of them and if he is skilled enough to follow every movement in melody and harmony, these subjective changes will be aurally perceptible. To this end, he has at his disposal many and varied means — provided he also has the skill. These means are: (1) The actual harmonic progressions, whatever the meter. The harmony must move easily and naturally, without great complexity or ponderous suspensions, if the mood is gentle or pleasant. If the mood is violent or recalcitrant, however, the progressions should move haltingly, and there should be fairly frequent modulations into more remote keys; the progressions should also be more complex, with frequent and unexpected dissonances, and suspensions that are rapidly resolved. (2) The meter, by means of which all kinds of movement may be imitated in general terms. (3) The melody and the rhythm, which are of themselves equally capable of portraying the language of every emotion. (4) Dynamic variations, too, contribute significantly to expression. (5) The choice of accompaniment, with particular regard to the choice of instruments and the way in which they interact, and (6) Modulations into, and extended passages in other keys.

The composer should carefully consider all these elements, judging the effect of each of them with care and precision; in this way, he will be in a position to express every emotion as accurately and as tellingly as possible. Despite the fineness of nuance that differentiates certain emotions, there are many emotions that are not beyond music's power to express. In the aria "Dalle labbre del mio bene," from the operetta *Europa Galante,* for example, Graun has expressed to perfection that kind of tenderness, combined with complete submission to the master's will, that is so eminently typical of an Ottoman seraglio. Here is triumphant proof that music has the capacity to express the most difficult emotions.

Nonetheless, careful thought and extreme diligence are called for if perfect expression is to be achieved, for this great composer and others of the front rank have frequently lapsed in the matter of correct expression. We would recommend anyone who wishes to achieve this essential artistic goal to take careful note of the foregoing remarks and of what is to follow.

Every piece of music must have a definite character and evoke emotions of a specific kind. This is so both of instrumental and vocal music. Any composer would be misguided if he started work before deciding on the character of his piece. He must know whether the language he is to use is that of a man who is proud or humble, bold or timid, violent or gentle. He must know if the character is a supplicant or one in authority. Even if he comes upon his theme by accident, he should still examine it carefully if he is to sustain its character throughout the piece. Having determined the character of his piece, he must put himself into the emotional state that he wishes others to experience. His best course of action is to imagine some drama, happening or situation that will naturally induce the kind of state that he has in mind; and if his imagination is sufficiently fired by this, he should at once set to work, taking care not to introduce a musical passage *[Periode]* or figure *[Figur]* that is out of character with the piece.

Many composers have been led astray by an overfondness for certain pleasant-sounding and skillfully contrived formulae that express particular emotions. It should be borne in mind that such repetitions are often detrimental to expression and are suitable only for certain obsessive emotions and passions. Other emotions, however, involve impressions that are constantly changing, variable, and transient. In such cases, frequent reiteration of the same expressive formula is unnatural.

If the composer is to set a given text to music, he should first of all study its true spirit, character, and mood. He should give detailed consideration to the circumstances and intentions of the person speaking; and he should determine the overall character of his vocal line. He should choose the most effective key, an appropriate tempo, rhythms that are intrinsic to the emotion, and intervals that are best suited to its ebb and flow. The expressive element characteristic of the piece [*dieses Charakteristische*] must prevail throughout, especially where the text calls for some specific emphasis.

Translated by Peter Le Huray and James Day

Music

A proper idea of this charming art must begin with an attempt to trace its origins in nature. Since we can in some degree observe the process of tracing its origins in nature daily, and since we are in the process of discovering how partly civilized people refine the raw material of song through the principles of taste, this task is less difficult than it might be. Nature has established a direct link between the ear and the heart; each emotion is expressed by particular sounds, each of which awakens in the listener's heart the original experience that gave rise to it. A cry of terror terrifies us; joyful sounds awaken happiness. The cruder senses — smell, touch, and taste — affect the body, not the soul; they arouse nothing but blind pleasure or displeasure; their energies are absorbed in enjoyment or revulsion. The visual and aural senses, however, affect the spirit and the heart. In these two senses lie the mainsprings of rational and moral behavior. The aural sense is certainly the more powerful of the two. Dissonance is far more easily perceived than is a clash of colors; the charming chromatic harmony of the rainbow is by no means as moving as a triad, for example. So the sense of hearing is by far the most effective path to the emotions. Who would claim that clashing or unharmonious colors have ever caused pain? But the ear can be so adversely affected by dissonance as almost to bring the listener to despair.

This is doubtless because the material that affects the aural nerves — air — is much coarser and more physical than ethereal light, which affects the eye. The aural nerves consequently transmit to the entire body the impact of the shock they receive. This is not the case with visual effects. Hence it is understandable that the body, and consequently the soul, can be intensely affected by sounds. Little thought or experience is needed to discover the power of sound; the most inobservant of men feel it. A man who is a prey to strong emotions similarly often tries to intensify them with cries of joy, rage, etc. Children and very primitive peoples likewise express themselves spontaneously, inflaming and intensifying not only their own emotions but those of others by means of a whole range of varying sounds. Although a sequence of such cries may not constitute an actual song, it clearly has the makings of song.

The point at issue here is the very close link that subsists between movement, rhythm, and sounds. The measured movement of sustained physical effort, which occurs with regular emphasis in a discernible repeated pattern, relieves monotony, assists concentration, and serves to enlighten tasks that would otherwise become tedious, such as carrying or dragging a heavy load or, as Ovid observed, rowing a boat. The relief is even greater, however, when the movement is rhythmically accentuated, i.e., when the smaller strokes that constitute each step or beat vary almost imperceptibly in strength and weakness, as is the case in a blacksmith's hammering, or a team threshing. This is how the burden of toil is lightened, as the pleasure derived from unity in variety facilitates the continuation of the task in hand.

Such rhythms and measures may be applied to a sequence of sounds, since they inevitably convey the notion of movement. This is the origin of accompanied song and it is the natural link between song and dance. So it is not at all surprising on reflection that even the most primitive peoples have discovered music and to some extent developed it.

Music is thus deeply rooted in man's nature. As a notated art, it has its own principles that must be observed to ensure the progress of the art and the composition of music of quality. The first thing that we must do, therefore, is dispose of a widespread and common misconception concerning the immutability of musical principles. The Chinese are said to have no taste for European music; Europeans, on the other hand, cannot stand Chinese music. This is said to be because music is not based on universal principles that are rooted in human nature. We shall see.

If music had no aim other than that of arousing fleeting impressions of joy, fear, or terror, then a simple spontaneous cry from a large crowd would suffice. The effect of a shout of jubilation or terror from a large crowd is violent, however undisciplined, dissonant, odd, or unruly the sound may be. Laws and principles are irrelevant here.

But such noises do not last long; they soon lose their impact and thus our attention. They would do so even if they were prolonged. If sounds are to affect us, they must be subject to meter. This is a common experience of all sensitive peoples, Indians, Iroquois,

Siberians, and ancient Greeks alike. Meter and rhythm provide order and regular measure, the basic principles of which are respected by all peoples. But as rhythm *[das Metrische]* is infinitely variable, each people has its own idea of rhythm, a fact that can be illustrated from the dance melodies of various peoples; but the universal rules of regularity and order are common to all . . . .

As we have seen, music is essentially a sequence of sounds that are excited by passionate emotion and that are capable of arousing, sustaining, and illustrating such emotion. Let us now investigate what makes music an art and the purpose that musical works can serve.

Music's aim is to arouse the emotions; this it does by means of sequences of sounds that are appropriate to the natural expression of the emotion; and its application must suitably conform to the intentions of nature in emotional matters. We must examine each of these points in more detail.

There is no doubt about music's purpose, for its first seeds certainly sprang from the pleasure that was experienced in prolonging and intensifying an emotional state. The expression of joy was apparently a first step toward music. The wish to lighten arduous toil was the second; this could be done in one of two ways: either passively, by diverting the attention from the burden to pleasurable things through variety in unity, or actively by exciting actual joy by means of rousing sounds and energetic movement. In the first case, music seeks to captivate or charm the senses; in the second, it seeks to stimulate bodily and spiritual powers. The music of nature *[die bloss natürliche Musik]* hardly ever seems to lead to tenderness, sadness, or anger. Once it was found, however, that these emotions could be forcefully portrayed in art and thus aroused, this was done. Moreover, as the moral character of individuals and nations alike can be powerfully affected by the various ways in which people express them, music can be said to contain an ethical element in so far as that element can be emotionally felt and expressed. And, in fact, national songs and their associated dances faithfully reflect the mores of the people who create them.

There is no justification, though, for the idea that music can influence the conceptual imagination *[Vorstellungskraft]* in matters that are altogether unrelated to emotion, or that are related to them only through cognitive reflection. Language was invented to express ideas and concepts; it is language that constructs and projects images in the imagination, not music. The portrayal of such images is altogether foreign to music's aim. It is not rational man, a thinking and imaginative creature, that music influences therefore, but man as a sentient being. However learned, correct, or well wrought, then, a composition may be, it is not a piece of genuine music if it fails to stimulate the emotions. All that the listener needs is a sensitive heart; with this he may judge whether a work is good or bad, even if he lacks all musical knowledge. If music reaches his heart, it has achieved its purpose, and whatever serves to achieve this aim is good. Leave the experts to judge whether the music might have done so more effectively had the composer not weakened or spoiled it through lack of taste or skill. For only such experts know the means to the end and can judge whether good or bad use has been made of them.

Those, then, who have mastered the art as well as those who are connoisseurs may need to be reminded of music's aim, since the former often seek applause by purely technical devices, by leaps, runs, and harmonies, which are perhaps difficult to manage but which communicate nothing. At the very most a singer or instrumentalist who has mastered such technical difficulties arouses a reaction in the audience similar to that aroused by a skillful tightrope dancer or bareback rider in full gallop. How much more natural it is to prefer the song of a real nightingale to an imitation.

Those who doubt the ancient stories of music's marvelous powers are either ignorant of, or insensitive to, good music. The emotions are excited, as is well-known, by the action of the nerves and by the rapid circulation of the blood. Music unquestionably and genuinely affects both. Since music involves the movement of air and the impact of air in the highly sensitive aural nerves, it affects the body; how, indeed, could it fail to do so, since it can shatter even inorganic matter — not merely fragile windows, but even strong walls? Why doubt, therefore, that it can affect sensitive nerves in a manner unparalleled by any other art, or that through the nerves it can stimulate a feverish, tormented pulsing of the blood; that it can even, as we have read in the transactions of the Paris Académie des Sciences, actually cure a musician of a fever? . . .

It must not be forgotten, however, that although music enjoys this evident advantage over the other arts, its effect is more transient. It is easier to recall things that have been read or heard in speech than it is to recall sound as such. So it is that poetry and painting leave a lasting impression even though the actual works are no longer before us. If a piece of music is to make a lasting impression, it must be frequently repeated. On the other hand, where an immediate but transient impact is desired, music is supremely effective.

It follows, then, that this divine art might be put to effective use in the service of politics. What an incomprehensible waste simply to treat music as a pleasurable pastime for the leisured! Is further proof required that as rich as an age may be in scholarship, mechanical ingenuity, and intellectual achievement, it can yet be very poor in common sense?

Translated by Peter Le Huray and James Day

Wilhelm Heinrich Wackenroder

The Marvels of the Musical Art
(1799)

Whenever I so very fervently enjoy how a beautiful strain of sounds suddenly, in free spontaneity, extricates itself from the empty stillness and rises like sacrificial incense, floats gently on the breezes, and then silently sinks down to earth again—then so many new, beautiful images sprout forth and flock together in my heart that I cannot control myself out of rapture.—Sometimes music appears to me like a phoenix, which lightly and boldly raises itself for its own pleasure, floats upward triumphantly for its own gratification, and pleases gods and men by the flapping of its wings.—At other times it seems to me as if music were like a child lying dead in the grave—*one* reddish sunbeam from heaven gently draws its soul away and, transplanted into the heavenly ether, it enjoys golden drops of eternity and embraces the original images of the most beautiful human dreams.—And sometimes,—what a magnificent fullness of images!—sometimes music is for me entirely a picture of our life:—a touchingly brief joy, which arises out of the void and vanishes into the void,—which commences and passes away, why one does not know:—a little, merry, green island, with sunshine, with singing and rejoicing,—which floats upon the dark, unfathomable ocean.

Ask the virtuoso why he is so heartily gay upon his lyre. "Is not," he will answer, "all of life a beautiful dream? a lovely soap bubble? My musical piece is the same."

Truly, it is an innocent, touching pleasure to rejoice over sounds,

over pure sounds! A childlike joy!—While others deafen themselves
with restless activity and, buzzed by confused thoughts as by an
army of strange night birds and evil insects, finally fall to the
ground unconscious—O, then I submerge my head in the holy,
cooling wellspring of sounds and the healing goddess instills the
innocence of childhood in me again, so that I regard the world
with fresh eyes and melt into universal, joyous reconciliation.—
While others quarrel over invented troubles, or play a desperate
game of wit, or brood in solitude misshapen ideas that, like the
armor-clad men of the fable, consume themselves in desperation;—
O, then I close my eyes to all the strife of the world—and withdraw
quietly into the land of music, as into the *land of belief,* where all
our doubts and our sufferings are lost in a resounding sea,—where
we forget all the croaking of human beings, where no chattering
of words and languages, no confusion of letters and monstrous
hieroglyphics makes us dizzy but, instead, all the anxiety of our
hearts is suddenly healed by the gentle touch.—And how? Are
questions answered for us here? Are secrets revealed to us?—O,
no! but, in the place of all answers and revelations, airy, beautiful
cloud formations are shown to us, the sight of which calms us, we
do not know how;—with brave certainty we wander through the
unknown land;—we greet and embrace as friends strange spiritual
beings whom we do not know, and all the incomprehensibilities
that besiege our souls and that are the disease of the human race
disappear before our senses, and our minds become healthy
through the contemplation of marvels that are *far more incomprehensible* and exalted. At that moment the human being seems to
want to say: "That is what I mean! Now I have found it! Now I
am serene and happy!"—

Let the others mock and jeer, who race on through life as if on
rattling wagons and do not know this land of holy peace in the
soul of the human being. Let them take pride in their giddiness
and boast, as if they were guiding the world with their reins. There
will come times when they will suffer great want.

Happy the one who, when the earthly soil shakes unfaithfully
under his feet, can rescue himself serenely on airy tones and, yielding to them, now rocks himself gently, now dances away coura-
geously and forgets his sorrows with such a pleasing diversion!

Happy the one who (weary of the business of splitting ideas
more and more finely, which shrinks the soul) surrenders himself

to the gentle and powerful currents of desire, which expand the spirit and elevate it to a *beautiful faith*. Such a course is the only way to universal, all-embracing love and only through such love do we come close to divine blessedness.—

This is the most magnificent and the most wonderful picture of the musical art that I can sketch out,—although most people will consider it to be empty dreaming.

But, from what sort of magic potion does the aroma of this brilliant apparition rise?—I look,—and find nothing but a wretched web of numerical proportions, represented concretely on perforated wood, on constructions of gut strings and brass wire.— This is almost more wondrous, and I should like to believe that the invisible harp of God sounds along with our notes and contributes the heavenly power to the human web of digits.

And how, then, did man arrive at the marvelous idea of having wood and metal make sounds? How did he arrive at the precious invention of this most exceptional of all arts?—That is also so remarkable and extraordinary that I want to write down the story briefly, as I conceive of it.

The human being is initially a very innocent creature. While we are still lying in the cradle, our little minds are being nourished and educated by a hundred invisible little spirits and trained in all the polite skills. Thus, little by little, we learn to be happy by smiling; by crying, we learn to be sad; by staring wide-eyed, we learn to worship whatever is exalted. But, just as in childhood we don't yet know how to handle the toy correctly, so too, we don't rightly understand how to play with the things of the heart and, in this school of the emotions, we still mistake and confuse everything.

However, when we have come of age, then we understand how to employ the emotions, whether gaiety or sorrow or any other, very skillfully where they are appropriate; and sometimes we express them very beautifully, to our own satisfaction. Indeed, although these things are actually only an occasional embellishment to the events of our usual lives, yet we find so much pleasure in them that we like to separate these so-called emotions from the complex chaos and mesh of the earthly creature in whom they are entangled and elaborate them particularly into a beautiful memory and preserve them in our individual ways. These feelings that surge up in our hearts sometimes seem to us so magnificent and grand that we lock them up like relics in expensive monstrosities, kneel down before them joyously, and, in our exuberance, do not know whether we are worshiping our own human heart or the Creator, from whom all great and magnificent things come.

For this preservation of the emotions, various splendid inventions have been made and, thus, all the fine arts have arisen. But I consider music to be the most marvelous of these inventions, because it portrays human feelings in a superhuman way, because it shows us all the emotions of our soul above our heads in incorporeal form, clothed in golden clouds of airy harmonies,—because it speaks a language that we do not know in our ordinary life, which we have learned, we do not know where and how, and that one would consider to be solely the language of angels.

It is the only art that reduces the most multifarious and contradictory emotions of our souls to the *same* beautiful harmonies, which plays with joy and sorrow, with despair and adoration in the same harmonious tones. Therefore, it is also music that infuses in us true *serenity of soul,* which is the most beautiful jewel that the human being can acquire—I mean that serenity in which everything in the world seems to us natural, true, and good, in which we find a beautiful cohesion in the wildest throng of people, in which, with sincere hearts, we feel all creatures to be related and close to us and, like children, look upon the world as through the twilight of a lovely dream.—

When, in my simplicity, I feel very blessed under open skies before God,—while the golden rays of the sun stretch the lofty, blue tent above me and the green earth laughs all around me,— then it is fitting that I throw myself upon the ground and, in loud jubilation, joyously thank heaven for all magnificence. But what does the so-called artist among men do thereupon? He has observed me and, internally warmed, he goes home in silence, lets his sympathetic rapture gush forth much more magnificently on a lifeless harp and preserves it in a language that no one has ever spoken, the native country of which no one knows, and that grips everyone to the core.—

When a brother of mine has died and, at such an event of life, I appropriately display deep sorrow, sit weeping in a narrow corner, and ask all the stars who has ever been more grieved than I,— then,—while the mocking future already stands behind my back and laughs about the quickly fleeting pain of the human being,—

then the virtuoso stands before me and becomes so moved by all this woeful wringing of the hands, that he re-creates this beautiful pain on his instrument at home and beautifies and adorns the human grief with desire and love. Thus, he produces a work that arouses in all the world the deepest compassion.—But I, after I have long forgotten the anxious wringing of the hands for my dead brother and then happen to hear the product of his sorrow,—then I exult like a child over my own so magnificently glorified heart and nourish and enrich my soul with the wonderful creation.—

But when the angels of heaven look down upon this entire delightful plaything that we call *art*,—then they must smile in tender sadness over the race of children on earth and over the innocent artificiality in this art of sounds, through which the mortal creature wants to elevate himself to them.

Translated by Mary Hurst Schubert

Johann Gottfried Herder

Music, an Art of Humanity
(1802)

Thus the "Critique of the Autonomous Aesthetic Judgment" spoke of poetry and rhetoric, of sculpture and architecture, of painting, decorative gardening, furniture, and clothing; music unhappily was left out of the fine arts, and to what end? It becomes "a beautiful play of sensations that are externally produced, and that yet must also be generally communicable; which fine art then can be nothing other than the *proportion* of the various *degrees* of the *attunement (tension)* of the sense to which the sensation belongs, that is, concern the *tone* of the same, and in the *broad* meaning of the word it *can* be divided into the *artful* play *with the tone* of the sensation of hearing and of that of vision, that is, into *music and the art of color.*" Since *every* sensation, not only that of tone, must have degrees, and consequently also degrees of the attunement of our sense organ, and *every* degree assumes proportions because it is a proportion itself; since further *all sensations have a sensorium commune,* and consequently a common standard of measure in us by means of which we calculate the sensations of the most various organs equivalently: nothing has here been said as far as music is concerned. *The art of color and the art of tone, the art of tone and the art of color* fully equated; as though colors without drawing can be set equal to tones as a medium of art; finally "a beautiful play of sensations that are externally produced, and that yet must also be generally communicable;" since everyone knows that the sensations excited by tones are least of all susceptible of this general apodictic communicability—what can be said about this? Back to our path!

We observed that:

1. In the whole of nature, all elastic bodies upon being struck or stroked *make known* (audibly or less audibly to us) their *interior,* that is, their excited and restorative forces. This we call *sound,* and more finely excited, *tonal sonority;* tonal sonority, which sets every similarly organized object into equivalent vibration, and in sensitive beings brings about an analogous sensation. We found:

2. That here also *man* is a *general participant,* an auditor of the universe, that he must lend his sympathy to every aroused being whose voice reaches him. According to observations his auditory organ, hidden most deeply from the outside, reaches most deeply into the interior of his head, approaching first of all his perceptive organ of common sense, and spreads out in such a way that, as experiments reveal, we hear almost with our whole body. We recalled:

3. That *every tone has its type of excitation, its significative power.* Not only does every tonally sonorous body, every natural thing used as an instrument, have at its disposal its type of sonority, but also every vibration *its* modulation and with this its own manner of acting on our feeling. We found:

4. That for our ear there is a *scale of tones* the steps of which are determined by one another, are inseparable from one another, but the vaulting curve of which, and with it our progressive course on this scale, is susceptible of many changes, and consequently in the hands of art is an instrument for the excitation of many kinds of diversified sensations; that these progressive courses and modulations, as sensations of the same creature, must recur in their kinds, but precisely through their recurrence, in the same or in a different fashion, give our inner elasticity impulse and exaltation, in short the efficacy that nothing else can give it so diversely, rapidly, and powerfully. The sensitive creature feels himself moved, that is, displaced from his rest and thus caused to restore this to himself through his own inner force. He feels himself moved, buoyed up, *in accordance with proportions,* consequently *pleasantly,* and cannot do otherwise than return to rest again in such a proportion. This is *music,* nothing else.

5. *Thus everything that sounds in nature is music;* it has its elements in itself; and demands only a hand to draw them forth,

an ear to hear them, a sympathy to perceive them. No artist has invented a tone or given it a power that it did not have in nature and in his instrument; he has discovered it, however, and with a sweet power has forced it forth. The composer has discovered progressions of tones, and forces them on us with a gentle power. Not "externally are the sensations of music produced," but in us; from the outside there comes to us only the universally moving sweet tonal sonority, which, harmonically and melodically excited, also excites harmonically and melodically whatever is susceptible of it.

6. In the same fashion we know that the *voice of each thing similar in kind communicates itself preeminently to what is similar in kind,* a consequence of the genetic concept of music in general. In the similar instrument the sounded tones echo back most intensely and purely. Thus also in the living creature. The voice of the species communicates itself sympathetically to the species, especially when it lives socially, in herds, as natural history demonstrates in countless examples. An utterance of one in anxiety summons all together, allows them, as long as it sounds, no peace; anxiously they commiserate and hurry to help. The tones of joy, of longing, summon the one they apply to just as powerfully. The original power of tone thus does not rest on the "proportion of the various degrees of the attunement of hearing" alone, as though the sensation belonged to the ear, which produced tones itself, isolated from creation; this is only the state of the dream or illness, which presupposes waking and health. The power of tone, the cry of the passions, belongs sympathetically to the whole species, to its bodily and mental constitution. It is the voice of nature, the energy of one deeply moved, announcing himself to the whole species for sympathy; it is *harmonious motion.*

7. Hence the *dance:* for since the tones of music are *temporal* vibrations, they animate the body, just as sensation measured, raised, and lowered them; the rhythm of their expression expresses itself through its rhythm. Hence also the gesturing bound up with music. Strongly moved, natural man cannot abstain from it; he expresses what he hears through appearances of his countenance, through swings of his hand, through posture and flexing. The dances of primitive and especially of warm, highly active peoples are all pantomimic. Also with the Greeks it was not otherwise;

they speak of music as the leader of the dance, of a dance of every motion of the soul.

8. Since accordingly music, dance, and gesture, as manifestations of a common energy, are intimately connected through a bond of nature, could the most natural of them, the *answering voice* of the one who is feeling, be absent from them? We join in where voices sound; the power of *choruses,* especially at the moment of their entrance and recurrence, is indescribable. Indescribable the loveliness of voices that *accompany* one another; they are one and not one; they abandon, seek, pursue, contradict, combat, strengthen, and annihilate one another, and awaken and animate and console and flatter and embrace one another again, until they finally die away in a single tone. There is no sweeter image of seeking and finding, of the dissensions of friendship and of reconciliation, of loss and of longing, of doubting and certain recognition, and finally of total sweet union and fusion than these two and many voiced tonal successions, tonal contests, wordless or accompanied by words. In the latter case the words are not inactive interpreters, as it were, of what that lovely labyrinth may mean, but fellow contestants acting within it.

9. It was in the nature of things that music *at first and for a long time clung to dances and songs,* not merely, say, as in thought, for the sake of better understanding, so that dance and song may yet say somehow to the person devoid of feeling what tones and tonal successions mean. Without feeling for them, however, he would not understand this connection. He who is without feeling for music cannot account for why to such words one fiddles the way one does or in general dances to tones. "Mad hopping and leaping! and how they tire themselves without purpose purposefully, that is, according to critical aesthetics! And why is she singing? She may say what she will; it is unnatural for one to sing in emotion; one speaks." About opera one has often spoken in this way, and called it *criticism;* and about wordless music no differently. "Que me veux-tu, sonate? The Adagio sounds beautiful and tender; but why does one not underlay words to it? And how the tones here chase wildly and madly after, through, over, under, and next to one another! The senseless thing is called Presto?" Now to the Presto indeed no words might be underlaid: for what nightingale, present in every voice, could whistle or slip through them?

10. For a much deeper reason than such a rationalization did

music long cling to dance and song, namely, because these are the outward manifestations of its type, *the equivalently natural expression of its energy,* of *buoyancy* in time, of *rhythm.* Just as one does not dance without music, so young people do not hear it without a desire to dance; it leaps up in their limbs and in their gestures. With a newspaper article no one thinks of music; but let us read a passage that is wholly and passionately the language of feeling; one wants to, one must read it aloud with tone and gesture. Tone and gesture summon music to it, just as reciprocally with sweet melodic passages one not only wishes for words but even without speech creates them himself in his feeling. This natural bond between tone, gesture, and word all peoples have recognized or felt, and have entrusted it with the whole expression of their feeling. What nature had bound together, indeed what in the expression of the various senses was one, they did not want to sunder forcibly. Hence Greek music remained true so long and gladly to dance, to gesture, to choruses, to dramatic representation, and these to it; as sisters of one descent they loved and completed one another, like expression and impression. In accordance with the decided excellence that we recognize in the dramatic and lyric poetry, and in general in the language—shaped through song and declamation—of the Greeks, we cannot conceive of their music—as far as it rules and leads dance, song, gestures, and words—and also of these arts corresponding to it, as sufficiently great and sensitive.

11. The *noble effect,* accordingly, that these arts so naturally belonging to one another produce in an ingenious combination is not to be doubted, since reliable evidence both from early times and still now in examples of musico-poetic peoples who dance and rejoice testifies to it and the nature of the matter itself demands it. For whom do the tones, for whom do the impassioned gestures of a voice that feelingly unites tones, gesture, and word not remain throughout the day ineradicably in the soul? Such a deep bond exists between gesture and tone, between voice and feeling, that in the moment of perception we attribute to the singer, believe of her, all that she so magically and naturally imparts to us. It is indeed, we say, now *her* words, *her* tones; the artist only provided the opportunity for the vivifier to reveal *her* subjectivity. What music and dance are capable of, Noverre's letters concerning them may say; and who does not know, even without action, only accom-

panied by *tones*, the power of poetic art? Besides the Italians of the past and the present, who has not been stirred in his entire soul by Handel's, Gluck's, and Mozart's magical tones?

12. There are *three realms* in particular in which word and tone, tone and gesture, inwardly bound to one another, act strongly: the realms of *reverence*, of *love*, and of *active power*. *Reverence* has all the feelings at its disposal, from failing weakness to the most encompassing force and omnipotence, from anxious sorrow to loud rejoicing. The simplest in words, tones, and gestures here designates and effects the greatest, the most. The realm of *love* also has its maximum in longing and succeeding, in strife and victory, in grief and joy. The tender is its character. *Power* finally changes nature; it forms and transforms through courage, through decision and action. Nod and execution is its watchword. In all three realms we possess the most admirable masterworks, with respect to which it would be an ungrateful offense and sign of unfeeling lack of taste to sacrifice one species to the others. To each let there remain *its* place, *its* time. Even the so-called pictorial music is in the right place not expendable, if subduing or arousing natural forces, like the voice of the invisible, it supports the potent word, vitalizes the daring decision. Also to playful, prankish music let there remain its value: for is not our most intelligent, most cheerful existence jest and joy?

13. All this in the meantime would be misunderstood if one wished to infer that *tone may never be permitted to separate from word or from gesture*, so that these had to accompany and interpret it in its every smallest step. Burdensome companions in that case; and what do they wish to interpret through word or gesture in every note of transition? To designate *thoughts* speech is given to us; *feelings* it only compiles, and expresses more of them through what it does not than through what it does say. A chattering feeling becomes intolerable; since this chatter intends precisely to replace it and thus shows it as inauthentic. Tones may pursue and overtake themselves, contradict and repeat one another; the flight and return of these magical spirits of the air is precisely the essence of the art that acts through buoyancy. Words that rush and stumble over one another, on the other hand, that snatch at every stroke of the bow, that gulp at every breath of air, are particularly for slowly speaking peoples a babbling unseemly to speech and music. Music also must have the freedom to speak alone, as indeed the tongue speaks in

its own right, and song and speech do not entirely employ the same instrument. Without words, merely through and in itself, music has shaped itself into an art of *its* kind. Pan, who on his reed pipe summoned the *echo* and required in addition no words, no gestures—He was Pan, summoner and announcer of the music of the universe. Apollo, who invented the lyre when the swan alone hearkened to him, became through himself and this lyre the founder of all the choruses of the Muses. Orpheus by the language of his strings moved Orcus; to the words of a mortal the Eumenides would not have hearkened.

You, then, you who scorn the music of tones as such and can derive nothing from it, have nothing to do with it without words! Keep away from it! Regard it as play in which "purposive-purposeless" instruments are exercised! But you, musicians, set down before your music hall in the fashion of Plato the words: "Let no stranger to the Muses enter!"

14. How difficult it became for music to separate itself from its sisters, words, and gestures, and to develop for itself as an art, is demonstrated by the slow course of its history. A special, compelling means was called for to make it independent and to sever it from external support.

With the Greeks, that is to say, music had guided poetry, serving it, and mostly therefore only in recitative; in types of execution it gained much in this way, but only as a servant under the rule of the poet. In the dance, where it seemed the mistress, it was commanded by the festival, the circle, the form, and gestural art of human beings. What helped it upward, that trusting its own strength, it lifted itself aloft on its own wings? What was the something that severed it from everything foreign, from sight, dance, gestures, even from the accompanying voice? *Reverence.* It is reverence that raises men and a gathering of men above words and gestures, for then nothing remains to their feelings but— tones. What do they not have, however, in these tones, that is, in the sensations adhering to them? What do they lack in this high, free realm?

15. Reverence does not want to see who sings; from heaven the tones come to it; it sings in the heart; the heart itself sings and plays. Just as the tone, then, freed from the struck string or from its narrow pipe, resounds freely in the heavens, certain that it is affecting every sympathetic being, and reechoing everywhere, in

the contest of the echo is born anew, is imparted anew: so reverence, borne aloft by tones, hovers pure and free above the earth, enjoying as one the universe, in one tone harmoniously all tones. And as in each little dissonance it has a sense of itself, sensing in the narrow compass of our few tonal successions and keys *all* the vibrations, motions, modes, and accentuations of the universe; is there still a question whether music will surpass in inner effect every art that clings to the visible? It *must* surpass them, as spirit does the *body:* for it is spirit, related to great nature's innermost force—*motion.* What visually cannot become communicable to man, the world of the invisible, becomes so to him in *its* fashion, in its fashion alone. It speaks to him, arousing, acting; he himself (he knows not how), without effort and so powerfully, acting along with it.

16. *Transient,* therefore, is every moment of this art and must be so: for precisely the *briefer* and *longer, stronger* and *weaker, higher* and *lower, more* and *less* is its *meaning,* its *impression.* In arrival and flight, in becoming and having been, lies the conquering force of tone and sensation. Just as the one and the other fuse with many, rise, sink, and are submerged, and on the taut line of harmony, in accordance with eternal, indissoluble laws, again rise up and act anew, so my heart, my courage, my love and hope. In contrast, every art of contemplation, which clings to circumscribed objects and gestures, even to local colors, although it at once shows all, is nevertheless grasped only *slowly,* and because nothing visible can sustain perfection, at the end rewards us with satiety, as though *outlasting* itself. On fleet tones come and fly away, you wandering spirits of the air; stir my heart and leave behind in me, through you, for you, an endless longing.

17. For the rest the strife over the *value* of the arts among themselves or with reference to the nature of man is at all times empty and meaningless. Space cannot be turned into time, time into space, the visible into the audible, nor this into the visible; let none take on a foreign field, but let it rule in its own the more powerful, the more certain, the more noble. Precisely because the arts in respect of their medium exclude one another, they secure their realm; united nowhere but in the nature of man, in the midpoint of our sensation. How this is to enjoy and arrange them depends on our taste, or much more on our ordering reason. If this, because between tones and colors an analogy can be conceived, wishes to

treat tone as colors, colors as tones, to see pictures in music, and to paint in pastel the pictures of poetry as the poet conveyed them: then let it do so. The arts themselves are innocent of this tastelessness of a spurious reason.

* * *

The "general valid and necessary judgments of the critical power of judgment on the connection of the fine arts in one and the same product, as also the comparison of the aesthetic value of the fine arts among themselves" will thus not busy us for long. If music is a *"play of tone,* as painting is an *art of color,* where in the first the question still remains whether it is to be considered as a fine or only as a pleasing art (like the art of cooking, say, like gambling and jesting:" then the critical assertion may not offend us that it "speaks without concepts *through* mere sensations that are produced externally, is *only* transient, and more enjoyment than culture (The play of ideas that is excited by it *incidentally* is only the effect of an *almost mechanical* association), that it therefore judged *through* reason has less value than any other of the fine arts. Hence it demands, like *every* enjoyment, *frequent* change, and does not endure *repeated* repetition without *creating* boredom." Contrary to all experience. Precisely music conveys and demands repetition most among all the arts; in none is *ancora* so often heard. A mere *decomposition* of the tones, that is, harmony, tires and must tire, because it always says the same thing, and in addition a very well-known one; *true music,* however, that is, melody, the buoyant line of the whole course of the tones, becomes precisely through its repetition more enjoyable; its effect can become intensified up to the point of rapture. Passages that move us inwardly we cannot hear enough. Oh, and they die away! Insatiably we then wish for their return, until they (so we intend) come with us and remain our soul. Images abandon us and grow faint; tones come with us as our innermost friends, who from childhood on cheered and raised us up, delighted and strengthened us. "When one estimates the value of the fine arts according to the culture that they bring to the soul, and takes as a standard the broadening of the capacities that must come together in the power of cognitive judgment, then music has the lowest place among the fine arts, because it *merely plays with sensations.*" Miserable music that does this; toneless heart that in all music hears only a play with sensations. . . .

If one was to gather together without all the fables the effects that tones and songs have produced on the human heart individually and in families, groups, and nations, a series of tales of wonder would raise music from the lowest position in which it was placed high aloft also in respect of the *culture of mankind*. "The ideas of music are of *transitory* impression; they are extinguished either entirely, or when they are repeated involuntarily by the imagination they are rather burdensome to us than pleasing." Miserable music that involuntarily returning becomes a burden! And a heart to which returning tones that once were lovely to it become a burden, in what state could this be? In dreams themselves there sounds to us nothing more celestial than music; it exceeds in charm all dreamed-of beautiful forms. The dying, finally, as examples show, are raised up from the earth by a tone heard inwardly.

Translated by Edward A. Lippman

Johann Nikolaus Forkel

Bach the Composer
(1802)

Bach's first attempts at composition, like all early efforts, were unsatisfactory. Lacking special instruction to direct him toward his goal, he was compelled to do what he could in his own way, like others who have set out upon a career without a guide. Most youthful composers let their fingers run riot up and down the keyboard, snatching handfuls of notes, assaulting the instrument in wild frenzy, in hope that something may result from it. Such people are merely Finger Composers—in his riper years Bach used to call them Harpsichord Knights—that is to say, their fingers tell them what to write instead of being instructed by the brain what to play. Bach abandoned that method of composition when he observed that brilliant flourishes lead nowhere. He realized that musical ideas need to be subordinated to a plan and that the young composer's first need is a model to instruct his efforts. Opportunely Vivaldi's *Concertos for the Violin,* then recently published, gave him the guidance he needed. He had often heard them praised as admirable works of art, and conceived the happy idea of arranging them for the clavier. Hence he was led to study their structure, the musical ideas on which they are built, the variety of their modulations, and other characteristics. Moreover, in adapting to the clavier ideas and phrases originally written for the violin, Bach was compelled to put his brain to work, and so freed his inspiration from dependence on his fingers. Henceforth he was able to draw ideas out of his own storehouse, and having placed himself on the right road, needed only perseverance and hard work to succeed. And how persevering he was! He even robbed himself of sleep to practice in the night what he had written during the day! But the diligence he bestowed upon his own compositions did not hinder him from studying the works of Frescobaldi, Froberger, Kerl, Pachelbel, Fischer, Strungk, Buxtehude, Reinken, Bruhns, Böhm, and certain French organists who were famed in those days as masters of harmony and fugue.

The models he selected—Church musicians for the most part— and his own disposition inclined him to serious and exalted subjects. But in that kind of music little can be accomplished with inadequate technique. Bach's first object, therefore, was to develop his power of expressing himself before he attempted to realize the ideal that beckoned him. Music to him was a language, and the composer a poet who, whatever the idiom he affects, must first of all have at his disposal the means of making himself intelligible to others. But the technique of his period Bach found limited in variety and insufficiently pliable. Therefore he set himself at the outset to refashion the accepted harmonic system. He did so in a manner characteristically individual and bearing the impress of his personality.

If the language of music is merely the utterance of a melodic line, a simple sequence of musical notes, it can justly be accused of poverty. The addition of a bass puts it upon a harmonic foundation and clarifies it, but defines rather than gives it added richness. A melody so accompanied—even though all the notes are not those of the true bass—or treated with simple embellishments in the upper parts, or with simple chords, used to be called homophony. But it is a very different thing when two melodies are so interwoven that they converse together like two persons upon a footing of pleasant equality. In the first case the accompaniment is subordinate, and serves merely to support the first or principal part. In the second case the two parts are not similarly related. New melodic combinations spring from their interweaving, out of which new forms of musical expression emerge. If more parts are interwoven in the same free and independent manner, the apparatus of language is correspondingly enlarged, and becomes practically inexhaustible if, in addition, varieties of form and rhythm are introduced. Hence harmony becomes no longer a mere accompaniment of melody, but rather a potent agency for augmenting the richness and expressiveness of musical conversation. To serve that end a simple accompaniment will not suffice. True harmony is the interweaving of several melodies, which emerge now in the upper, now in the middle, and now in the lower parts.

From about the year 1720, when he was thirty-five, until his death in 1750, Bach's harmony consists in this melodic interweaving of independent melodies, so perfect in their union that each part seems to constitute the true melody. Herein Bach excels all the composers in the world. At least, I have found no one to equal him in music known to me. Even in his four-part writing we can, not infrequently, leave out the upper and lower parts and still find the middle parts melodious and agreeable.

But in harmony of this kind each part must be highly plastic; otherwise it cannot play its role as an actual melody and at the same time combine with the other parts. To produce it Bach followed a course of his own, upon which the textbooks of his day were silent, but which his genius suggested to him. Its originality consists in the freedom of his part writing, in which he transgresses, seemingly, at any rate, rules long established and to his contemporaries almost sacred. Bach, however, realized their object, which was simply to facilitate the flow of pure melody on a sound harmonic basis, in other words, successive and coexistent euphony, and he succeeded with singular success, though by unfamiliar means. Let me explain my meaning more closely.

Between simple intervals there is little difficulty in deciding whether the second note must rise or fall. And in regard to phrases, or sections of a phrase, if we analyze their structure and follow out their harmonic tendency, their resolution is equally clear. But this sense of destination may be provoked in each part by different intervals. As we have observed already, every one of the four parts must flow melodically and freely. But to secure that result it will be necessary to introduce between the notes that begin a phrase and establish its general atmosphere other notes that often are not consonant with those employed in the other parts and whose incidence is goverened by the accent. This is what we call a *transitus regularis et irregularis*. Each part starts from a fixed point, and returns to it, but travels freely between them. No one has made more use of such progressions than Bach in order to color his parts and give them a characteristic melodic line. Hence, unless his music is played with perfect fluency, occasional passages will sound harshly and we may be tempted to accuse him of exaggeration. But the charge is ill founded. Once we play them as Bach intended them, such passages reveal their full beauty and their attractive though bizarre dissonance opens up new vistas in the realm of sound.

But, to speak in detail of Bach's transgression of recognized rules: To begin with, he admitted octaves and fifths provided they sounded well; that is, when the cause of their being forbidden did not arise. Everybody knows that there are positions in which they sound well, and others when they should be avoided, owing to the harsh effect or thin harmony they produce. Bach's octaves and fifths never produce bad or thin harmony, and he was very definite as to when they could and could not be used. In certain circumstances he would not permit hidden fifths and octaves even between the middle parts, though we exclude them only between the outer parts. Yet, on occasion he used them in such a barefaced manner as to puzzle the beginner in composition. But their use very soon commends itself. Even in the last revision of his early compositions we find him altering passages, which at first sight appear impeccable, with the object of enriching their harmony and without scrupling to use hidden octaves. A remarkable instance occurs in the first part of the "Well-tempered Clavier," in the E major Fugue, between the fifth and fourth bars from the end. I regret to this hour that, on looking over the later text, from which Hoffmeister and Kühnel's edition of that work is printed, I was so foolish as to reject Bach's amended reading there, merely because the harmony is unorthodox though more pleasing. I stupidly preferred the older, more correct, and harsher reading, though in the later text the three parts run easily and smoothly. And what more can one demand?

Again, there is a rule that every note raised by an accidental cannot be doubled in the chord, because the raised note must, from its nature, resolve on the note above. If it is doubled, it must rise doubled in both parts and, consequently, form consecutive octaves. Such is the rule. But Bach frequently doubles not only notes accidentally raised elsewhere in the scale but actually the *semitonium modi* or leading note itself. Yet he avoids consecutive octaves. His finest works yield examples of this.

Again, Bach's statement that "over a pedal point all intervals are permissible that occur in the three scales" should be regarded rather as an expansion than a violation of the recognized rule. In general what is called an organ point is merely a retarded close. Bach, however, did not hesitate to employ it in the middle of a piece; a striking example occurs in the last gigue of the "English Suites." On a first hearing this gigue, imperfectly rendered, may not sound well. But it grows more beautiful as it becomes more familiar, and what seemed harsh is found to be smooth and agreeable, until one never tires of playing and hearing it.

Bach's modulation was as original and characteristic as his harmony, and as closely related to it. But the two things, though closely associated, are not the same. By harmony we mean the concordance of several parts; by modulation, their progression through keys. Modulation can take place in a single part. Harmony requires more than one. I will endeavor to make my meaning clearer.

Most composers stick closely to their tonic key and modulate out of it with deliberation. In music that requires a large number of performers, and in a building, for instance a church, where the large volume of sound dies away slowly, such a habit shows good sense in the composer who wishes his work to produce the best possible effect. But in chamber or instrumental music it is not always a proof of wisdom, but rather of mental poverty. Bach saw clearly that the two styles demand different treatment. In his large choral compositions he bridles his exuberant fancy. In his instrumental works he lets himself go. As he never courted popularity, but always pursued his ideal, Bach had no reason to suppress the nobility of his inspirations, or to lower their standard for public consumption. Nor did he ever do so. Therefore every modulation in his instrumental work is a new thought, a constantly progressive creation in the plane of the chosen keys and those related to them. He holds fast to the essentials of harmony, but with every modulation introduces a new suggestion and glides so smoothly to the end of a piece that no creaking of machinery is perceptible; yet no single bar—I might almost say no part of a bar—is like another. Every modulation bears a strict relationship to the key from which it proceeds, and springs naturally from it. Bach ignored, or rather despised, the sudden sallies by which many composers seek to surprise their hearers. Even in his chromatic passages his progressions are so smooth and easy that we are hardly conscious of them, however extreme they may be. He makes us feel that he has not stepped outside the diatonic scale, so quick is he to seize upon the consonances common to dissonant systems and combine them to his sure purpose.

Translated by Charles Sanford Terry

The Genius of Bach

It is surely unnecessary to ask whether that artist is a genius who, in every form of his art, has produced masterpiece after masterpiece, of an originality that sets them above the achievements of all other ages, distinguished also by a wealth of originality and agreeableness that enslaves every hearer. The most fertile fancy, invention inexhaustible, a judgment so nice as to reject intuitively every irrelevant and jarring detail, unerring ingenuity in employing the most delicate and minute resources of his art, along with an unrivaled technique—these qualities, whose expression demands the outpouring of a man's whole soul, are the signboards of genius. The man who cannot find them in Bach's music either is not acquainted with it at all or knows it imperfectly. One needs to be steeped in it thoroughly to appreciate the genius of its author. For the greater the work the closer study is demanded for its apprehension. The butterfly method, a sip here and there, is of little use.

But admirable as were the gifts Bach received from nature, he could never have become an accomplished genius had he not learned betimes to avoid the rocks on which many artists, some of them perhaps not less gifted than he, too often founder. I will communicate to the reader some scattered thoughts on the subject and conclude this essay with an indication of the characteristics of Bach's genius.

Even the largest natural gifts, coupled with the strongest propensity for a particular art, offer no more than fruitful soil on which that art may thrive by patient cultivation. Industry, the true begetter of every art and science, is an indispensable factor. Not only does it enable genius to master technique, but it stimulates the critical and reflective faculties also. The very ease with which genius acquires and applies the apparatus of musical composition frequently entices it to leap over root principles in its plunge into deeper waters, or to fly before its wings are grown. In such a case, unless genius is guided back to neglected fundamentals and forced to build itself upon the great examples of the past, it will inevitably expend its treasure uselessly and never attain to its promised dimensions. For it is an axiom, that real progress can never be made, nor the highest perfection be attained, if the foundations are insecure. If arduous heights are to be achieved, the easier obstacles must first be approached and overcome. Guided by his own inexperience no one ever can hope to become great. He must profit by the practice and example of others.

Bach did not founder on this rock. His soaring genius attended an equally ardent industry that incessantly impelled him, whenever he found his own equipment insufficient, to seek guidance from others. Vivaldi and his concertos were the first from whom he sought counsel. From them he turned to the principal organ and clavier composers of the period. Nothing is more intellectually stimulating than counterpoint, and the composers Bach studied were distinguished by their mastery of it, as their fugal writing attests. Hence Bach's diligent study and imitation of them pointed his taste and imagination to perceive wherein himself was lacking and what steps were needed to take him farther in his art.

A second rock upon which genius often comes to grief is the public's undiscriminating applause. To be sure, I do not undervalue public approval or commend without reserve the remark of a Greek teacher to his pupil, "You performed badly, otherwise the audience would not have applauded you." Yet is is nonetheless true that many artists are thrown off their balance by exaggerated and often unmerited plaudits, particularly in their early careers before they have acquired self-discipline and sound judgment. The public merely asks for what it can understand, whereas the true artist ought to aim at an achievement that cannot be measured by popular standards. How, then, can popular applause be reconciled with the true artist's aspirations toward the ideal? Bach never sought applause, and held with Schiller:

> Kannst du nicht allen gefallen durch deine That und
> dein Kunstwerk,
> Mach' es wenigen recht; vielen gefallen ist schlimm.

Like every true artist, Bach worked to please himself in his own way, obeying the summons of his own genius, choosing his own subjects, and finding satisfaction only in the approval of his own judgment. He could count on the applause of all who understood good music, and never failed to receive it. Under what other conditions can sound works of art emerge? The composer who debases his muse to the popular mood either lacks real genius or, having it, abuses it. For to catch the ear of the public is not a difficult task and merely connotes an agreeable facility. Composers of that class are like artisans who frankly fashion their goods to suit their market. But Bach never condescended to such artifices. The artist, in his judgment, is the dictator of public taste, not its slave. If, as often happened, he was asked to write something simple for the clavier he would answer, "I will do what I can." He would choose an easy theme. But when he began to develop it he always found so much to say that the piece soon became anything but simple. If his attention was drawn to the fact, he would answer smilingly, "Practice it well and you will find it quite easy. You have as many good fingers on each hand as I have." Nor was he prompted in this by mere contradictoriness, but exhibited the true artist spirit.

It was, in fact, the artist temperament that led Bach to make the great and sublime his goal. For that reason his music is not merely agreeable, like other composers', but transports us to the regions of the ideal. It does not arrest our attention momentarily but grips us the stronger the oftener we listen to it, so that after a thousand hearings its treasures are still unexhausted and yield fresh beauties to excite our wonder. Even the beginner who knows but the ABC of his art warms with pleasure when he hears Bach's music and can open his ear and heart to it. It was the true artist spirit, too, that guided Bach to unite majesty and grandeur of design with meticulous care for detail and the most refined elegance, characteristics that we rather seek, perhaps, in works whose object is merely to give pleasure. Bach held strongly that if the strands are imperfect, the whole design is faulty. His genius is sublime and impressive, and he never condescends to be frivolous even when he touches the lighter forms of art.

To conclude: it was the union of astounding genius and indefatigable application that enabled Bach to widen at every point the domain of musical expression. His successors have failed to maintain the art at the level to which he raised it. If Bach was more successful, if he was able to produce great work of convincing beauty and imperishable as a model for those who came after him, we owe it as much to his application as to his genius.

This man, the greatest orator-poet that ever addressed the world in the language of music, was a German! Let Germany be proud of him! Yes, proud of him, but worthy of him, too!

Translated by Charles Sanford Terry

E. T. A. (Ernst Theodor Amadeus) Hoffmann

Beethoven's Instrumental Music
(1813)

When we speak of music as an independent art, should we not always restrict our meaning to instrumental music, which, scorning every aid, every admixture of another art (the art of poetry), gives pure expression to music's specific nature, recognizable in this form alone? It is the most romantic of all the arts—one might almost say, the only genuinely romantic one—for its sole subject is the infinite. The lyre of Orpheus opened the portals of Orcus—music discloses to man an unknown realm, a world that has nothing in common with the external sensual world that surrounds him, a world in which he leaves behind him all definite feelings to surrender himself to an inexpressible longing.

Have you even so much as suspected this specific nature, you miserable composers of instrumental music, you who have laboriously strained yourselves to represent definite emotions, even definite events? How can it ever have occurred to you to treat after the fashion of the plastic arts the art diametrically opposed to plastic? Your sunrises, your tempests, your *Batailles des trois Empereurs,* and the rest, these, after all, were surely quite laughable aberrations, and they have been punished as they well deserved by being wholly forgotten.

In song, where poetry, by means of words, suggests definite emotions, the magic power of music acts as does the wondrous elixir of the wise, a few drops of which make any drink more palatable and more lordly. Every passion—love, hatred, anger, despair, and so forth, just as the opera gives them to us—is clothed by music with the purple luster of romanticism, and even what we have undergone in life guides us out of life into the realm of the inifinite.

As strong as this is music's magic, and, growing stronger and stronger, it had to break each chain that bound it to another art.

That gifted composers have raised instrumental music to its present high estate is due, we may be sure, less to the more readily handled means of expression (the greater perfection of the instruments, the greater virtuosity of the players) than to the more profound, more intimate recognition of music's specific nature.

Mozart and Haydn, the creators of our present instrumental music, were the first to show us the art in its full glory; the man who then looked on it with all his love and penetrated its innermost being is—Beethoven! The instrumental compositions of these three masters breathe a similar romantic spirit—this is due to their similar intimate understanding of the specific nature of the art; in the character of their compositions there is none the less a marked difference.

In Haydn's writing there prevails the expression of a serene and childlike personality. His symphonies lead us into vast green woodlands, into a merry, gaily colored throng of happy mortals. Youths and maidens float past in a circling dance; laughing children, peering out from behind the trees, from behind the rose bushes, pelt one another playfully with flowers. A life of love, of bliss like that before the Fall, of eternal youth; no sorrow, no suffering, only a sweet melancholy yearning for the beloved object that floats along, far away, in the glow of the sunset and comes no nearer and does not disappear—nor does night fall while it is there, for it is itself the sunset in which hill and valley are aglow.

Mozart leads us into the heart of the spirit realm. Fear takes us in its grasp, but without torturing us, so that it is more an intimation of the infinite. Love and melancholy call to us with lovely spirit voices; night comes on with a bright purple luster, and with inexpressible longing we follow those figures that, waving us familiarly into their train, soar through the clouds in eternal dances of the spheres.

Thus Beethoven's instrumental music opens up to us also the realm of the monstrous and the immeasurable. Burning flashes of light shoot through the deep night of this realm, and we become aware of giant shadows that surge back and forth, driving us into narrower and narrower confines until they destroy *us*—but not the pain of that endless longing in which each joy that has climbed aloft in jubilant song sinks back and is swallowed up, and it is only in this pain, which consumes love, hope, and happiness but does not destroy them, which seeks to burst our breasts with a many-voiced consonance of all the passions, that we live on, enchanted beholders of the supernatural!

Romantic taste is rare, romantic talent still rarer, and this is doubtless why there are so few to strike that lyre whose sound discloses the wondrous realm of the romantic.

Haydn grasps romantically what is human in human life; he is more commensurable, more comprehensible for the majority.

Mozart calls rather for the superhuman, the wondrous element that abides in inner being.

Beethoven's music sets in motion the lever of fear, of awe, of horror, of suffering, and wakens just that infinite longing that is the essence of romanticism. He is accordingly a completely romantic composer, and is not this perhaps the reason why he has less success with vocal music, which excludes the character of indefinite longing, merely representing emotions defined by words as emotions experienced in the realm of the infinite?

The musical rabble is oppressed by Beethoven's powerful genius; it seeks in vain to oppose it. But knowing critics, looking about them with a superior air, assure us that we may take their word for it as men of great intellect and deep insight that, while the excellent Beethoven can scarcely be denied a very fertile and lively imagination, he does not know how to bridle it! Thus, they say, he no longer bothers at all to select or to shape his ideas, but, following the so-called demonic method, he dashes everything off exactly at his ardently active imagination dictates it to him. Yet how does the matter stand if it is *your* feeble observation alone that the deep inner continuity of Beethoven's every composition eludes? If it is *your* fault alone that you do not understand the master's language as the initiated understand it, that the portals of the innermost sanctuary remain closed to you? The truth is that, as regards self-possession, Beethoven stands quite on a par with Haydn and Mozart and that, separating his ego from the inner realm of harmony, he rules over it as an absolute monarch. In Shakespeare, our knights of the aesthetic measuring-rod have often bewailed the utter lack of inner unity and inner continuity, although for those who look more deeply there springs forth, issuing from a single bud, a beautiful tree, with leaves, flowers, and fruit; thus, with Beethoven, it is only after a searching investigation of his instrumental music that the high self-possession inseparable from true genius and nourished by the study of the art stands revealed.

Can there be any work of Beethoven's that confirms all this to a higher degree than his indescribably profound, magnificent Symphony in C minor? How this wonderful composition, in a climax that climbs on and on, leads the listener imperiously forward into the spirit world of the infinite! . . . No doubt the whole rushes like an ingenious rhapsody past many a man, but the soul of each thoughtful listener is assuredly stirred, deeply and intimately, by a feeling that is none other than that unutterable portentous longing, and until the final chord—indeed, even in the moments that follow it—he will be powerless to step out of that wondrous spirit realm where grief and joy embrace him in the form of sound. The internal structure of the movements, their execution, their instrumentation, the way in which they follow one another—everything contributes to a single end; above all, it is the intimate interrelationship among the themes that engenders that unity which alone has the power to hold the listener firmly in a single mood. This relationship is sometimes clear to the listener when he overhears it in the connecting of two movements or discovers it in the fundamental bass they have in common; a deeper relationship that does not reveal itself in this way speaks of other times only from mind to mind, and it is precisely this relationship that prevails between sections of the two allegros and the minuet and that imperiously proclaims the self-possession of the master's genius.

How deeply thy magnificent compositions for the piano have impressed themselves upon my soul, thou sublime master; how shallow and insignificant now all seems to me that is not thine, or by the gifted Mozart or that mighty genius, Sebastian Bach! With what joy I received thy seventieth work, the two glorious trios, for I knew full well that after a little practice I should soon hear them in truly splendid style. And in truth, this evening things went so well with me that even now, like a man who wanders in the mazes of a fantastic park, woven about with all manner of exotic trees and plants and marvelous flowers, and who is drawn further and further in, I am powerless to find my way out of the marvelous turns and windings of thy trios. The lovely siren voices of these movements of thine, resplendent in their many-hued variety, lure me on and on. The gifted lady who indeed honored me, Capell-meister Kreisler, by playing today the first trio in such splendid style, the gifted lady before whose piano I still sit and write, has made me realize quite clearly that only what the mind produces calls for respect and that all else is out of place.

Just now I have repeated at the piano from memory certain striking transitions from the two trios.

* * *

How well the master has understood the specific character of the instrument and fostered it in the way best suited to it!

A simple but fruitful theme, songlike, susceptible to the most varied contrapuntal treatments, curtailments, and so forth, forms the basis of each movement; all remaining subsidiary themes and figures are intimately related to the main idea in such a way that the details all interweave arranging themselves among the instruments in highest unity. Such is the structure of the whole, yet in this artful structure there alternate in restless flight the most marvelous pictures in which joy and grief, melancholy and ecstasy, come side by side or intermingled to the fore. Strange figures begin a merry dance, now floating off into a point of light, now splitting apart, flashing and sparkling, evading and pursuing one another in various combinations, and at the center of the spirit realm thus disclosed the intoxicated soul gives ear to the unfamiliar language and understands the most mysterious premonitions that have stirred it.

That composer alone has truly mastered the secrets of harmony who knows how, by their means, to work upon the human soul; for him, numerical proportions, which to the dull grammarian are no more than cold, lifeless problems in arithmetic, become magical compounds from which to conjure up a magic world.

Despite the good nature that prevails, especially in the first trio, not even excepting the melancholy largo, Beethoven's genius is in the last analysis serious and solemn. It is as though the master thought that, in speaking of deep mysterious things—even when the spirit, intimately familiar with them, feels itself joyously and gladly uplifted—one may not use an ordinary language, only a sublime and glorious one; the dance of the priests of Isis can be only an exultant hymn. Where instrumental music is to produce its effect simply through itself as music and is by no means to serve a definite dramatic purpose, it must avoid all trivial facetiousness, all frivolous *lazzi*. A deep temperament seeks, for the intimations of that joy that, an import from an unknown land, more glorious and more beautiful than here in our constricted world, enkindles an inner, blissful life within our breasts, a higher expression than can be given to it by mere words, proper only to our circumscribed earthly air. This seriousness, in all of Beethoven's works for instruments and for the piano, is in itself enough to forbid all those breakneck passages up and down for the two hands that fill our piano music in the latest style, all the queer leaps, the farcical capriccios, the notes towering high above the staff on their five- and six-line scaffolds.

On the side of mere digital dexterity, Beethoven's compositions for the piano really present no special difficulty, for every player must be presumed to have in his fingers the few runs, triplet figures, and whatever else is called for; nevertheless, their performance is on the whole quite difficult. Many a so-called virtuoso condemns this music, objecting that it is "very difficult" and into the bargain "very ungrateful."

Now, as regards difficulty, the correct and fitting performance of a work of Beethoven's asks nothing more than that one should understand him, that one should enter deeply into his being, that—conscious of one's own consecration—one should boldly dare to step into the circle of the magical phenomena that his powerful spell has evoked. He who is not conscious of this consecration, who regards sacred music as a mere game, as a mere entertainment for an idle hour, as a momentary stimulus for dull ears, or as a means of self-ostentation—let him leave Beethoven's music alone. Only to such a man, moreover, does the objection "most ungrateful" apply. The true artist lives only in the work that he has understood as the composer meant it and that he then performs. He is above putting his own personality forward in any way, and all his endeavors are directed toward a single end—that all the wonderful enchanting pictures and apparitions that the composer has sealed into his work with magic power may be called into active life, shining in a thousand colors, and that they may surround mankind in luminous sparkling circles and, enkindling its imagination, its innermost soul, may bear it in rapid flight into the faraway spirit realm of sound.

Translated by Oliver Strunk

Arthur Schopenhauer

From *The World as Will and Representation* (1819)

Music—the Unique Art

We have now considered all the fine arts in those general terms relevant to our purpose, beginning with architecture, whose aim as such is to crystallize the will's objectification at the lowest level of its visible aspect. Here it reveals itself as something circumscribed by law, a ponderous striving of inert matter incapable of cognition, yet even at this stage revealing internal conflict and strife, namely, between gravity and rigidity. . . . We concluded our exposition with tragedy, which, at the highest level of the will's objectification, brings that very conflict before our eyes on a fearful scale and with fearful clarity. Yet there is still one fine art that has of necessity been excluded from consideration, since in the systematic exposition of our theory there was no suitable place for it.

This art is music. It stands quite apart from all the others. In it, we do not perceive an imitation or a copy of some idea of the things that exist in the world. Even so, it is such a great and eminently splendid art, it creates such a powerful reaction in man's inmost depths, it is so thoroughly and profoundly understood by him as a uniquely universal language, even exceeding in clarity that of the phenomenal world itself, that we must certainly look for more in it than Leibniz's "exercitium arithmeticae occultum nescientis se numerari animi," even though Leibniz was quite right, in that he was speaking only of immediate and external significance. However, if music were no more than this, the satisfaction it affords would be akin to what we experience when we correctly solve a mathematical exercise and it could not be that intimate joy with which we see the innermost depths of our being expressed. Looking at the matter, then, from the point of view of aesthetic effect, we must seek a much deeper and more serious significance, one that relates to the innermost nature of the world and of ourselves, a significance whereby the numerical relationships into which music may be analyzed are held to be not what music is but only what it symbolizes. We may infer by analogy from the other arts that it must relate to the world in some sense or other as a representation does to what is represented, as a copy does to a model; for all the arts possess this character. Music's effect on us is on the whole similar to theirs, but stronger, more immediate, effective, and inevitable. The way in which it relates to the world must also be very profound, infinitely true and really striking, since it is immediately and universally comprehensible; and hence there is a certain infallibility about it in that its form can be reduced to certain definite rules, expressible in numerical terms, from which it may not deviate at all without altogether ceasing to be music. Nonetheless, the point of comparison between music and the world, the relationship in which the one stands to the other as an imitation or copy lies hidden very deep. Music has been performed in all ages without there being any accounting for this relationship. Content with directly responding to it, people renounce abstract understanding of any such direct response.

How Music Relates to the Will

(Platonic) ideas are the adequate objectification of the will; the object of all the other arts is cognition of these objectifications by means of the representation of individual objects (for that is what works of art themselves always are), and this is possible only when some change takes place in the subject reacting to them. Thus the other arts all objectify the will only indirectly, i.e., by means of ideas, and as our world is nothing but the appearance of a multiplicity of ideas, through entry into the *principium individuationis* (the form of cognition available to the individual as such), so music, which bypasses ideas, is also totally independent of the phenomenal world; it simply ignores the world, and it could in some sense continue to exist even if the world did not, something that cannot be said of the other arts. Music, in other words, is just as *immediate* an objectification and image of the entire *will* as the world itself is, as immediate, in fact, as those ideas are that in their multiplicity of appearances constitute the world of individual objects. Music is thus in no sense, like the other arts, the image of ideas, but the image of the *will itself*, which also takes objective shape in ideas; and for this very reason the effect of music is far more powerful and penetrates far more deeply than that of the other arts; for they communicate only shadows, whereas it communicates the essence. Since, however, the same will takes objective shape in ideas as in music, only rather differently in each case, there must therefore be, not perhaps an immediate resemblance, but at any rate a parallel, an analogy, between music and ideas, whose appearance in variety and imperfection constitutes the visible world. The demonstration of this analogy will, as an illustration, make it easier to understand this explanation, which the obscurity of the subject has made difficult.

The Analogy between Music and the Phenomenal World

I recognize in the deepest notes of harmony, in the fundamental bass, the lowest level of the will's objectification, inorganic nature, the mass of the planets. All the high notes, light and more rapidly dying away, should clearly be considered as arising out of the secondary vibrations of the deep fundamental, vibrations that simultaneously and gently sound whenever the fundamental does. It is a harmonic law that only those upper notes may coincide with a bass note that really form a consonance with the bass note's upper partials (its *sons harmoniques*). Now this is analogous to the fact that all natural bodies and structures must be regarded as having been developed step-by-step from the mass of the planet, which both engenders and supports them; and the upper notes stand in the same relationship to the fundamental bass. Depth of pitch has a threshold beyond which no further sound can be heard—this is analogous to the fact that material cannot be perceived unless it has form and quality; in other words, without its being the expression of some power that cannot be more explicitly defined. In this power, however, an idea is expressed. It is also analogous in a more general sense to the fact that no matter can be totally independent of the will. Hence from sound as such a certain degree of pitch is inseparable just as a certain degree of expression of the will is from matter. The fundamental bass is thus to us in harmony what inorganic nature is in the world—the crudest mass on which everything is based and from which everything arises and develops. Further, I recognize in the combination of those subsidiary parts *[Ripienstimmen]* generated by the harmonic texture that lies between the bass and the leading melodic part, the entire step-by-step sequence of ideas in which the will objectifies itself. The parts lying closest to the bass are the lowest of those steps—bodies that are still inorganic, yet well able to express themselves in sound: the higher parts symbolize for me the world of plants and animals. The specific intervals of the scale parallel the specific degrees of objectification of the will and the separate species in nature. Deviations from arithmetical correctness in intervals occasioned by any kind of tempered scale or chosen tonality are analogous to individual deviations of a type from a species; furthermore, out-of-tune notes that do not correspond to a true interval may be compared to monstrous hybrids of two animal species or of man and animal. But all these bass and subsidiary parts that constitute the harmonic texture lack that coherence in progression that the upper part alone has, moving as it does in rapid and fluent runs and figures, whereas the others move more ponderously and lack any internal coherence. The deep bass moves most ponderously of all and represents mass in its crudest form; it rises and falls only in wide intervals, in thirds, fourths, and fifths, never stepwise, unless it is a transposed bass in double counterpoint. This slow gait is also physically essential; a rapid run or trill low down in inconceivable. The inner parts that move more rapidly, but still without melodic coherence or any sense of progression, parallel the animal world. The incoherent movement and the circumscribed part writing of all inner parts is analogous to the fact that, in the entire nonrational world, from crystal to perfect animal, no being has a truly coherent sense of self-awareness to shape its life into a significant whole, nor does it experience a succession of spiritual developments. None perfects itself by development of character [*Bildung*]; everything remains according to its kind, eternally static and determined by fixed laws. Finally, in melody, in the high, singing, principal part, which dominates the whole and progresses freely in a single, uninterrupted, coherent, and meaningful idea from start to finish, a complete entity in itself, I recognize the highest stage of the objectification of the will, the conscious life and strife of man. Just as he alone, being endowed with reason, is always aware of the past and the future, so that his material existence is complete, coherent, conscious, and of infinite potential, so *melody* alone has a significant, purposeful coherence from start to finish. Consequently, it tells the story of the will as illuminated by self-awareness, the will that imprints on the phenomenal world its successive actions. But melody expresses still more: it reveals the will's secret history, portrays its every movement, its every endeavor, everything that reason comprehends under the broad pejorative concept of emotion, being incapable of further abstraction. Thus it has always been claimed that music is the language of emotion and passion, just as words are the language of reason. . . .

Translated by Peter Le Huray and James Day

Georg Friedrich Wilhelm Hegel

From *The Aesthetics*
(1835)

Music and the Other Arts

αα. The representational arts are concerned with objective plastic beauty. They portray the human being in its universal and idealized form as a unity and avoid specifically individual detail that might otherwise compromise the coherence of the representation. Music must achieve its aim differently. The representational artist needs only to bring to light the idea that is veiled in the material shape, and the form that is already latent in it. Hence, each particular and essential individual feature simply adds more precise interpretative detail to a complete form that is already in the artist's mind, because an imprecise notion of the content for which he must find a shape is already latent there. For example, in a work of plastic art a human figure in a given situation will need a body, or hands, or feet or a trunk, or a head with specific expression and in a certain position, together with certain other shapes, and other circumstantial details. Each of these features depends on the others, so that each can combine with the others to produce an overall pattern of which it is an indispensable part. The development of the theme in this case merely involves a more detailed working of the given material. The more detailed the development of the resulting image before us, the more concentrated the unity and the more coherent the precise interrelationship of the parts. If the work is a genuine work of art, the more exact the detail the greater the unity of the whole. Now of course inner organization and overall coherence are equally essential in music, because each part depends on the existence of the others; but in this case, the material is developed rather differently, and the term *unity* has a more restricted meaning.

ββ. A musical theme should have a meaning that is complete in itself. If it is now repeated or developed by means of broader contrasts and a wider range of technical procedures, repetitions, key changes, developments in foreign keys, and so on, these procedures may easily strike us as irrelevant, since they belong more properly to the field of technical musical procedures and to the appreciation of harmonic ingenuity and resourcefulness. Nothing of all this is required nor communicated by the theme itself. In the representational arts, on the other hand, the execution of detail—the whole process, indeed, of going into detail itself—becomes a matter rather of delineating the content more and more precisely and analyzing it more searchingly. Yet it cannot really be denied that even in a musical composition some content can be expressed through the more obvious relationships, contrasts, tensions, transitions, complexities, and resolutions, that the themes undergo, now being expanded, now added to, now treated in alternation, the one theme now absorbing the other, now hurrying on, now changing, disappearing, reappearing elsewhere, now seemingly overwhelmed, and then triumphantly reemerging. But even in this case, such development does not achieve any deeper and more concentrated unity, as in sculpture and painting, but a unity that constitutes more of an expansion, a broadening, an extension, a digression, and eventual return. The thematic content may well be the unvarying point of departure, but it does not bind the whole together as it can do in the representational arts, especially those aspects of it that confine themselves to the portrayal of the human organism.

γγ. Music, in contrast to the other arts, enjoys enough in the way of inner formal freedom to be able more or less to abandon the content, the material at its disposal. The recall of a theme at will is, as it were, an act of self-realization on the artist's part, i.e., a discovery of the fact that *he* is the artist, having the power to proceed as his fancy takes him. All the same, improvisation is in this respect manifestly different from a finished piece of music intended as a coherent whole. In improvisation, freedom from restraint is an end in itself; the artist can, amongst other things, demonstrate his freedom to weave well-known melodies and passages into his extempore creation, he can display them in new lights, revealing their detail, he can lead to new ones, and progress even further from his starting point, diversifying his material ever more and more.

On the whole, however, a piece of music may either be developed fairly strictly (it thus in a manner of speaking achieves a unity more akin to that of the plastic arts); it may on the other hand be developed according to the intensity of the artist's feelings, by episodes that depart to a greater or lesser degree from the original, using such means as capricious variations of tempo, by the use of sudden pauses that are then swept aside as the rushing torrent resumes its course. While, then, the painter or sculptor should be recommended to study the forms of nature, the musician has no parallel field of study at his disposal, save for the forms that have already been developed that would have to be adhered to. The limitations and boundaries within which music must operate are largely predetermined by the nature of sound itself; this does not relate as closely to the content of what is being expressed as in the other arts. There is accordingly a great deal of room for freedom in the subjective manipulation of these materials.

This is the main aspect in which music differs from the objectively representative arts.

γ. *Thirdly*, on the other hand, music is most closely related to *poetry*, since both arts affect the senses through the use of the same medium—sound. There are nonetheless considerable differences between even these two arts, both in the way they make use of sound and in the methods of expression that they adopt. If then a text is a poetic work of art in its own right, music can be expected to add but little to it. The dramatic choruses of the ancients are a case in point, for in these music merely played a subordinate role. But if, on the other hand, music is given greater autonomy, the text must necessarily have slighter poetic value and must deal only with general emotions and broad imaginative concepts. A poetic exposition of profound thoughts will no more make a good text for music than will descriptions of natural physical objects or descriptive poetry in general. The texts of songs, operatic arias, oratorios, and suchlike may well be quite mediocre and of little technical and poetic merit. The poet should be self-effacing if the musician is to be given proper scope for his imagination. In this respect the Italians such as Metastasio have shown great skill. Schiller's poems are, of course, in no way intended to be set to music, and are clearly cumbersome and useless for such a purpose. Wherever music is skillfully developed, little or nothing can be understood of the text anyway, especially the way our German language is pronounced. It is plainly unmusical to focus one's interest on the text. Thus an Italian audience gossips, eats, and plays cards, and so on during the less-important scenes of an opera, but when an important aria or some other important piece of music begins, everyone is all attention. We Germans, on the other hand, concentrate our main attention on what happens to the operatic princes and princesses, and to their servants, squires, confidants, and lady's maids, and on what they say. Even now there are probably many people who perhaps regret the flow of the action whenever a tune starts up, and seek relief in chatter. In sacred music, too, the text is usually either a well-known credo or perhaps a compilation of excerpts from the psalms, the words being intended only as an excuse for a musical commentary. The music is thus something to be performed for its own sake; it is not designed to reinforce the impact of the text, but only rather its general substance, much in the way, perhaps, the painting selects it subject matter from biblical history.

Musical Interpretation of Content

We may ask in what *second* respect music *interprets [Auffassungs-weise]* things differently from the other arts when it seizes on and expresses a particular content, either as an accompaniment to a text, or independently of it. I have already suggested that of all the arts music has the greatest potential freedom not only from a specific text, but also from specific content. Music therefore achieves satisfactory expression by means of a closed sequence of combinations, variations, contrasts, and communication, all of which are part of the musical world of sound. But in such a case the music will be empty and meaningless and unworthy of consideration as art, since it lacks spiritual content and expression, which are essential to art. Music rises to the level of true art only when the sensuous element of sound in its innumerable combinations expresses something that is suitably spiritual. Such content may be more precisely expressed in words, or it may be felt more intuitively *[empfunden]* through the harmonic relationships and melodic animation of the notes themselves.

α. In this respect music's true task is to bring that content to life in the listener's *subjective inner consciousness,* not to present it either as a general and conscious mental *imaginative concept,* or a specific latent physical *shape*—even if such shape were artistically possible. Music has the difficult task of realizing in sound this life and movement in which it has its being, or of fusing with the words and imaginative concepts expressed, clothing them in sound in order to throw fresh light on them to stimulate a reaction in us and engage our sympathy.

αα. The inner consciousness itself thus becomes the form in which music contrives to embody its content. It can thus assimilate and clothe in the form of emotion whatever gets through to it. It is for this reason, though, that music must avoid imitating visual objects and must confine itself to making the listener more clearly aware of the workings of his inner self *[die Innerlichkeit dem Innern faßbar zu machen].* It may do this by causing the substantial inner depth of a particular content as such to penetrate the depths of our being. It may, on the other hand, choose to mirror the life and movement of a specific idea [*Gehalt*] in one individual *subjective* inner consciousness, so that this subjective inner consciousness thus becomes its own object.

ββ. The special characteristic relating the abstract inner consciousness most closely to music is *emotion,* the self-extending subjectivity of the ego. Emotion does in fact gravitate toward some content, but it still leaves this content confined within the ego unconnected with anything external and is not thereby formally connected with it. In this way, emotion always remains only the outward covering of the content. It is this field in which music operates.

γγ. From here music extends it range to cover every *specific* emotion of the soul, every degree of happiness, merriment, humor, moodiness, rejoicing, and jubilation; similarly such things as the various degrees of anxiety, trouble, sadness, mourning, care, pain, longing, and finally such things as awe, supplication, and love become part of the true sphere of musical expression.

β. The sounds of "Ahs" and "Ohs" that function as interjections, cries of pain, sobs, and laughter, are the most direct and vital nonartistic expression of the emotions and the states of soul. The soul thereby draws attention to and gives expression to its objective existence in a manner midway between birdsong, in which the bird projects itself in song, without any practical result, and derives pleasure from so doing, and withdrawal to the subconscious and to the world of inner thought itself.

Natural interjections of the kind, though, are not music, for unlike the sounds of speech they are of course not articulate, conscious symbols [Zeichen] of imaginative concepts. They thus express no predetermined content under the guise of a universal concept, but they give expression through sound of a mood and emotion that the sound itself directly symbolizes. Expressions of the kind afford the heart relief. Nonetheless, such relief is not aesthetic relief. Music, however, by means of specific tonal relationships must express emotions, purging them of intemperance and crudity.

γ. Thus music may well originate in interjections, but only when the interjections are properly shaped does it become music. In this sense music must artistically refine its raw material to a greater degree than painting and poetry do before that material can be used to express some spiritual content. Only later shall we need to look more closely at the manner in which tonal resources are employed; for the moment I shall simply repeat the observation that musical notes in themselves may differ enormously in type and quality, and may divide into or combine in the most varied kinds of compatible, essentially contrasting, related, or unrelated patterns. These contrasts and combinations, and the different ways in which they move and change, the way they are presented, progress, and conflict, resolve and dissolve into nothing, reflect to a greater or lesser degree the inner nature both of a particular content and of the emotions that are absorbed [sich bemächtigen]. Hence tonal relationships of a specific kind are now understood and given shape, expressing a conventionalized code what is latent in the depths of the spirit as specific content.

But the element of sound thus shows itself to be more closely related to the fundamental inner nature of a given content than any of the phenomenal material considered so far. This is because sound is not [befestigen] associated with spatial patterns, nor does it assume material substance in the form of differentiated objects that are extended in space. Sound operates [anheimfallen] much more within the ideal dimension of time. There is thus no question of any differentiation between simple inner being and the objectively physical. The same is true of the emotional form assumed by any content of the kind music is best suited to express. For in contemplation and mental conception, as the self-conscious processes of thought, a necessary distinction is immediately evident between the contemplating, conceptualizing, thinking ego and the contemplated, visualized, or thought-of object. In the process of feeling, however, the difference is eliminated, or rather it never arises, the content being inextricably part of the texture of the inner self as such. So whenever music is placed at the service of poetry, and conversely, whenever poetry combines with, clarifies, and interprets music, music cannot give objective shape to thoughts and imaginative concepts, nor can it try to project them in the way that they are conceived by the consciousness as concepts and thoughts. Music must either, as we have said, stimulate the emotions to react to tonal relationships, relationships that bear some inner connection with the basic nature of this content, or else it must seek to express more faithfully the emotion itself that the content may arouse. It is by means of notes then that music matches and mirrors the inner nature *[verinnigen]* of poetry as both the author and the listener *experience* it.

Translated by Peter Le Huray and James Day

Bettina von Arnim

Beethoven
(1832)

I very much wanted to make [Beethoven's] acquaintance during my brief stay; but no one wanted to lead me to him, on account of his odd humor and because he was said to be unsociable. I had to seek him out myself; he had three residences, in the city, just outside town, and in the country. I found him on the top floor of a tall house; in the anteroom a piano lay on the ground, and next to it an inferior bedstead with a straw sack and woolen blanket. The manservant said: "That is the gentleman's lair." I walked in; he was sitting at the piano. I approached him and spoke loudly and closely into his ear (for he was deaf): "My name is *Brentano*." He smiled, extended his hand to me without standing up, and said: "I have just written a beautiful song for you." He sang "Do You Know the Land," not melodiously, not sweetly; his voice was harsh, resonating out beyond cultivation and pleasing sound through its outcry of passion. He asked me: "Well, how do you like it?" I nodded in approval; he sang it again with that fire that is fanned by the awareness of imparting its ardor. He then looked at me triumphantly; he saw that my cheeks and eyes were glowing and said naively: "Aha!"—And now he sang the words: "Do not go dry, tears of eternal love! Oh, to even the half-dried eye, how desolate, how dead does the world appear!" Then he wrote this sentence in characters on a writing board that he carried in his pocket, while allowing me to smooth out his disheveled hair. He kissed my hand, and when I wanted to leave he came with me.

Along the way he said: "Music is the climate of my soul; there it flourishes and doesn't spring up merely as weeds, as with the thoughts of others who call themselves composers; but few comprehend what a throne of passion each individual piece of music is—and few know that passion is itself the throne of music." And he went on speaking in this way, as though I had been his confidante for years.

*   *   *

People were amazed to see me enter hand-in-hand with the unsociable Beethoven into a gathering of more than forty people who were seated at a table eating. He took a seat without ceremony, said little, presumably because he was deaf, and twice took his writing board out of his pocket, writing a few characters on it. After the meal the entire party climbed up to the turret of the house to survey the surrounding countryside. After everyone had come down and he and I were alone again, he pulled out the board, looked it over, wrote and crossed something out, and then said: "My song is finished." He reclined on the window ledge and sang it out entirely, into the breezes. Then he said: "That has quite a sound, doesn't it? It belongs to you, if it pleases you, I wrote it for you; you stimulated me to do it, I read it in your eyes as though it were written there." He came by every day for as long as I stayed in Vienna. A lady from the party, one of the premier pianists, performed one of his sonatas. After he had listened for a while, he said: "That's not right." Then he sat down himself at the piano and played the same sonata, which could be called superhuman.

He gave me some messages for Goethe, saying how he treasured him above all others. They became acquainted the following year, in Teplitz. Goethe paid him a visit; he played for him, and when he saw that Goethe seemed deeply moved, he said: "O sir, I didn't expect that of you. Several years ago in Berlin I also did a concert, I gave it everything I had, felt that I had really accomplished something, and hoped for considerable applause. But, behold, just when I had expressed my greatest enthusiasm, there was not the slightest hint of applause. That was too much for me; I didn't comprehend it. However, the puzzle then solved itself in that the whole Berlin audience was quite sophisticated and, having been deeply moved, tottered toward me with wet handkerchiefs in order to assure me of its gratitude. That was quite immaterial to a coarse enthusiast like myself; I realized that I'd had a romantic, but not artistic audience. But from you, Goethe, I won't accept this. When your works were going through my mind it deposed the music, and I was proud enough to want to glide along on the same heights as you; but for the life of me I didn't know how, and at the very least, were I to do it myself in your presence, the enthusiasm would have to have a totally different impact. Surely you must know how good it feels to be applauded by many hands; if you don't want to acknowledge me and value me as your equal, then who should do it?—By what pack of beggars am I to let myself be appreciated?" With this he backed Goethe into a corner, who at first had no idea how he should make up for this, because he clearly felt Beethoven was right.—The empress and Austrian dukes were in Teplitz, and Goethe enjoyed much recognition on their part; in particular, it was no small matter to his heart to show his devotion to the empress. He conveyed this to Beethoven in solemnly modest words. "Oh, what is this?" said Beethoven. "You don't have to do it that way, you're not doing anything good, you have to hit them squarely over the head so they see what they have in you, otherwise they won't notice it. There is no princess who recognizes a Tasso longer than the shoe of vanity is pinching her. I handled them differently. When I was supposed to give lessons to Duke Rainer, he left me waiting in the antechamber. For that I wrenched his fingers apart but good, and when he asked why I was so impatient I said: he had lost the time I spent waiting outside, and I had no more time to waste. After that he didn't leave me waiting again, indeed, had he done so I would have shown him that this is an act of foolishness that only reveals their bestiality. I said to him: they could give someone a medal, but that doesn't make the person the slightest bit better. They can make someone a court advisor or privy councillor; but they can't make someone into a Goethe or Beethoven. Therefore, that which they can't make, and which they themselves are a long ways from being—they must learn to have respect for that, it's healthy for them.—Then, while out walking, the empress and the dukes approached them along with the entire court. Whereupon Beethoven said: "Just hold on to my arm tightly, they have to make room for us, not we for them."—Goethe didn't share this opinion, and the matter became unpleasant for him. He freed himself from Beethoven's arm and situated himself along the side, hat in hand, while Beethoven, with arms held down, walked right on through the dukes, tipping his hat only slightly, while they moved to both sides to give him room and greeted him in a friendly way. He stood on the far side and waited for Goethe, who had bowed deeply while letting them pass. Now he said: "I waited for you, because I honor and respect you, the way you deserve to be treated; but you paid them too much homage."—Afterwards Beethoven came walking up to us and told us the whole story and was as happy as a child that he had teased Goethe in this way.—The quotations are all literally true, nothing essential has been added; Beethoven himself told it this way several times, and in more than one respect it mattered a lot to me. I told the story to the duke of Weimar, who was also in Teplitz and teased him (Goethe) mightily without telling him where he got it from.

Translated by Michael Gilbert

Eduard Hanslick

"Content" and "Form" in Music
(1854)

Has music a content?
    Since people first gave thought to music, this has been the question most passionately debated. It has been answered categorically in both the affirmative and the negative. Eminent people, mostly philosophers, have affirmed the contentlessness of music: Rousseau, Kant, Hegel, Herbart,* Kahlert, etc. Of the numerous physiologists who support this view, Lotze and Helmholtz are the most important and for us are noteworthy for their musical cultivation. Much the more numerous faction is on the other side in the debate, arguing for the content of music. These are the real musicians among writers, and the majority of people are of the same general conviction.

It seems a little odd that precisely those who are conversant with the technical principles of music are least able to break away from the error of a view that contradicts those principles, for which failure one might more readily excuse the abstract philosophers. This is because, on this point, many musical writers are more concerned with doing what they consider honor to music than they are with truth. They attack the doctrine of the contentlessness of music, not as one opinion against another, but as heresy against the articles of faith. The rival view seems to them a shameful mis-

---

*Robert Zimmermann has most recently, in his *Allgemeine Aesthetik als Formwissenschaft* (Vienna, 1865), on the basis of Herbart's philosophy, rigorously worked out the formal principle for all the arts, including music.

conception, crude blasphemous materialism: "What? The art that exalts and inspires us, to that so many noble souls dedicate their lives, the art that can serve our most sublime ideas—should it be burdened with the anathema of contentlessness? Is it a mere clockwork chime of the senses, mere empty tinkling?" With that kind of vociferation, which they usually let off with both barrels, although one part of it has nothing to do with the other, nothing can be either disproved nor proved. This is not a point of honor, not a token of sectarianism, but simply a matter of knowledge of truth. To arrive at this we must, above all, be clear about the concept under dispute.

It is the mixing up of the concepts of content *[Inhalt]*, subject *[Gegenstand]*, and material *[Stoff]* that has in this connection caused and still causes so much unclarity, since each uses for its own concept a different term or attaches different ideas to the same word. *Content* in its original and proper sense means what a thing holds, what it includes within itself. In this sense, the tones out of which a piece of music is made, which as its parts constitute it as a whole, are the content itself. Nobody is willing to accept this answer, dismissing it out of hand as something altogether self-evidently wrong, because we usually confuse *content* with *subject*. When we raise the question of the content of music, we have in mind the idea of subject (subject matter), which, as the ideal conception of the work, stands directly opposed to the tones as it material ingredients. In this sense of *material*, however, as the subject matter or topic dealt with in the work, music in fact has no material. Quite rightly, Kahlert vigorously argues that verbal descriptions of music should not be provided, as is not the case with painting, although he is wrong where he goes on to say that such verbal descriptions might in some cases provide "a remedy for failure to achieve aesthetic pleasure." But it can clarify our question, which is: What is the content of music? If music actually had a content in this sense, i.e., a subject, the question about the "what" of a composition would necessarily have to be answered in words. An "indefinite content," which everyone can have a different opinion about and which everyone can only feel but not reproduce in words, is not at all a content in the present sense.

Music consists of tonal sequences, tonal forms; these have no other content than themselves. They remind us once again of architecture and dancing, which likewise bring us beautiful relationships without content. However each person may evaluate and name the effect of a piece of music according to its individuality, its content is nothing but the audible tonal forms; since music speaks not merely by means of tones, it speaks only tones.

Krüger, who is by far the best-informed proponent of musical "content" against Hegel and Kahlert, maintains that music merely presents another side of the same content that belongs to the other arts, painting, for example. "Every plastic form," he says, "is static. It allows not action, but rather past action or the essence of action. Thus the painting does not tell us that this is Apollo conquering; rather it shows the conquerer, the enraged combatant," etc. He says that music, on the contrary, "gives the verb to that motionless plastic substantive, the activity, the inner surge. If, in the case of painting, we have recognized as true motionless content such attributes as 'enraged' or 'amorous,' than no less should we recognize, in the case of a piece of music, the true dynamic content: [Someone or something] rages, loves, rushes, surges, storms." This latter is only half-true. Music can rush, surge, and storm, but it cannot love and be angry. These are inwardly felt passions. We here refer the reader back to our second chapter.

Krüger continues by comparing the definiteness of painted content with the content of music. He says: "The visual artist represents Orestes pursued by Furies, as is made evident by the externals of Orestes' body: In eye, mouth, brow, and posture is the expression of flight, melancholy, despair; close to him are the shapes of the accursed Furies, who have him in their power in sovereign, dreadful grandeur, likewise externally visible in fixed outlines, features, postures. The composer represents Orestes being pursued, not in static outline, but from the point of view opposite to that of the visual artist: He sings of the horrors and trembling of his soul, of the impulse to struggle and flee," etc. In my view, this is entirely false. The musician cannot represent Orestes in the one way or the other; indeed, he cannot represent Orestes at all.

It is not a valid objection that the visual arts are likewise unable to present to us the particular historical personage and that, unless we brought to it our knowledge of the actual historical situation, we would not be able to identify the painted shape as the individual. Certainly the painting is not Orestes, the man with these experiences and these biographical particulars; only the poet can represent these, because only the poet can narrate. Nevertheless, the *Orestes* painting unmistakably shows us a youth of aristocratic features, in Greek attire, with fear and mental anguish in his countenance and bearing: it shows us the hideous shapes of the goddesses of vengeance pursuing and tormenting him. What, in music, compares in definiteness with that visible (abstracted from the historical) content of the painting? Diminished sevenths, themes in the minor, tremolando bass, and the like: in short, musical forms that could equally signify a woman instead of a young man, pursued by bailiffs instead of Furies; jealous, vengeful, tortured by physical pain—anything imaginable, if we will grant that the piece signifies anything.

We have already established that, if we are to discuss the content and the representational capacity of music, we must base our discussion only on instrumental music. Surely nobody will so far forget this as to suggest that Orestes in Gluck's *Iphigenia* is a counterexample to the above. This Orestes comes not from the composer but from the poet's words, the actor's figure and mimicry, the designer's costumes and staging: these produce the complete representation. What the composer contributes is perhaps the most beautiful thing of all, but it is the very thing that has nothing to do with the creating of the actual Orestes: song.

Lessing has explained with wonderful clarity what the poet and the visual artist make out of the story of Laocoön. The poet presents by means of language the historical, individually distinct person Laocoön, whereas the painter and sculptor present an old man with two boys (of particular age, appearance, costume, etc.) crushed by the fearful coils of the serpent, the death agony shown in facial expression, attitude, and gesture. Lessing says nothing about the musician, as well he might not, since the musician can make precisely nothing out of the Laocoön story.

We have already indicated how closely the question of the content of music is related to its situation with regard to natural beauty. The musician encounters no such prototype for his art as assures the other arts of the definiteness and recognizability of their content. An art that lacks prototypal natural beauty has, strictly speaking, no external shape. The original of its form of manifestation is nowhere to be found, hence we can have no concept of it. This art (i.e., music) reiterates no subject matter already known and given a name; therefore it has no nameable content for our thinking in definite concepts.

When we talk about the content of a work of art, we can really only make sense if we attach a form to it. The concepts of content and form mutually determine and complement each other. Where in thought a form does not seem separable from a content, there exists in fact no independent content. But in music we see content and form, material and configuration, image and idea, fused in an obscure, inseparable unity. This peculiarity of music, that it possesses form and content inseparably, opposes it absolutely to the literary and visual arts, which can represent the aforementioned thoughts and events in a variety of forms. Out of the story of William Tell, Florian made a historical novel, Schiller a drama, and Goethe began working on it as an epic. In all these cases, the content is the same; the difference is in the prose. Aphrodite rising out of the ocean is the identical content of innumerable painted and carved artworks, which are not confused with one another because of their form. In music there is no content as opposed to form, because music has no form other than the content. Let us consider this more closely.

The independent, aesthetically not further reducible unit of musical thought in every composition is the theme. The ultimate determinations that one ascribes to music as such must always be manifest in the theme, the musical microcosm. Listen to any principle theme you like, say, that of Beethoven's Symphony in B Major. What is its content? Its form? Where does the one end and the other begin? We hope we have made it clear that no specific feeling is the content of the movement and that this will be no less apparent in the present concrete example. So what shall we say is the content? The tones themselves? Of course. But they are already formed. What shall we say is the form? Again, the tones themselves, but they are forms already fulfilled.

Every attempt in practice to separate form from content in a theme leads to contradiction or caprice. For example, if we repeat a theme on another kind of instrument or at a higher octave, does this alter the theme's content or its form? If, as usually happens, we say the latter, all that remains as content of the theme is the series of intervals as such, as the layout of notation in the score as it presents itself to the eye. But this is not a musical determination but an abstraction. It is like looking at the same view through windows with panes of many colors. The view is red, blue, yellow, etc. This, however, changes neither the content nor the form of the view, only the color. Such innumerable changes of color of the same forms, from the most dazzling contrast to the most delicate nuances, are entirely characteristic of music. And they constitute one of the richest and most highly developed aspects of its effectiveness.

A melody originally sketched for piano, which someone then orchestrates acquires thereby a new form, but not form for the first time: it is already a formed conception. Still less would one want to assert that a theme changes its content through transposition and retains it form, since this view is doubly contradictory: the hearer would at one and the same time have to say that he recognizes the content as similar, but it sounds different.

Of course, in the case of whole compositions, particularly extended ones, we are accustomed to speaking of their form and content. This is not the original, logical sense of these concepts, but a particularly musical signification. By the "form" of a symphony, overture, sonata, aria, chorus, etc., we mean the architectonic of the combined components and groups of notes out of which the piece is made. Hence, more precisely, we mean the symmetry of these parts in their sequence, contrast, repetition, and development, in which case we understand the content to be the themes worked up into such an architectonic. Therefore there can be here no more question of a content as "subject," but, solely of a *musical* content. Hence, in connection with complete musical works, the words *content* and *form* are used not in the purely logical, but in an artistic sense. If we want to subsume these concepts under the concept of music, we must proceed not with the complete (and therefore fully assembled) artwork, but with its ultimate, aesthetically not further reducible, nucleus. This is the theme or themes. In these, form and content in no sense suffer themselves to be separated. If we want to specify the "content" of a theme *[Motiv]* for someone, we will have to play for him the theme itself. Thus the content of a musical work can be grasped only musically, never graphically: i.e., as that which is actually sounding in each piece. Since the composition follows formal laws of beauty, it does not improvise itself in haphazard ramblings but develops itself in organically distinct gradations, like sumptuous blossoming from a bud.

This bud is the principle theme, the actual material and content (in the sense of subject matter) of the whole tonal structure. Everything in the structure is a spontaneous continuation and consequence of the theme, conditioned and shaped by it, controlled and fulfilled by it. It is as if it were a logical axiom, the rightness of which we take in at a glance, but which needs to be challenged and expounded by our intelligence in order for us to see what happens in the musical development of it, analogously to a logical demonstration. The composer puts the theme, like the principal character in a novel, into different situations and surroundings, in varying occurrences and moods—these and all the rest, no matter how sharply contrasted, are thought and shaped with reference to it.

Accordingly, we will perhaps call "contentless" that most spontaneous kind of preludizing in which the player, relaxing more than working, launches forth into chords, arpeggios, and rosalias, without allowing an autonomous tonal configuration to come distinctly to the fore. Such free preludes are neither recognizable nor distinguishable as individuals; we might say that they have (in the wider sense) no content because they have no theme. The theme or, rather, the themes of a piece of music are therefore its essential content.

For a long time in aesthetics and criticism, due significance has not been given to the principal themes of compositions. After all, however, the theme reveals the mind that produced the whole work. When a Beethoven begins the *Leonore* overture or a Mendelssohn, his *Fingal's Cave,* then every musician, without hearing another note of the piece, must recognize which palace he stands before; but when we are confronted by the sounds of a theme like that of Donizetti's *Fausta* overture or Verdi's *Louise Miller,* we need penetrate no further into the work to know that we are in the neighborhood pub. In Germany, both theory and practice put a disproportionate value upon the musical development of a theme, as opposed to *thematic substance.* But whatever does not (explicitly or implicitly) lie ready in the theme cannot later be organically developed. And it is perhaps attributable less to lack of skill in thematic development than to lack of symphonic efficacy and fecundity of themes that our time has produced no more Beethovenian works.

Regarding the question of the *content* of music, we must take particular care not to use the word in its laudatory sense. From the fact that music has no content in the sense of "subject matter," is does not follow that music lacks *substance.* Clearly "spiritual substance" is what those people have in mind who fight with sectar-

ian ardor for the "content" of music. . . . Music is play *[Spiel]* but
not frivolity *[Spielerei]*. Thoughts and feelings run like blood in
the arteries of the harmonious body of beautiful sounds. They are
not that body; they are not perceivable, but they animate it. The
composer composes and thinks. He composes and thinks, however,
at a remove from all objective reality, in tones. This is obvious,
but it must be expressly repeated here, because it is all too often
denied and violated by the very people who acknowledge it in
principle. They think that composing is the translating of some
kind of conceptual content into tones. But the tones themselves are
the untranslatable, ultimate language. Indeed, from the very fact
that the composer is forced to think in tones, it follows that music
has no content, while every conceptual content must be capable of
being thought in words.

Although we have, in our investigation of *content*, had to exclude all music composed to specified texts as contradictory to the
pure concept of music, yet the masterworks of the vocal repertoire
are absolutely necessary for the assessment of the *substance* of
music. From simple song to the most elaborate opera and the time-
honored religious celebration with church music, music has never
ceased to accompany and thus indirectly to exalt the most cher-
ished and significant activities of the human spirit.

Along with our vindication of the notion of the ideal substance of
music, a second result must be emphasized. The subjectless formal
beauty of music does not preclude its productions from bearing
the imprint of individuality. The manner of artistic treatment, like
the invention of this or that particular theme, is in each case
unique: it can never be dissolved into a higher unity, but remains
an individual. Thus, a theme by Mozart or Beethoven stands on
its own feet as firmly and unadulteratedly as a stanza by Goethe,
a dictum of Lessing's, a statue by Thorwaldsen, or a painting by
Overbeck. Autonomous musical concepts (i.e., themes) have the
trustworthiness of a quotation and the vividness of a painting: they
are individual, personal, everlasting.

For this reason, we cannot share Hegel's view regarding the sub-
stancelessness *[Gehaltlosigkeit]* of music. Yet it seems to us even
more erroneous that he attributes to this art only the articulation
of the "unindividualized inner self." Even from Hegel's musical
standpoint, which disregards the essentially formative and objective
activity of the composer, interpreting music as free renunciation

of subjectivity, the "unindividualizedness" itself does not follow, since the subjectively producing mind shows itself as essentially individual.

Elsewhere, we have touched upon how individuality leaves its mark by means of the choice and treatment of different musical elements. Regarding the accusation of contentlessness *[Inhaltslosigkeit]*, music has content, but musical content, which is a not inconsiderable spark of the divine flame, like the beauty of any other art. But only by firmly denying any other kind of "content" to music can we preserve music's substance. This is because from indefinite feelings, to which as best such a content is attributable, no spiritual content derives; rather, in each composition, the content derives from its particular tonal structure as the spontaneous creation of mind out of material compatible with mind [i.e., the tones].

Translated by Geoffrey Payzant

Friedrich Nietzsche

From *Richard Wagner in Bayreuth*
(1876)

The spirit of Hellenic culture lies in infinite dispersion upon our present age: while forces of all kinds exert their pressure and people offer themselves the fruits of the modern sciences and skills as means of exchange, the image of the Hellenic is dawning again with pale features, as yet quite distant and ghostlike. The earth, which has hitherto been orientalized enough, yearns again for Hellenization; though whoever wishes to assist her in this, must be quick, fleet-footed, in order to bring together the most diverse and distant points of knowledge, the most remote regions of talent, in order to traverse and be in command of all these so immensely spread-out fields. And so it is that a series of counter-Alexanders has now become necessary, who possess the greatest strength, the strength to pull together and connect, to fetch the furthest threads and preserve the fabric from being blown apart. Not to loosen the Gordian knot of Greek culture, as Alexander did, such that its ends fluttered off to the far corners of the globe, *but rather to tie it together again, after it was undone—that is now the task*. In Wagner I perceive such a counter-Alexander: he captures and closes together that which was scattered, weak, and indolent; he possesses, if a medical expression be allowed, an astringent power: and in that he belongs among the great forces of culture. He has command over the arts, religions, the histories of different peoples, but is nevertheless the opposite of a polyhistor, of a mind that only collects and arranges things. For he molds things together, he animates those things that have been gathered together; he is a *simplifier of the world.* One will not be confounded by such an idea if one compares this most general of tasks, which his genius has set before him, with the much narrower and more immediate one that people tend to think of first in association with the name Wagner. People expect from him a reform of the theater; assuming he were to succeed at this, what would this accomplish for that higher and greater task?

Well, with that, modern man would be changed and reformed; so necessarily does one thing hinge upon another in our modern world, that if but one nail is removed, the building shakes and falls. What we are stating here with apparent exaggeration about Wagner's reform would be expected from any other genuine reform as well. It is utterly impossible to produce the highest and purest effect of theatrical art without renewing in all places, in morals and the state, in education and commerce. Love and justice, empowered here at a single juncture, namely, in the realm of art, must in accordance with the law of their inner necessity spread further and cannot retreat back into the motionless state of their earlier chrysalization. Merely in order to grasp the extent to which the position of our arts in relation to life symbolizes the degeneration of this life, the extent to which our theaters are an insult to those who build and attend them: merely to grasp this, one must completely reorient one's thinking and be able to see the customary and everyday as something very unusual and complex. A strange clouding of judgment; a poorly concealed mania for diversion, for entertainment at any price; philistine considerations, pretense, and playacting with the seriousness of art on the part of its practitioners; brutal greed for profit on the side of its purveyors; the hollowness and mindlessness of a society, which thinks of the masses only to the extent it needs them or considers them a threat and goes to theater and concerts without ever being reminded of their responsibilities: all of this together forms the musty, pernicious atmosphere of today's conditions of art. And if one becomes accustomed to this, as our educated people have, one fancies it necessary to breathe this bad air for the sake of one's health, and is then badly off when forced by some constraint or other to temporarily do without it. In reality there is but *one* way to convince oneself in short order of just how vulgar, indeed how peculiarly and intricately vulgar our theater institutions really are: just hold them up for comparison to the onetime reality of the Greek theater! Assuming for a moment that we knew nothing of the Greeks, perhaps we could not get at our circumstances at all and one would consider such objections, as they were first raised on a large scale by Wagner, to be the daydreams of people who are at home in the land of at-home-nowhere. Perhaps one would say: given the way people are, such art is sufficient and proper—and they've never been otherwise!—But of course, they *have* been otherwise, and even now there are people who aren't satisfied by the present institutions of art. And this is precisely what the fact of Bayreuth demonstrates. Here you find well-prepared and consecrated spectators, the profound emotion of people who are at the pinnacle of happiness and precisely in this feel their entire being drawn together, in order to empower themselves toward greater and higher volition. Here one finds the most devoted sacrifice of artists and the spectacle of all spectacles, the victorious creator of a work, in itself the quintessential embodiment of a wealth of victorious artistic deeds. Does it not almost seem like magic to be able to encounter such a phenomenon in our present age? Must not those who have the opportunity to take part in and witness this already be transfigured and renewed, in order to transfigure and renew henceforth in other areas of life? Has a safe harbor not now been found, beyond the wild waves of the sea? Doesn't there lie a stillness here, spread out over the waters?

*   *   *

. . . To us, Bayreuth signifies the morning devotion on the day of battle! One could not do us a greater injustice than to assume that we are concerned here solely with art; as though it counted only as a means of salvation and narcosis, with which to dissociate oneself from all of the other, miserable conditions of our time. In the image of the tragic artwork of Bayreuth, we see precisely the battle of the individual with all those things that confront him as ostensibly unconquerable necessity: with power, law, origin, pacts, entire orders of things. Individuals cannot possibly live more beautifully than when, in the battle for justice and love, they ripen and sacrifice themselves unto death. The gaze with which the mysterious eye of tragedy looks upon us is not a slackening and body-binding form of magic, even though it demands stillness, as long as it looks at us; for art is not there for the battle itself, but rather for the quiet moments beforehand and in the midst thereof, for those moments of retrospect and anticipation when one grasps the symbolic, when a refreshing dream approaches us with a feeling of gentle fatigue.

Translated by Michael Gilbert

The Case of Wagner
(1888)

To *the artist of decadence:* there we have the crucial words. And here my seriousness begins. I am far from looking on guilelessly while this decadent corrupts our health—and music as well. Is Wagner a human being at all? Isn't he rather a sickness? He makes sick whatever he touches—*he has made music sick*—

A typical decadent who has a sense of necessity in his corrupted taste, who claims it as a higher taste, who knows how to get his corruption accepted as law, as progress, as fulfillment.

And he is not resisted. His seductive force increases tremendously, smoke clouds of incense surround him, the misunderstandings about him parade as "gospel"—he has not by any means converted only the *poor in spirit.*

I feel the urge to open the windows a little. Air! More air!—*

That people in Germany should deceive themselves about Wagner does not surprise me. The opposite would surprise me. The Germans have constructed a Wagner for themselves whom they can revere: they have never been psychologists; their gratitude consists in misunderstanding. But that people in Paris, too, deceive themselves about Wagner, though there they are hardly anything anymore except psychologists! And in St. Petersburg, where they guess things that are not guessed even in Paris! How closely related Wagner must be to the whole of European decadence to avoid being experienced by them as a decadent. He belongs to it: he is its protagonist, its greatest name.— One honors oneself when raising him to the clouds.

For that one does not resist him, this itself is a sign of decadence. The instincts are weakened. What one ought to shun is found attractive. One puts to one's lips what drives one yet faster into the abyss.

Is an example desired? One only need observe the regimen that those suffering from anemia or gout or diabetes prescribe for themselves. Definition of a vegetarian: one who requires a corroborant

---

Luft! Mehr Luft! Goethe's last words are said to have been: *Licht! Mehr Licht!* "Light! More light!"

diet. To sense that what is harmful is harmful, to be *able* to forbid oneself something harmful, is a sign of youth and vitality. The exhausted are *attracted* by what is harmful: the vegetarian by vegetables.* Sickness itself can be a stimulant to life: only one has to be healthy enough for this stimulant.†

Wagner increases exhaustion: that is why he attracts the weak and exhausted. Oh, the rattlesnake-happiness of the old master when he always saw precisely "the little children" coming unto him!‡

I place this perspective at the outset: Wagner's art is sick. The problems he presents on the stage—all of them problems of hysterics—the convulsive nature of his affects, his overexcited sensibility, his taste that required ever stronger spices, his instability that he dressed up as principles, not least of all the choice of his heroes and heroines—consider them as physiological types (a pathological gallery)!—all of this taken together represents a profile of sickness that permits no further doubt. *Wagner est une névrose.*§ Perhaps nothing is better known today, at least nothing has been better studied, than the protean character of degeneration that here conceals itself in the chrysalis of art and artist. Our physicians and physiologists confront their most interesting case in Wagner, at least a very complete case. Precisely because nothing is more modern than this total sickness, this lateness and overexcitement of the nervous mechanism, Wagner is *the modern artist par excellence,* the Cagliostro of modernity. In his art all that the modern world requires most urgently is mixed in the most seductive manner: the three great *stimulantia* of the exhausted—the *brutal,* the *artificial,* and the *innocent* (idiotic).**

---

*Wagner was a doctrinaire vegetarian, and Nietzsche's brother-in-law, Bernhard Förster, copied Wagner's vegetarianism along with his anti-Semitic ideology; so did Hitler. Nietzsche wrote his mother about Förster: "For my personal taste such an agitator is something impossible for closer acquaintance. . . . Vegetarianism, as Dr. Förster wants it, makes such natures only still more petulant" (*Briefe an Mutter und Schwester* [letters to mother and sister, Leipzig, 1909], no. 409; for further quotations from letters about Förster see Kaufmann's *Nietzsche,* chapter 1, section III).

†For parallel passages in Nietzsche's other works, see the last three pages of chapter 4, section I, in Kaufmann's *Nietzsche.*

‡Allusion to Matthew 19:14, Mark 10:14, Luke 18:16.

§"Wagner is a neurosis."

**The words *idiot* and *idiotic* occur frequently in Nietzsche's writings—after his discovery of Dostoevsky early in 1887. See Kaufmann's *Nietzsche,* chapter 12, note 2, where the relevant passages are cited.

Wagner represents a great corruption of music. He has guessed that it is a means to excite weary nerves—and with that he has made music sick. His inventiveness is not inconsiderable in the art of goading again those who are weariest, calling back into life those who are half-dead. He is a master of hypnotic tricks, he manages to throw down the strongest like bulls. Wagner's *success*—his success with nerves and consequently women—has turned the whole world of ambitious musicians into disciples of his secret art. And not only the ambitious, the *clever,* too.— Only sick music makes money today; our big theaters subsist on Wagner. [. . .]

*   *   *

Let us recover our breath in the end by getting away for a moment from the narrow world to which every question about the worth of *persons* condemns the spirit. A philosopher feels the need to wash his hands after having dealt so long with "The Case of Wagner."—

I offer my conception of what is *modern.*— In its measure of strength every age also possesses a measure for what virtues are permitted and forbidden to it. Either it has the virtues of *ascending* life: then it will resist from the profoundest depths the virtues of declining life. Or the age itself represents declining life: then it also requires the virtues of decline, then it hates everything that justifies itself solely out of abundance, out of the overflowing riches of strength. Aesthetics is tied indissolubly to these biological presuppositions: there is an aesthetics of *decadence,* and there is a *classical* aesthetics—the "beautiful in itself" is a figment of the imagination, like all of idealism.—

In the narrower sphere of so-called moral values one cannot find a greater contrast than that between a *master morality* and the morality of *Christian* value concepts: the latter developed on soil that was morbid through and through (the Gospels present us with precisely the same physiological types that Dostoevsky's novels describe), master morality ("Roman," "pagan," "classical," "Renaissance") is, conversely, the sign language of what has turned out well, of *ascending* life, of the will to power as the principle of life. Master morality *affirms* as instinctively as Christian morality *negates* ("God," "beyond," "self-denial"—all of them negations). The former gives to things out of its own abundance—it transfigures, it beautifies the world and *makes it more rational*—the latter impoverishes, pales, and makes uglier the value of things, it *negates* the world. *World* is a Christian term of abuse.—

These opposite forms in the optics of value are *both* necessary: they are ways of seeing, immune to reasons and refutations. One cannot refute Christianity; one cannot refute a disease of the eye. That pessimism was fought like a philosophy, was the height of scholarly idiocy. The concepts "true" and "untrue" have, as it seems to me, no meaning in optics.—

What alone should be resisted is that falseness, that deceitfulness of instinct that *refuses* to experience these opposites as opposites— as Wagner, for example, refused, being no mean master of such falsehoods. To make eyes at master morality, at *noble* morality (Icelandic saga is almost its most important document) while mouthing the counterdoctrine, that of the "gospel of the lowly," of the *need* for redemption!—

I admire, incidentally, the modesty of the Christians who go to Bayreuth. I myself wouldn't be able to endure certain words out of the mouth of a Wagner. There are concepts that do *not* belong in Bayreuth.—

What? A version of Christianity adapted for female Wagnerians, perhaps *by* female Wagnerians—for Wagner was in his old days by all means *feminini generis?* To say it once more, the Christians of today are too modest for my taste.—

If Wagner was a Christian, then Liszt was perhaps a church father!—The need for *redemption,* the quintessence of all Christian needs, has nothing to do with such buffoons: it is the most honest expression of decadence, it is the most convinced, most painful affirmation of decadence in the form of sublime symbols and practices. The Christian wants to be *rid* of himself. *Le moi est toujours haïssable* [The ego is always hateful].

Noble morality, master morality, conversely, is rooted in a triumphant yes said to *oneself*—it is self-affirmation, self-glorification of life; it also requires sublime symbols and practices, but only because "its heart is too full." All of *beautiful,* all of *great* art belongs here: the essence of both is gratitude. On the other hand, one cannot dissociate from it an instinctive aversion *against* decadents, scorn for their symbolism, even horror: such feelings almost prove it. Noble Romans experienced Christianity as *foeda superstitio* [an abominable superstition]. I recall how the last German of noble taste, how Goethe experienced the cross.

One looks in vain for more valuable, more *necessary* opposites.—

But such falseness as that of Bayreuth is no exception today. We are all familiar with the unaesthetic concept of the Christian *Junker*. Such *innocence* among opposites, such a "good conscience" in a lie is actually *modern par excellence*, it almost defines modernity. Biologically, modern man represents a *contradiction of values;* he sits between two chairs, he says yes and no in the same breath. Is it any wonder that precisely in our times falsehood itself has become flesh and even genius? that *Wagner* "dwelled among us"? It was not without reason that I called Wagner the Cagliostro of modernity.—

But all of us have, unconsciously, involuntarily in our bodies values, words, formulas, moralities of *opposite* descent—we are, physiologically considered, *false.*— A *diagnosis of the modern soul*—where would it begin? With a resolute incision into this instinctive contradiction, with the isolation of its opposite values, with the vivisection of the *most instructive* case.— The case of Wagner is for the philosopher a *windfall*—this essay is inspired, as you hear, by gratitude.—

Translated by Walter Kaufmann

Friedrich von Hausegger

A Popular Discussion of *Music as Expression* (c. 1885)

You have invited me most congenially to summarize the most important aspects of my views on music in popular fashion. Attempting such a popular exposition of aesthetic theories can make one hesitant. One is accustomed to directing aesthetics toward a horizon situated as far as possible from the popular realm. Does the same not hold true for music in its performance? Is it not generally maintained that specialized knowledge is required not only for the understanding of music but for its enjoyment as well? And nevertheless, we must confess that it was precisely the popular element in music—that which directly stirs the soul without first necessitating aid of an expert nature—which has constantly remained victorious, and not seldom in struggle against academic criticism. We observe this strange spectacle, that precisely the significant and vital receive no attention on the part of musical criticism, indeed, on the contrary, they have encountered for the most part misunderstanding and hostility. This permits the conclusion that there is a force at work in music that does not coincide with what is accessible to academic criticism as a standard of judgment, and that precisely this force, which has hitherto escaped the scientifically critical eye, is the key factor in the further development of the art of music.

Is there no way to get at this force? Are we at all entitled to speak of the value of a "science" for art, when precisely what has always constituted the effectiveness of art eludes its critical observation? One simply must confront this question, and it has also awakened in my soul that kind of anguish of which it is said it is the necessary precondition of every fruitful thought. Helplessly the eye wandered around among various systems of notation; the ear searched for laws of consonance and dissonance; the sounding tone was examined in terms of what mysterious powers of nature it concealed within; similar natural phenomena were called upon for assistance, and the advice of history was sought. In whichever direction these observations turned, it was the law that justified the phenomenon; however, that internally moving force, in which the law irresistibly expresses itself before it is recognized in the forms of the phenomenon—that invisible force with which music stirs our soul without first directing it to theories and knowledge— it has not found a place within the limits of what the scientific study of music has presented for consideration and discussion.

Into this time of need fell the impressions of the works of Richard Wagner and the study of Schopenhauer. The latter conceives of music as an objectification of the will, like the world itself. This sentence, which in its composure gives rise to a certain temptation, accords to music a place in the life of the world in which it appears elevated far above what music as an academic field was capable of ascribing to its peculiarities and virtues. And what Schopenhauer had sensed took on tangible incarnation in the mighty creative work of Wagner, as well as illumination and depth in Wagner's published views.

In music, one is not dealing merely with lines, signs, vibrations, and tonal stimuli. Its understanding grows out of the deepest urges of the soul. What becomes audible in it is a language we need to master just as little as the language of the emotions that expresses itself in so eloquent and convincing a manner in the play of facial expression and gestures as well as the intonation of words. In accordance with its deepest essence, music is expression.

The conception of music as a language of feeling is not new, but it lacked any tangible scientific basis. Consequently, Hanslick was able to contest this notion successfully in his highly controversial treatise *Vom musikalisch Schönen* (On the Musically Beautiful). The very vague concept of emotion, open to the most varying interpretations, affords no handle for conducting a scientific investigation. The scientifically accessible intermediary factor existing between the tonal forms, as they have developed in the course of history, and the corresponding emotions, was missing. Neither the imaginative interpretations of the adherents of emotion theory, nor research in the areas of acoustics and physiology have been able to establish the vital connection.

Given this situation, it is understandable that science, oriented toward precise research, decided to leave off with those phenomena accessible to its observations and experiments, and not only to do without an investigation into deeper causes, but rather to deny such causes altogether. At which point there came advice from other positions not accessible to the specialists. In particular, it was Wagner, whose unique gifts and broad learning led him to the observation of the relations between language, gesture, and music.

Language and gesture were originally manifestations of emotional stimulation. Only over the course of time did language become a means of mutual communication and bodily movement useful for some external purpose as work. In the process, however, both the tonal movement inherent in language, as well as gesture, to the extent it does not serve some particular external purpose, retained the quality of being expression, that is, of bearing witness to emotional stimulation that is linked with them. To be certain, this quality is present today only in reduced measure, and special attention must be focused upon it for it to be recognized at all. It is also effective without being especially recognized.

The intonation of the spoken word gives this the emphasis through which the speaker seeks to achieve a sense of emotional participation for his communications. The accompanying gesture supports this effort. The observer possesses an incredibly refined and immediately activated capacity to understand this form of expression. The sounds of anger, jubilation, melancholy, the nuances of astonished exclamation, of flattering address, of reproach, of inquiry—these are never misunderstood, even when the content of the words spoken is unclear or was not understood. The same thing applies to gesture. What might the cause of this reciprocal effect be, which in all likelihood has been observed so little precisely because it is so general and appears so natural that it hardly occurs to anyone to discover something striking about it? There can be no cause other than that the emotional stimulation of our fellow human beings and their expression are the object of a special interest that asserts itself involuntarily.

The less practice there is with controlling sound expressions and gestures, the stronger they express themselves. Thus, strong utterances of this type can be found in the uneducated, children, and natives, and were most certainly a trait of primitive peoples. It is such utterances that, in the attention they stimulate, call forth a unique reciprocal effect between the emotional perceptions of people. Indeed, the perfection of the human race in general can be attributed to this and its underlying ability. But if we are to get beyond such general assertions, we must ask ourselves how this reciprocal effect can be explained physiologically.

One can witness the phenomenon that forms of expression one observes communicate themselves instinctively to the observing person as well. For example, in the presence of an angry person one will, without wanting to, assume the facial expression of anger, just as the expression of joy in the face of another will also be reflected in our own. Our bodies as well are involuntarily affected by the gestures of a passionately excited person. With the expressive forms of anger, joy, etc., the associated emotional state engages itself automatically. This is an often-attested fact. Thus we come to the result, that through both sound utterances and gestures, to the extent these proceed from emotional stimulation, these emotional states are transferred to others. However, a certain sensation of pleasure is associated with the state of emotional stimulation that then engages itself if it is not suppressed by something like displeasure aroused by the source of stimulation, or a diversion of interest caused by the same. An actuating stimulus that follows no external purpose but rather is an outbreak of the life drive has a pleasurable effect in and of itself. One such actuating activity is play, in which Schiller recognized the origin of art.

The natural wish to awaken and heighten this unique feeling of pleasure leads one to seek emotional stimulation of this sort. As painfully as we are moved by the suffering of others, their struggle with fate, their defeat—if all of that is portrayed by an actor, it is an object of pleasure for us. Why? We experience the emotional stimulation awakened in us by the dramatic performance as a heightened sensation of existence, without being affected by facts arousing displeasure, which otherwise are wont to cause correspondingly unpleasant feelings. We are only watching a play, and it is only of significance to us to the extent that it stirs up our innermost being toward a heightened experience of life.

What appears clearly before the eyes in a play also lends to the other arts, especially music, their own unique effect. Specifically, in music the same elements can be found with which the actor makes his impact—sound and gesture—but in refined form. Sound has clarified itself into tone; and the motions of gesture correspond to rhythm. It is most interesting to pursue the historical process explaining this development; but that would lead beyond the scope of the present discussion. Hence I refer you to my book that deals with these matters in greater detail: *Music as Expression.* This much is certain: contemporary music as well, even in its most sublimated forms, must follow the laws that give the character of expression to sound and gesture if it is to find understanding and favor.

In spite of all of the artistic elaborations music has undergone, indeed with which it began and continued for some time in the West (from the art of the Dutch on down to J. S. Bach), it has nevertheless returned to simple melody, which could be veiled but never entirely covered up. The great result of the historical development of Western music is sovereign melody: melody, which in its expressive meaning coincides with what sound and gesture seek to communicate; but which in addition to this makes use of expressive means that are clarified, heightened, and enriched by a marvelous process.

Is our present-day music not perceived in the same way as the language of sound and gesture? Not only song, but instrumental music as well, acting as an imitation and heightening of vocal music, as it were, stimulates us to physical movement, often in striking fashion. A beautiful melody affects the muscles of the throat, a thrilling rhythm brings the body into corresponding motion. There are listeners who are so unable to escape the force of this effect that they involuntarily sing along and follow the rhythm of the music with their bodily movements. Only the habit of controlling our forms of expression, together with the multitude of distracting impressions brought with it by modern life, lead us to limit these manifestations of music's impact to a certain degree and mostly bring about immediately suppressed dispositions.

If we investigate that which presents itself to us as melody, i.e., as a combination of tones corresponding to our requirements in its essential conditions, we arrive at the result, no longer surprising to us, that the laws according to which melody is constituted with respect to intervals and time sequence coincide with those laws operating in the human organism that govern bodily forms of expression. The effective phrases occurring in melody correspond to the intonations of expressive speech; rules of accentuation are common to both speech and music; and the rhythmic structure of melody is, like that of language, dependent upon the organization of human organs. The segments of melody correspond to breathing movements, its rhythm to the bodily gestures determining and accompanying sound expression, and its reduction to an equal measured pulse to the beating of the heart. If one analyzes a melody that characteristically stimulates a given emotional state, one will find that in its tonal structure, rhythm, and time measure it coincides with the physical expressions that make themselves felt in the human body in the same emotional state. Series of tones that distance themselves from the sound and gesture of human expression remove themselves in equal measure from being received into the life of the emotions, and consequently deprive themselves of the unique effect that determines the value of music. For this reason, movement in music limits itself to the range drawn from the human pulse. The lowest number of pulses are 30 to 40 per minute, and the highest 200. The limiting oscillation settings of the Mälzel metronome are 40 and 208 pulses per minute.

We may therefore contend that what moves us so deeply in music, what confers upon it its meaning, what opens itself to our understanding, is human expression, albeit in a marvelously clarified and refined form. It is this that we thirst for, whereas the sensual stimulus of sound, if it does not serve to support such expression, is capable of offering us only momentary delight, not lasting satisfaction. It is a peculiar confirmation of the viewpoint set forth here that in the practice of music, the effort is always present to remind us that we are dealing with an expressive declaration unique to the human being as such. This is true to the greatest degree in the case of singing, which presents itself as an expression of the personality appearing before our eyes and participating otherwise through facial expression and gesture. But instruments as well must be handled by humans, and the listener has to internalize this if its impact is not to limit itself to a fleeting sensual stimulus. Only our capacity for abstraction and powers of imagination, which supplement the impressions of a tonal structure perceived as human forms of expression with the image of the personality imparting himself in it, allow us to look apart to a certain degree from the outer appearance of a person revealing himself through artistic activity, though never to the extent that one could dispense entirely with the person's accompaniment or performance. Attempts to remove the performers from the sight of the listeners during musical performances have never produced satisfactory results. It would be no great accomplishment to invent a machine that would surpass everything of which humans are capable in terms of precision, power, endurance, ease—in short, all those virtues that leap into our senses. And yet! Can an artistically sensitive person imagine a time in which the machine, in spite of its greater capacity, could supersede the practicing artist? Why not? The adherents of the theory of "sounding forms in motion" would have to be at a loss for an answer. We, however, will not lack an explanation: for the simple reason that the tonal form itself does not exhaust the essence of music, because this form seeks to be perceived as expression and as such must be conceived in association with a self-expressing personality.

Thus, we have attributed the significance and value of music to the fact that it is a refined and to a marvelous degree clarified expression of emotional states that is understood by the listener as the expression of such states and perceived as a heightening of his sensation of existence, as an awakening of his inner life. In tracing this conception of music further, we are led to ask the artist as well as the enjoying recipient what actually transpires in them while producing or enjoying a work of art. My treatise *The Transcendent World of the Artist* is devoted to the investigation of this highly interesting process of the soul as well as its psychological and philosophical significance.

Translated by Michael Gilbert

Thomas Mann

Coming to Terms with Richard Wagner
(1913)

I can never forget what I owe to Richard Wagner in terms of artistic pleasure and artistic understanding—no matter how far I move away from him in spirit. As a prose writer, story teller, and psychologist I had nothing immediate or practical to learn from that practitioner of symphonic theater, whose poetic impact, like that of Klopstock, goes beyond the realm of the particular, and whose prose style was always a source of embarrassment to my love. But of course the arts are only different manifestations of art itself, which is the same in all its forms; and Wagner need not have been the great blender of the arts that he was in order to have exercised an instructive and nourishing influence on every form of artistic endeavor. What also gave my relationship to Wagner a certain immediacy and intimacy was the fact that secretly I always saw and loved in him—notwithstanding the claims of the theater— a great *narrative* artist. The recurrent motif, the self-quotation, the symbolic phrase, the verbal and thematic reminiscence across long stretches of text—these were narrative devices after my own heart, and for that very reason full of enchantment for me; and I acknowledged at an early age that Wagner's works had a more stimulating influence on my youthful artistic aspirations than anything else in the world, filling me constantly with a longing, envious and infatuated, to produce something similar, if only on a small and modest scale. And indeed, it is not difficult to catch a whiff of the spirit that informs the *Ring* in my own *Buddenbrooks,* that epic pageant of the generations, linked together and interwoven by leitmotifs.

For a long time all my artistic thinking and practice was over-shadowed by the name of Wagner. For a long time it seemed to me that all artistic desires and ambitions must conduce inevitably to that mighty name. At no time, however—not even in the days when I never missed a single performance of *Tristan* at the Munich Hoftheater—could my professions *about* Wagner ever have been seen as a profession of faith *in* Wagner. As a thinker and personality he seemed to me suspect, as an artist irresistible, if also deeply questionable in terms of the nobility, purity, and wholesomeness of his influence; and never did I surrender my youthful heart to him with the same trusting abandon with which I yielded to the spell of the great poets and writers—those of whom Wagner felt entitled to speak, almost pityingly, as "literary writers." My love for him was a love devoid of belief, for it has always seemed to me pedantic to insist that one cannot love without also believing. It was a liaison, an affair—skeptical, pessimistic, clear-sighted, spiteful almost, yet full of passion and indescribable charm. Wonderful hours of deep and solitary happiness amidst the theater throng, hours filled with frissons and brief moments of bliss, with delights for the nerves and the intellect alike, and sudden glimpses into things of profound and moving significance, such as only this incomparable art can afford!

But today I no longer believe—if indeed I ever did believe—that the stature of a work of art is to be measured in terms of the unsurpassability of its artistic resources. And I have the impression that Wagner's star is in the descendant in the skies of the German mind.

I am not talking about his theory. If it were not something so completely secondary, not so wholly a retrospective and superfluous glorification of his own talent, then his creative work would undoubtedly have become just as untenable as the theory: and nobody would have taken it seriously for a moment without the work, which appears to validate it as long as one is sitting in the theater, but which in fact validates nothing but itself. Has *anybody* ever seriously believed in this theory, I wonder? In this amalgam of painting, music, words, and gesture that Wagner had the nerve to proclaim as the fulfillment of all artistic ambition? In a hierarchy of genres in which *Tasso* would rank below *Siegfried*? Are Wagner's writings on art actually read, in fact? And whence this lack of interest in Wagner the writer? Is it because his writings are propaganda rather than honest revelation? Because their comments on his work—wherein he truly lives in all his suffering greatness— are singularly inadequate and misleading? This must suffice by way of excuse. But it is true enough: there is not much to be learned about Wagner from Wagner's critical writings.

No, I am talking about his mighty oeuvre proper, which has currently attained the peak of its popularity with the bourgeois public—about his art as a taste, a style, a particular mode of sensibility. Let us not be deceived by the loud applause of the young people standing in the theater stalls. The truth is that among the better-educated youth of today there is much criticism of Wagner, much instinctive, albeit unvoiced mistrust, and indeed—let us be frank—much indifference toward Wagner. How could it be otherwise? Wagner is nineteenth century through and through, he is *the* representative German artist of that epoch, which will live on in the memory of mankind as great (perhaps) and ill-starred (for certain). But if I try to imagine the artistic masterpiece of the twentieth century, I see something that differs radically—and favorably, it seems to me—from that of Wagner: something conspicuously logical, well formed and clear, something at once austere and cheerful, no less imbued with strength of purpose, but more restrained, refined, more healthy even in its spirituality—something that does not seek its greatness in the monumentally baroque, nor its beauty in the sweep of emotion. A new classicism, I believe, is on the way.

Even so, whenever some chord, some evocative phrase from Wagner's work impinges all unexpected on my ear, I still start with joy; a kind of homesickness, of nostalgia for my youth, comes upon me; and once again, as of old, my spirit succumbs to that clever and ingenious wizardry, full of yearning and cunning.

Translated by Allan Blunden

Thomas Mann

Hans Pfitzner's *Palestrina*
(1918)

I have heard Hans Pfitzner's musical legend, *Palestrina*, three times now, and remarkably easily and quickly I made this difficult and audacious production into my own, my intimate possession. This work, something ultimate, consciously ultimate, from the sphere of Schopenhauer and Wagner, of romanticism, with its characteristics reminiscent of Dürer and Faust, its metaphysical mood, its ethos of "cross, death, and grave," its mixture of music, pessimism, and humor—it is completely "to the point," to the point of this book, its appearance at this moment brought me the consolation and blessing of complete sympathy, it agrees with my innermost idea of humanity, it makes me positive, releases me from polemics, and in it my feeling has been offered a great object it can gratefully join with until, healed and reassured, it is ready to create again itself; seen from this work, repulsiveness lies in an unreal light.

Did Pfitzner's musical poem have something new to say to me? Hardly. But I must have wanted to the point of languishing to hear what was deeply and intimately familiar, to make it my own again; yes, the extraordinary effect it immediately had on me at that first morning performance before an amphitheater of experts to whom I in no way belong, the rapidity with which I absorbed it, can only be explained by an unusual tension of preparedness and receptivity that the times, the hostility of the times, had brought forth in me. I shy away from an analysis, not only because I basically hate the effect of finality that the critical word produces, but especially because dissection means division, a sequence of observation, the separation of the intellectual and the artistic elements, for example, by which I am afraid of damaging the whole. Naturally there is nothing but unity here. But art is strong in and for itself, and it also overpowers those who would taboo the intellectual will it serves if they understood it. The product of a melancholically alienated way of thinking that is at odds with the times can be strong, happy, and victorious through the talent that helps it to triumph over the minds of thousands. In the process it happens then, of course, that something is taken—and probably even taken with the artist's consent—for talent, art, and pure stylization, which is really something quite different, something psychologically far more immediate. These archaic fifths and fourths, these organ sounds and liturgical finales—are they nothing but mimicry and historical atmosphere? Do they not demonstrate at the same time a psychological tendency and intellectual inclination in which one must, I fear, recognize the opposite of a politically virtuous tendency and mood? Let us put the question aside! Talent is what conquers. Let us admire it!

What great artistry, in combination with the most nervous agility, penetrating harmonic audacity with a pious ancestral style! One knows the master school where this was learned. The psychologically modern element, all the refinement of this insertion of harmonic retardations, how purely organically it joins itself to what is musical milieu, what, therefore, is humble-primitive, Middle Ages, frugality, the breath of the grave, crypt, and skeleton, in this romantic musical score! The charming theme of Ighino, which is repeated most beautifully in the prelude to the third act, I immediately locked into my heart—this melodious symbol of the personality of a child full of wistfulness and loyalty who gladly leaves what is splendid and new and remains sympathetic to the old. The passage is wonderful; I believe the most subtle and the sweetest part of the work is connected with it. How much the work gains simultaneously in chasteness and in the power of deliverance when it is painfully born out of the music, when the music paints those agonies and inhibitions of the soul from which the final element, the difficult word, breaks free and strives upward: for example, in the rhythmically incomparable measures that prepare Ighino's entry and outburst, "The old father's grief . . ." And what breast that was still breathing quietly would not suddenly—and inevitably, over and over—be shaken by sobs when the pure voice of the child sings of Palestrina's glory, his "genuine glory—

> that quietly and in time
> Enveloped him like a festive raiment?"

A blessed-lyrical moment whose beauty gains self-confidence as the melodic passage is immediately repeated in lighter instrumentation. Very late, in the third act, it is touched on once more by way of allusion: there where Ighino assures his father that one will still speak of him in the most distant future; and with envy one perceives again here, as in other places, what possibilities of unification and of ingenious or intimately thoughtful deepening the Wagnerian-motif artwork provides.

Again, I am leaving aside all ethical and intellectual considerations in order for the present to admire exclusively the aesthetic powers and merits of the work. I survey the extensive but artistically compactly filled scenario of the first act, and find that it is joined together unusually beautifully and easily, in fortunate necessity. The conversation of the boys is followed by the emotional scene between Palestrina and the prelate; immediately there is the "predecessor" scene, faded and filled with ghostly sounds of the past, this heartfelt vision, the deep, struggling conversation in the night of a living person, piously and nobly filled with tradition, with the masters ... they disappear, from distress and darkness the lonely one cries upward, then the angel's voice rises up heart-stirringly into the *Kyrie,* the tired one's hour of grace begins, he bends his ear to the shadowy mouth of his dead sweetheart, light bursts from the depths, the endless choruses break out in the *Gloria in excelsis,* to the accompaniment of all their harps they sing to him of perfection and peace. Then the high tension is resolved, everything becomes pale, Palestrina hangs exhausted in his armchair, and now? Could it be possible to close this act without exhaustion, an act that is a true celebration in honor of painful artistic genius and an apotheosis of music, after it has risen to such visions? To bring forth another effect that even exceeds such a climax? What joy to see how this is possible, how such a possibility has long been prepared with that exquisite, permissible, yes, imperative and enthusiastic cleverness, circumspection, and politics of art! Pay attention! Through the window of Palestrina's work-room one becomes aware of the cupolas of Rome. Very early, as early as the end of the first scene, when Silla, the promising pupil who sides with the Florentine futurists, looks out over Rome and takes leave of the conservative old nest with pleasantly ironical phrases, the orchestra, after the majestically sweeping motif of the city, begins a moderately strong, monotonous dinning in seconds that seems as if it will never end, and whose purpose, for the moment, is undiscoverable. The people exchanged amazed and smiling looks at this strange accompaniment, and there was no one who would have prophesied any dramatic future to this whimsically nonsensical idea. Pay attention, I say! Since then more than an hour has gone by in reality, but by illusion a whole night, and a world of things has happened. The disappearing angelic glory has left earthly dawn behind, the day is rising rapidly in a red glow over the cupolas outside, there is Rome, its powerful theme announced clearly and ostentatiously in the orchestra—and then, truly, the forgotten dinning of yesterday evening starts up again, it is like a ringing, yes, they are bells, the morning bells of Rome, not real bells, only imitated by the orchestra, but in such a way as massive swinging, resounding, droning, and dinning church bells have never been imitated artistically before—a colossal swinging of daringly harmonized seconds in which, as in the roar of a water-fall that one's ears cannot master, every kind of pitch and vibration, the thundering, roaring, and crashing, mix with the greatest string falsetto, exactly as it is when hundreds of resounding bells seem to have set the whole atmosphere into vibration and to want to blow up the firmament. It is an enormous effect! The master, who is slumbering at the side in his chair, the holy city in a purple glow that, as it shines through the window, glorifies the pitiful locale of nocturnal creative ecstasy, and in addition the powerful resounding of the bells that only retreats when the boys, who have had a good night's sleep, collect the sheets of music that are spread around the room and exchange a few lines; and that then resumes its powerful course again until the curtain falls.

I admire as a compositional beauty the way in which the powerful figure of Cardinal Borromeo, this boisterous patron, combines the clerical-intellectual world of Palestrina with the world of reality, the world of the second act. But this second act, standing as it does in its turbulent colorfulness between the first and the third, is itself a compositional beauty. Contrary to the aesthetic judgment of most people, I enjoy this impossibility made possible, in a pure drama of ideas that is, if not "plot," then at least an intellectually illuminated, colorful event. Life in the light of thought—what better thing can art provide us, what more entertaining? I have actually heard the opinion: Meyerbeer, historical opera. This is completely erroneous. To tell everything—perhaps I was personally better prepared than others to avoid this misunderstanding; perhaps I had long been well acquainted with the main intention here: to let the idea speak through historical detail, and only in this way to give this detail dramatic tension. At any rate, every reproof here attacks the whole work, the conception. One may believe that the idea of this composition: art, life, and art again, was the earliest fog, the first thing that the poet actually *saw*.

Pessimism and humor—I have never perceived their correlation more strongly and never more sympathetically than in the face of the second Palestrina act. The optimist, the reformer, in a word, the politician, is never a humorist; he is lofty-rhetorical. The pessimistic moral philosopher, however, whom one likes to call today quite figuratively the "aesthete," will behave toward the world of will, reality, guilt, and practical affairs with a natural preference for humor; as an artist he sees them as picturesque and amusing, in sharp contrast to the quiet dignity of intellectual life: and only in this contrast rests the dramatic nature of the council scenes in which the product of that exuberant night that we experienced, Palestrina's mass, becomes an object of political negotiation. Truly, what type of life and reality would be more grotesque, tumultuous, and funny in the sense of this contrast than politics? The second act is nothing other than a colorful and affectionately studied satire on politics, specifically on its immediately dramatic form, the parliament. That it is a parliament of clerical men increases the ridiculousness and lack of dignity to the extreme. Admittedly, music is original passion; and therefore the orchestral prelude, perhaps the most splendid musical piece of the evening, has a completely stirring effect: this crashing, storming, falling, breathtaking agitation, the most admirable moment of which is the fourfold, gasping onset of the main motif, tragically illustrates Palestrina's statement about the "movement that life constantly whips us into." It is a description, only too full of experience, of the dreadful Samsara. And still it is precisely this fundamental passion of the music that together with the human element creates the overpoweringly funny part. I am thinking of the figure of the patriarch Abdisu of Assyria and the sounds of unimagined and fantastic absurdity with which the orchestra accompanies his sacerdotal jubilation over "*the* day" and "*this* work," and his mildly unsuccessful parliamentary speech. Never at all has the moving comedy of doddering old age and venerable innocence been so thoroughly perceived and raised to such a special effect.

Say what you will, the act is entertaining. The richness of accents, the sharpness of the types, the transparency of ideas, lend it the sublime charm of victorious art. The spritely Bishop of Budoja, the unbridledly arrogant Spaniard, the conceited Cardinal Novagerio, in whose role the torture motif does its infamous work: life is in motion, art plays lights upon it, gathers it to its highest energy—and what a homecoming, then, to *art itself,* to the tidy cell of the creative artist, to the world of loneliness and of loyalty. The Pope sings hexameters—a singularly grand idea. The final note is of resignation and peace, "musical thought" on the harmonium, only lightly disturbed by distant, rapid *evvivas* to the chirping of the mandolins. And quietly the orchestra speaks the final word that was also the initial word, and is a secret.

I have not said anything yet about Pierluigi Palestrina, the musical hero of the work. I loved his figure from the moment he stepped with the prelate through the narrow door of his little room, the figure of the medieval master, of the artist, as popular romanticism does not at all dream of him, quiet, modest, simple, without claim to "passion," subdued and composed, wounded inside, dignified by suffering. I see him as, with his gentle, already-graying head to one side, he lifts his hand slightly toward the young pupils and says, "Be pious and quiet." Infinite sympathy wells up. "Be pious and quiet!" How should a person obliged to create a work of art not be pious and quiet? Or should such a person perhaps run out into the street and make political gestures? But if this figure of an artist is not romantic in the cheap sense—it is still *romanticism,* simply by forming the lyrical center of the poem. Romantic art tends to be "backward pointing" in two senses: not only to the degree that it is, as Nietzsche says, "applied history," but also because it turns reflexively-reflectingly back toward the subject. Conversely, at least, all art that has art and the artist as its subject—no matter how skeptical-ironical the treatment of the subject

may be—all *confessional* art, therefore, is *romantic* art; and especially here, even if also for some additional reasons, especially as
an artistic confession, and indeed as one of the most ruthlessly
radical type, *Palestrina* is a romantic work of art. But as far as
politics is concerned, let one not hope that it has been dispensed
with! Has it *never* been dispensed with, even though we were not
aware of it? [. . .]

There is in the *Palestrina* score a theme—it is probably actually
the most important of all, and once we had almost started to talk
about it—the significance of which is not immediately clear and
that cannot easily be given a name, such as, for example, the Emperor Ferdinand and the council motifs, or the motifs of the cities
of Rome, Bologna, and Trent. It is a melodic figure of extraordinary
beauty, consisting of two measures that are presented, as it were,
with sadly aware precision, to which a nobly perceived cadence is
added that rises high up and returns to the dominant, decoratively
accompanied by a final flourish of sixteenths. It appears as early
as in the overture at the end of Palestrina's own archaic theme,
and its reappearance always accompanies or creates moments of
spiritual and poetic significance. It dominates the musical scene
when the cardinal encourages the tired master to create the preserving and crowning work; it resounds also when the predecessors
announce to him "the sense of the times" and that of his own life;
and it forms, in an un-Wagnerian, untheatrical way, the quietly
resigned conclusion of the whole work. What, then, does it mean?
Undoubtedly it belongs to Palestrina's personality. It is the symbol
for a part of his character, or for his character in a certain connection: the symbol of his artistic fate and of his temporal situation,
the metaphysical statement that he is not a beginning, but an end,
the motif of the "capstone," the look of melancholy, the look back-
wards. But I have not yet said where this theme is *also* expressed:
there, you see, where Lucretia's passing is mentioned—truly and
unmistakably it forms the symphonic undercurrent to Ighino's sentence: "He became dark and empty"; therefore it is also at the
same time the symbol of Palestrina's psychological condition after
the death of his wife, the symbol of his love that is turned backward
or rather downward to the shadow kingdom, the love that proves
to be the inspiring force in that creative, miraculous night; it is, all
in all, the magically melodious sounding formula for his special

type of productivity, a productivity of pessimism, of resignation and of longing, a romantic productivity.

On a summer evening between the second and third *Palestrina* performances we were sitting on a garden terrace, discussing the work by making obvious comparisons with the *Meistersinger* both as a drama about an artist and as a work of art in general; we compared Ighino with David, Palestrina with Stolzing and Sachs, the mass with the prize song; we talked of Bach and of Italian church music as stylizing forces. Pfitzner said: "The difference is expressed most clearly in the concluding scenic pictures. At the end of the *Meistersinger* there is a stage full of light, rejoicing of the people, engagement, brilliance, and glory; in my work there is, to be sure, Palestrina, who is also celebrated, but in the half-darkness of his room under the picture of the deceased one, dreaming at his organ. The *Meistersinger* is the apotheosis of the new, a praise of the future and of life; in *Palestrina* everything tends toward the past, it is dominated by *sympathy with death*." We were silent; and in his manner, the manner of a musician, he let his eyes move directly upward into vagueness.

It is not readily understandable why his last word shook and astounded me so much. Not that it was on material grounds a surprise for me; it was of course completely consistent. What startled me so was the formulation. "Sympathy with death." I did not believe my ears. It was my expression. Before the war I had begun to write a little novel, a type of pedagogical story, in which a young person, landed in a morally dangerous locale, found himself between two equally quaint educators, between an Italian literary man, humanist, rhetorician, and man of progress, and a somewhat disreputable mystic, reactionary, and advocate of antireason—he had the choice, the good youngster, between the powers of virtue and of seduction, between duty and service to life and the fascination of decay, for which he was not unreceptive; and the turn of phrase, "sympathy with death," was a thematic constituent of the composition. Now I heard it word for word from the mouth of the *Palestrina* composer. And not pointedly at all, in a completely improvised way, it seemed, he had only spoken the words to give matters their correct name. Was this not quite remarkable? In order to characterize his elevated musical work properly, this important contemporary had, with absolute necessity, hit upon an expression of my ironical literary work. How much brotherhood comes read-

ily from contemporaneousness itself! And how much similarity in
the direction of intellectual work is necessary for two intellectual
workers, who, distant from one another, live in completely different artistic spheres, outwardly without connection, to agree upon
the same literary symbol for whole spiritual complexes!

"Sympathy with death"—not a phrase of virtue and of progress.
Is it not rather, as I said, the formula and basic definition of all
romanticism? And that beautiful, nostalgic-fateful Palestrina motif,
which we could not name at first, could it be the motif of creative
sympathy with death, the motif of romanticism, the *final word* of
romanticism? The artist who sang Palestrina was the same one
who made such a strong impression on Romain Rolland in Basel
as the evangelist in the St. Matthew Passion. At night at his table
he looked grippingly like the author: with this, the confessional
stamp of the whole performance became complete. It was not so
much a matter of the culmination of Italian church music, as rather
of the "capstone" of the structure of romantic opera, of the wistful
end of a *national* artistic movement that finished gloriously with
Hans Pfitzner, according to his own insight.

Translated by Walter D. Morris

August Halm

On Fugal Form, Its Nature,
and Its Relation to Sonata Form
(1913)

What a fugue is, what a sonata is, it does not seem possible to say, but only what takes place in each of the two forms, what each calls for: a definition of the fugue or the sonata has up till now, to my knowledge, neither been formulated nor discovered.

Essential to the fugue is a contrapuntal mode of thought and the equal claim of each voice to the theme. The first of these, the independent conduct of the voices so that each one has its own meaningful course, can indeed exist in every musical form; it can even dominate another form, for example, the sonata form. Thus Beethoven designed his Sonata for Piano and Violin in A Minor, Opus 23, essentially in three voices and in this made an attempt—not too happy, to be sure—at a contrapuntally voiced sonata. We should expect the polyphonic style more in sonatas for string quartet or string trio, where each of the four or three voices is represented in its own right by one player, who as a musical intelligence might well lay claim also to a part already meaningful in itself, whether this would then be superior or subordinate or equal in rank to its partners. The facts teach us that even without this mentality a quartet can manage to exist; in classical quartets in the best instances there is a mixed contrapuntal and homophonic character. The fugue by contrast permits no choice in this respect: counterpoint is its vital element. Each voice participates to approximately the same degree as the rest in the main theme; and this may not fall to it only, so to speak, as a favor, but it is the right of each voice to join in representing the main idea. Here, however, in the right to do so, lies also its duty to be constantly in readiness for this important role, and this readiness again lies in its continuously guarded self-esteem: it must impose on itself at all times an existence that is answerable to itself and meaningful. It can well on occasion defer and listen to the activity of the other voices in order after a time to fall to work again—but it may not, so long as it is a participant in the play, abandon its own sense, or lead any existence, therefore, that is explained and justified only by its "mere dependence." When one voice is crowned with the chief idea, the others alongside it may not appear impoverished and poorly clothed, but must seem to be peers who are worthy at any moment of the crown, if indeed, thanks to the greater freedom of motion at their command, they do not assume a still more beautiful and noble attitude than is possible for the bearer of the main theme, for this is not seldom like a severe, undecorated costume, or better, like a simpler form of existence, which only on the basis of the fugue sprouts into the grandeur of the fuller blossoms.

We regard the three-part fugue as normal in construction; its first group is devoted to the main key, its second to the relative of this, and its third group to the subdominant key, while the dominant in each instance is always used for the "answer" of the theme so that the tonic (as the dominant of the subdominant) again comes into its own for the close. After this third group (or "development") and in accordance with the length and animation of the piece, an organ point that prepares for the conclusion on the dominant of the tonic and in addition probably a coda also will be desired or necessary; that is a question that is resolved by the properties of the individual piece, not by the nature of the fugue.

This grouping seems to aim more at harmonic fullness than that of the chief form of the sonata. The latter provides a fifth-related or third-related key for the group of the second theme; the restatement is according to rule reserved for the main key. By contrast, great and really unrestricted freedom is permitted for the group of the development; besides this, the domination of a definite key within a group, with its larger expansion and with the broader unfolding of its content, is no longer a strict rule. In practice, therefore, the sonata permits the greater richness of harmonic event; the fugue, on the other hand, has the harmonically richer schema, it arrives at a greater selection through its basic arrangement. This selection is rational to a high degree, it takes into consideration the closest relationships, which is to say the most solid and fruitful connections. Next-related keys are those that have the greatest inclination to interconnect; it is thus only natural that these ties are consummated or rather permitted in a piece.

It is equally only natural, indeed, that warmth arises in this way, that things do not proceed neutrally. If I play in F major, the related dominants C major and B-flat major and the relative key D minor are constantly on the watch, so to speak; their entrance is an event that is awaited, indeed desired, the fulfillment of a longing that in the final analysis we may ascribe not only to us but also to the musical form, if only we are capable of feeling something with music, of conferring upon it a soul. And here a more severe critique would now have to affirm a deficiency in Bachian music. This event, namely, is absent in his fugues. When Bach opens a new group, it often takes place without our noticing it; we doubtless hear that after a development in F major another arrives in D minor—but we follow nothing of this; no determined intensification, no agitation, no trembling announces an important happening, a decisive act; he who does not hear the keys themselves will seldom notice anything of the fact that here something special is afoot. If he needs F major, Bach brings this up "with a relaxed hand"; he *imparts* F major. The fugue he produces has contrapuntal but not formal mastery; it is formally correct, but no more. Its voices indeed live, but its form still does not, it has no soul and no will, it does not long for, does not hope and rejoice. Here lay the possibility of a true progress of the fugal form; a further possibility connected with this was that of lending the individual groups different characters; and both could lead to a more broadly expanded fugue—that in itself is also progress.

A good fugue that lasts ten minutes, in other words, is worth more than two good fugues of five minutes each, provided that each, in correspondence with its content, has its correct length. To set up the necessary larger context is always also the greater accomplishment, just as it is also the more difficult task.

That is was reserved for more recent art to differentiate the groups of the fugue seems to me to be more a matter of chance than that another advance appeared only with advanced harmony: that, namely, of more vigorously comprehended form, as this reveals itself in the manner of introducing the new group. We can see the immediate explanation of the latter in the enriched harmonic means, which permit climaxes that were foreign to Bach; while on the contrary no such direct basis is evident for the fact that Bach did not treat the different groups also in a different manner, did not place them under the dominion of different characters. With more penetrating inward deliberation we shall indeed go back to the immanent will of his art, to the artistic disposition, to find the one basis for both.

For instead of assuming that Bach lacked the capacity to use harmony for climaxes, it makes much more sense to believe that this lay far from his artistic intentions. He did not have harmonic, but contrapuntal climaxes: the multiplied and weightier relationships of the melodic factors, of the "voices," are for him the high point of a piece. In view of the enormous harmonic wealth that he commanded, of the intrepidity in his manner of deploying it, which indeed even today is able to astonish and even alarm the listener, we should hardly call the technical possibility also into question for him. Indeed Bach secured his greatest artistic merit in the field of harmony, not counterpoint. As a master of counterpoint Bach is an eclectic or collector, a summary figure, and at the same time, to be sure, an improver and perfecter; but as a master of harmony he learned basically only from himself without having in this an actual model, he invented *architectonic harmony,* found and directed its powers and virtues as they were needed for construction, for coherence and articulation, for the vaulting of large arches. "Johann Sebastian Bach, the Germans' greatest harmonist": so reads an inscription under an old picture of the master. That is much more correctly said than it was meant, for under the designation "harmonist" only the musician or composer in general was understood.

The impression of Bülow that, placed alongside Bach, Handel appears as a dilettante, is certainly grounded above all in the harmonic superiority of Bachian music. Here it is doubtless a matter of taste to think either that Bach exhausted himself in the one great invention, or that the other, that of *dramatizing harmony,* to venture this very much misunderstood expression, was just not of interest to him.

It is not by chance that the greatest master of the classical sonata also forced great progress on the fugue. For it was surely progress when the different groups were treated differently by Beethoven and their entrance also shaped itself into an event. To offer change is still no virtue, but it certainly is such to differentiate and to articulate. Both are basically *one* advance that has its origin in the will to expression, to more thorough representation. Distinction of the individual parts was necessary when the form spread out, and the more expansively formed fugue also had to manifest more distinct high points and climactic curves. In the fact that it makes possible such growth of form might lie the final and deepest musical meaning of the whole harmonic development that gives our so-called modern music its stamp even though its immediate goal may lie in another field. Even though, in specific terms, what was won was placed for the most part in the service of intensified and refined "expression," indeed, even though it had been invented to this end, we know nevertheless since Anton Bruckner's revelations how it really serves and abets music. Bruckner is the first absolute musician of great style and finished mastery since Bach, the creator of dramatic music—of the art that combated and vanquished the music drama. If the fugue sought to be fertilized by the spirit of new music, it had to find contrast, leaving thematic unity intact, in the manner of treating the theme.

Most fugues begin with the main theme, and indeed this is presented by one voice without accompaniment. It is self-understood that no unpleasant state of insufficiency may be produced by this. Thus the musical idea must be self-assured and without the demand for an accompaniment; it must carry its intelligibility and worth in itself; no uneasiness, no fear of being alone may adhere to it.

Still more: the theme must really refuse to accept an "accompaniment." For the best fugue themes accompaniments simply cannot be thought of at all; sufficient unto themselves, they tolerate no support; they insist on being either alone or among equals. That means: there must already be alive in themselves the wish for independent companions on their way; they not only permit the independence of others, but it is their pride to demand it; in musical terms: they are by nature contrapuntally disposed and directed to counterpoint.

Here and there we meet with an attempt to evade this natural demand: we hear themes that at first present themselves to us unintelligibly, and reveal their form, their sense only in full harmonic illumination or even as elucidated by a countertheme. That may be pretty, interesting, or provocative of intimations, as a riddle and an indistinct whisper can be pretty or interesting: but in the last analysis there is little gained by such things for musical art. If we know the riddle's solution, the end and goal of the path, the magic that can inhere originally in such places fails and there remains over only the actual value. Consequently soundness, solidity is the most important thing for a fugue theme; if above and beyond this it is also blessed with beauty, so much the better. But what we commonly call "interesting," what aims at surprise, let us rather keep distant from the fugue: surprises wear out; they are hostile to the whole style of the fugue, to its uninterrupted course, and in the theme itself, which is destined to be repeated often, of thoroughly doubtful advantage, mostly even of undoubted harm. The theme is to convince, not to persuade, not even to conquer; a median measure, a certain reserve is particularly to be expected of it, which concerns the rhythmical element. Sudden gestures, brusque commands, and arousing calls such as Beethoven often uses in opening his sonatas would be of little use in a fugue; they would soon be intolerable. Here at least refinement and when possible cultivation in thematic construction is much more demanded. How much of such cultivation is achieved in Bach's best themes—even if we may also hear these being picked up simply and almost as though by chance on the boulevard—to show that calls for a special study.

The answer to the theme—more correctly stated, the answering form of the theme—the special laws of which belong to the theory of composition, stands (as already mentioned) in the dominant of the key in which the theme was presented. In this constant change of fifth-related keys there lies the danger of a certain heaviness and obstinacy of the pace and flow of the harmony and at the same time an obstacle to chromaticism, which can be considered the essential element of recent harmony; unobstructed there really remains only melodic chromaticism as Bach often makes use of it, even somewhat more often than we of the present day are fond of, who see more in this manner only play, or in the most favorable circumstance a preliminary play, or prelude *[Vorspiel]*, since we have come to know the seriousness and the fecundity of true, or harmonic, chromaticism. Also the theme itself is bound by this condition; it cannot distance itself far from the main key, apart from the fact that constantly repeated transitions would tire us much more than solid persistence in normality does. To what extent freedom may still be achieved within this constraint, to what degree, that is, the interludes can be burdened with the chromatic element—that will be decided by the question of how far a harmonically "modern" fugue is possible in general. The fugato sections in sonatas or symphonies may hardly be cited here as decisive. An occasional episodic fugato within another form is an essentially different thing from a fugue; that is already clear in the fugato sections of the classical composers. Thus the fugal section in the Finale of the G-minor Symphony of Mozart is of rather good effect within the contrapuntally impoverished piece as a whole; if it stood in a true fugue it would seem on the contrary quite miserable. The whole question of life and nourishment, so to speak, is asked in a different way in the fugue than it is in a fugato.

In any event if the fugato does not have the style of the fugue it nevertheless has its technique, and thus to illuminate a peculiarity of fugal themes we can invite the comparison of the forms that a theme first has as a sonata theme and then assumes as the theme of a fugato. We often find in Beethoven the inclination to introduce fugal technique in the developments of his sonatas or symphonies. Here it is striking that the composer avoids the hasty and indeed even the clear termination of the theme. Just think of the first movement of the Sonata for the Hammerklavier and of the Finale of the A Major Sonata Opus 101. The fugue theme, more explicitly, must demand extension; its melody is indeed spun out when the next voice announces the theme, and the voice that first had the theme is here in particular not permitted to discontinue either externally or internally; caesuras must simply be avoided, since not all the sounding voices may have a caesura at the same time. "Infinite melody" rules in the fugue. Now the newly entering voice produces a caesura by its entrance: accordingly the first voice must here strictly restrain itself from a close, at least from a vigorous close with a "masculine ending." Bülow decided after some doubt how far the theme of the D Minor Fugue of Bach (*The Well-Tempered Clavier,* vol. 2) proceeds; but Bach intentionally veiled the end of this theme in darkness just as he does with other themes.

The reader who takes this treatise in earnest will not find it improper if I refer here to one of my fugues composed for string orchestra. Its theme closes with a suspension and the resolution of the suspension in the dominant, of which the natural resolution to the tonic, however, is then withheld; in its place there appears an eighth rest and only after this does the melody continue, as the dominant is taken up again. Here the caesura is evaded or rendered ineffectual by the harmonic tension, which continues the breath across the pause. If in place of the pause there followed a close on a stressed tonic, that would be subject to censure as an unquestionable error. The otherwise beautiful G-sharp Minor Fugue of Bach in the first book of *The Well-Tempered Clavier* suffers somewhat throughout from the cadence of the theme, which is to be sure not strikingly energetic but nevertheless perfect, and the repeated appearance of which gives the whole piece something of a steplike divided character, something of a terrace form, which little becomes a fugue in particular.

In the first theme of the first movement of the Hammerklavier Sonata as transformed for fugal use, it is also worth noting that the huge leap from the upbeat to the first accented note was reduced to a modest fourth. That was called for by fugal technique, which demands simple intelligibility from the theme, and to this there belong readily comprehensible intervals, namely, natural as well as small ones. To have widely spaced tones in different "registers" in a conversation of three or four independently propelled voices would tear the theme apart because of the changing tone colors; how difficult to grasp even the leap of a sixth can be in a theme when it lies in a middle voice we can see, for example, in the B-flat Major Fugue of the first book of *The Well-Tempered Clavier*. Beethoven evaded this restrictive rule with sufficient if indeed not perfect success in the beginning of the theme of the fugal finale of the same Hammerklavier Sonata, which because of the abruptly broken off and strikingly hammered first note as well as the trill on the second note powerfully penetrates and bores into the consciousness of the listener.

For the sake of completeness we would still have to speak of the length of the theme, which should as little exceed the limit of comprehensibility as the spatial dimension. Here, however, this limit is less easy to set than for the compass, since the memory for long stretches can indeed be strengthened. In spite of this we can without hesitation call many themes too long, especially when the composer himself feels them to be too long, when his patience soon fails to carry out such a theme fully, just as in the *Hammerklavier* finale the composer obviously saw himself burdened by the long theme. But a fugue with impatience in its weft yields no durable texture. Precisely a patient power or a powerful patience is much more the signature of the fugue. There can be no fugue without trust in the theme, indeed without love for it.

Finally a certain neutrality, a moderate line is called for in the theme by the circumstance that it will be taken up by the soprano as well as by the bass and by the middle voices. Because of this the rapidity of motion of the theme is also confined within somewhat narrower limits than with other forms since low tones are unwieldy by nature—which might be helped by the augmentation of the theme in the bass. But even for the sake of easy intelligibility the theme is held to a moderate motion. A special property of a theme that is favorable for a complete fugue is finally its capacity for transformation into minor or major, which is called for by the group of the relative key.

If we summarize what has been said, we find that a fugue theme must renounce many attractive features that we prize in a sonata theme or a rondo theme; the whimsical, the surprising, the persuasive, even the impassioned is here a danger or a defect that grows with each repetition. A fugue theme is precisely no "inspiration," but a state of musical order; a simply natural, solid, perhaps also sober formulation; or an artful one when it is more worked out and differentiated in its forces of motion—at any rate achieved more by selection of what is most sound or by intellectual effort than merely by "inspiration." How much positive artistic virtue and strength is demanded for this we can easily make clear to ourselves by our own attempts as well as by the comparison of standard sonata themes with good fugue themes; indeed we are hardly able to imagine the themes of the fugato sections adduced above as themes of a correct fugue; they are too slight for this! They would not stand from the start so imperturbably and self-assuredly before us as is fitting for a fugue theme; precisely the duty of a responsible beginning would have deprived them of their status as themes of a fugal interlude.

Translated by Edward A. Lippman

Hans Breuer

The *Wandervogel* Movement and Folk Song
(1919)

The favorite songs of the *Wandervogel* movement have changed as often as Parisian fashions: the beer song, the bushel (harvest) song, the air, *Moritat* ballads, and gymnastics (*Turner-*) songs. Finally, the folk song came along, quietly and unassumingly. But it didn't actually *come;* it *stayed*—remained behind as the sole viable remnant of those early times with their concocted songs. And as the years wove folk song after folk song into our ranks, we recognized more and more, that here, quietly, a new and special world was coming into being for our *Wandervogel* movement. Ever more clearly and sharply profiled, the folk song raised itself up from among the tangled mass of those quickly wilting creatures, proudly, as the splendid rose tree stretches its thorny wood over the inferior grasses.—With that the painter created a profound symbol.—Now it is there, and only the idle question remains: *why* did it of necessity come to us?

Let us look first at our *Wandervogel* outings. What role does the folk song play on our excursions? We'll take some brief episode as an example.

We once lay there upon the old, flower-shaded terraces of the bishop's palaces in Meersburg. It was a marvelous, sultry summer evening. Before us rested Lake Constance, dark and deep. Far off on the opposite shore a few lights were already blinking. So still was the evening. Now and then a fish splashed upon the warm water. There was much poetry in the expansive landscape, and, as though sung by itself, we heard from a distance:

Dear herdsman, stay in the lake—

And we tuned our lutes (guitars) and softly hummed along:

> There were two kings' children
> They liked each other so
> They couldn't come to each other
> That water was much too wide—
> That water was much too wide.

And the evening drank the song into itself as a thirsty person would drink quenching balsam.—And there was much melancholy in the soft harmonies, but that was also the content of this seldomly great landscape picture. Draped in the night, the old castle lay with its memories of Droste [Annette von Droste-Hülshoff]; there were the dark waters, the summer night and the little lights beckoning on the far shore—all of this in tune with the basic character of this song.

Two women came along, dressed in an old-fashioned manner, who had stood still and listened.—They then interrupted the stillness: "Oh, would the gentlemen please sing another!" "Not tonight," we replied, "but early tomorrow we'll come up to the castle (it was the women from the castle) and strike one up for you." For we didn't want to do a single song more that day; the one was enough. This one song had given us much for the evening, one more would have destroyed everything; it was the essence, the consummate expression of this poetic wandering hour.

Decorated with red sashes, we went up to the castle the next morning. "The gentlemen are already expected," whispered the old gatekeeper with import. And now, all step confidently and with singsong into the resounding gateway hall—but here we must break off. It would be too much to tell all of the beautiful things we experienced there.

And so it is in practice: with singsong we enter our quarters at a peasant's house; in the early morning by the hearth, by flickering candlelight, a short, sad Swabian tune with the words "Must I then head out to the little town"; and then out in the forest a fresh hunters' song. Upon returning, the city gate echoes again with the sound of "Bi-Ba-Basel" and the bratwursts of the innkeeper summon forth the "Silly Gourmand" from our never-tiring throats. We intone a solemn "Ave Maria" to the setting sun, but then add:

Farewell and good night,
Now it is time to close,
For I must go.

And thus, out of every wandering hour outdoors there comes
the sound of a folk song; it is the most immediate language of all
our experience.

But the folk song is also our most honest language.

All of those concocted songs, which came and went, were sin-
cerely alien to the essence of the *Wandervogel* movement. There are
beer cheers, which at the point of drunkenness pound in incendiary
fashion through the empty rooms of the skull; there are Teutonic-
haired bard songs about the breasts of men, the drinking horn
and the love of gymnastics—*coffea maxima*—there is touching,
sentimental stuff, comparable to those sweet oleographs; there are
cobbler boy and proletarian marches. And there is an entire dung-
heap of comic music-hall songs, there is the *Büchsenfrühling,*
vaudeville trash, and Berlino-Styrian shouting music for the phonograph. But scarcely one "song," one genuine song, no matter how
short, has come from the big-city people.

And for that reason, because there is nothing better, one takes
this cheap stuff out into the countryside, contaminates the good
old singing spaces, and drives the folk song out of its home. It is
a good thing for us, that, after briefly losing our way, we quickly
come to the realization that outside of the city all of this rubbish
is no more than empty, insipid gibberish, false and mendacious to
the core. Out there beneath a blue sky, where the larks beat their
wings, there resounds only what has grown and come to be out
there:

I went through a grass green forest,
There I heard the birds singing.

What was felt by the people out there and, captured poetically,
found sincere expression in folk song, this can only find its proper
resonance with us in our wandering, in climbing over mountain
and valley, where the birds and flowers greet us.—There is no
Wandervogel youth so devoid of feeling that on occasion some folk
tune had not especially stirred him: whether it be in May, when

all sing and wander, be it upon an old mountain castle, overgrown with wild roses, or on some fantastic moonlit night!

Conversely, of course, many a good folk song sounds coarse and uncouth in a velvet boudoir. Whispering the *Specksalat* ("bacon salad") on velvet pillows is just as senseless as belting out or whistling a Handelian largo in a roadside ditch. After all, one does not take silk bedding out into the hay.—The folk song belongs out beneath the open sky, on country roads and in the rooms of peasants; there it sounds self-evident and natural.

For us Germans, the folk song has a very special language, one reminding us of home; it is more understandable yet to us than the silent view of the landscape's forms and shapes. What grips our innermost being more: the sad picture of frozen flowers in the springtime or the deep melancholy of the old minor-mode tune?—

> A frost fell in the spring night
> It fell upon the tender little blue flowers.
> They are wilted . . . withered.

A dark cloud remains silent to most eyes, but everyone hears and understands the lament in that gloomy melody—

> A dark cloud moves in
> . . . .
> And if you don't come soon, dear sun,
> Then all in the green wood will decay,
> And all of the weary flowers
> Will face a weary death.

The folk tune transmits much to the ear that the eye outwardly does not see.

And so the surrounding world gradually comes alive for the *Wandervogel* youth; and by wandering and singing so finely of the mourning mountain and valley, of the deep Rhine and the floating little ship, of the proud linden tree in the deep valley, of the rushing water and the mill wheel, of Miss Nightingale and the little flowers, the age-old sacred bonds of nature gradually reconnect themselves for him, bonds the unhappy course of time once tore asunder. The tree that was ripped out of its motherly ground has again taken root. And man—having sprung forth himself from the womb of nature—gradually finds himself again in his primordial relatives; he understands their language; he has again become natural.

In the folk song, the *Wandervogel* youth is in the company of a natural man, who yearns for and dreams as yet of a full, whole humanity, one that with its pithy roots still drinks nourishment from the ground of its all-relatedness. And all those who today stream forth into the open from the desolate walls of their city houses, driven like the crusaders by some forboding urge, to them the folk song yields much more than the masses: an—their—ideal human being.

What the *Wandervogel* youth is searching for out there, that stands written in the folk song! One can indeed say: *the folk song is the consummate expression of our* Wandervogel *ideals.*

And for that reason our slogan is: *Honor the folk song, you* Wandervogel *youth! Recognize in it and with it your true nature! Recognize yourself!*

But recognize as well what distant times have worked and created in you; recognize what is in you of those precious fragments of that old, half-broken culture vessel. Recognize your German essence, your unique character, derived from the immortal works of your ancestors.—Why are we of the *Wandervogel* movement such romantics?—We, too, have grown weary of the barbarism of the façade-bakers and the vile potpourri of urban art and life forms. Here, as well, the rule applies: get your feet back on the old, solid ground and then—go on building! Nothing speaks to the heart of our people more than its songs; in the folk song lives the precipitate of our entire German history.

To the *Wandervogel* youth, casting his dreaming gaze searchingly over the fortress ruins graying with age, filled with a yearning for deeds and proud ideals—to him, these most venerable stones become a ballad:

> There lies in Austria a castle,
> That is quite well built
> Out of silver and reddish gold,
> With walls of marble stone.

And something beckons from the barren, crumbled balcony, and the July wind softly laments the pain of the proud, beautiful noble lady:

—All of that happened for my sake,
Be still.

It is life itself that to this day flows through those stones, like
they, corroded and crumbled by centuries; but these are precious,
sacred remains: German becoming, German dreams, the soul of
the German people. Here are the true roots of our strength, not
in the German hurrah and the German record-setting craze—the
distinctive sign of our national malaise. Here, there opens up for
the *Wandervogel* youth a deep look into the work of the century,
work on our spiritual legacy. And that might perhaps contribute
to the beginnings of an organic cultural development.

And the farmer, to whom we sing these old songs again, arrives
as well at a better recognition of himself. The city has deluded the
country folk, through false magic it has made them blind to all of
the beautiful and good things that as yet live beneath them. But
the peasant, too, wants to be fashionably urban and in the process
forgets the good old art forms, ways, and customs, above all the
folk song.—But now the *Wandervogel* youth come out of the cities
and sing to the peasant: "Into the hay, hurray, hurray, three lilies,
and the musketeers are merry brothers." And the farmer hears that
with pleasure, that sounds as though it were coming from within
his own soul, and he suddenly discovers that he still carries much
of this precious heritage within himself, his eyes are opened; the
old, solid peoples' song has reacquired its rights to a homeland.—
This is no theory, it is already accomplished fact. Whoever does
not believe it should go sometime to the Heidelberg forestrangers'
families by Klingen Pond, or to the streets of Neckargemünd, where
year in and year out *Wandervogel* youth parade through. There
one hears again: "Bi-Ba-Basel" and "The Hunter in the Green
Wood" and many other beautiful folk songs.—And it can be said
that no one is called in such measure to bear these blessings than
the *Wandervogel* youth. Through his way, which is to wander, he
is, so to speak, the parliamentarian of peace between the city and
the country. The *Wandervogel* youth, who in the evening sits with
his guitar amidst the peasant family, who sings their old songs and
inspires their beautiful homes, who praises the wonderful earthen
dishes on their walls, the solid oak chests and cutout chair backs,
he gives his people more than all of the peoples' education experiments forced and imposed from above. For he restores to them

their pride and faith in themselves, and that is the backbone of all progress. In this way the mission of our *Wandervogel* movement is growing and deepening; we not only receive for our boys, we give something back. And that is the higher aim!—

Let the banners fly, let the black, heathen griffin pennant wave. We are a proud *Wandervogel* movement! Hail!

Translated by Michael Gilbert

Max Weber

Technical, Economic, and Social Interrelations between Modern Music and Its Instruments
(1921)

Origins of the Strings

Our string instruments that are akin to those of antique culture and known in a primitive form to the Chinese and other music systems, represent the convergence of two different species of instruments. On the one hand, they are descendants of the violin-like string instruments native to the Orient and the tropical regions, provided with a resonant body made of one piece (originally the shell of the tortoise with skin stretched above it).

The lyre known from Otfried in the eighth century that consisted of one, later three and more strings, belonged to these instruments as did the *rubeba* (rebeck) imported from the Orient during the crusades and used extensively in the eleventh, twelfth, and thirteenth centuries. This instrument was well adapted to traditional music. It was able to produce the diatonic church modes including the *B Moll* (B minor). However, it was not properly of progressive nature. Neither the resonance nor the cantilena was ready to be developed beyond narrow limits.

These instruments were confronted by string instruments with a resonant body built as a composite and provided with special string parts (frets). These made possible the formation of the resonant body necessary for an unhindered manipulation of the bow and its optimal equipment with the modern resonance bearers (bridge, sound post). For the effectiveness of string instruments shaping of the resonant body is decisive. A string merely firmly strung without a vibrating body does not produce a musically useful tone.

The creation of resonant bodies is a purely Occidental invention, the specific motive for which can no longer be ascertained. It seems to be related to the fact that the handling of wood in the form of boards and all finer carpenter's and wooden inlay work is much more typical of Nordic peoples than those of the Orient.

The Hellenic plucked string instruments with their resonant bodies, which in comparison with those of the Orient were already built artistically, were subject, thus, after their migration north, to very early further improvement precisely in those respects. The first instruments with raised borders were still of rather primitive kind. The one stringed *trumscheit* that probably originated from the monochord had a resonant board body with transmission of the vibrations by means of a sound post and produced by means of simple technical devices a strong, trumpet-like increased sound. Tone production did not take place mechanically but through fingered manipulation. Only experts could produce other than first harmonics. Without doubt because of its very tonal limitations, the instrument reenforced modern tone feeling. The wheel lyre *(organistrum)*, a keyboard instrument with raised borders, produced the diatonic scale, but it also possessed bourdon strings tuned in fifths and fourths. Like the *trumscheit* it was domesticated in the monasteries of the early Middle Ages.

Whether wheel lyres were originally in the hands of jongleurs cannot be established, but they were never the instruments of noble amateurs. Next to the lyre among the instruments important to the jongleurs later belongs the Germanic and Slavic fiddle, which is already found in the ninth century. It was the instrument of the Nibelungen heroes. For the first time on it, the neck was formed as a separate part supplying the sturdiness needed for its use in a modern fashion.

The fiddle (called by Hieronymus of Moravia *"vielle"*) originally had two unison strings (for the third accompaniment) and bourdon strings or none of this kind depending on whether artistic or popular music was to be performed. From the fourteenth to the eighteenth century it also had frets. As long as the requirements of orchestra music did not take possession and transform it, the instrument had increasing harmonic importance. Because of its technique and hardiness it became the bearer of folk tunes.

Evolution of String Instruments under the Influence of the Bards

Social organizational factors contributed additional forces to the evolution of the strings. The Gaelic crwth, important as the instrument of the bards, was originally plucked and later played. The rules for playing it were subject to regulation through congresses of bards (as, for example, the Congress of 1176). It is the first of many string instruments with a bridge and holes through which the hand may be passed. Subjected to continuous technical improvement, it became harmonically useful after the addition of the bourdon strings. The crwth is today considered to be the ancestor of the fiddle with raised borders.

Professional organization secured the musical influence of the bards. This in turn was a basic factor in the continuous improvement and typification of their instruments. These instruments were indispensable for the advancement of music.

Furthermore, technical improvements in the construction of string instruments were connected, toward the end of the Middle Ages, with the musical guild organizations of instrumentalists that in the Sachsenspiegel were still treated as having no legal rights. This guild organization appeared in the thirteenth century, providing a fixed market for the manufactured instruments, helping standardize their types.

Still other social factors are represented in the gradual acceptance of instrumentalists beside the singers in the bands of hierarchy, of princes, and of communities. Established instrumental roles became the rule only in the sixteenth century. This gave to the production of instruments an even more productive economic foundation. Since the fifteenth century in close connection with humanistic music theorists, the attempt was made to provide instruments ready to be played in orchestras. The separation of the high and low viols was executed at least with the French *ménétriers* of the fourteenth century.

The Great Instrument Makers and
the Modern Orchestra

The numerous species of viols still found in the seventeenth and eighteenth centuries with very different, often very numerous stringing, recalling the rapid increase of strings on the Hellenic kithara, were a product of uninterrupted experimentation especially in the sixteenth century. It was also encouraged by the individually varied traditional practices and pretensions of the leading orchestras. These numerous types of viols vanished in the eighteenth century in favor of the three modern string instruments: the violin, viola, and cello. The superiority of these instruments was unambiguously demonstrated by violin virtuosity first appearing in full bloom since Corelli, and through development of the modern orchestra.

The violin, viola, and cello became the instruments for a special modern organization of chamber music, the string quartet as it was definitely established by Joseph Haydn. They constitute the kernel of the modern orchestra. They are a product of persistent experiments of the manufacturers of instruments from Brescia and Cremona.

The gap between the performance capacity of these instruments, which were in no way improved since the beginning of the eighteenth century, and their predecessors is very striking. Speaking with some exaggeration, the string instruments of the Middle Ages did not permit the legato playing that in our view is specific to them, although the ligatures of old mensural notation permit us to conclude they existed. The sustaining of tones, increasing or decreasing volume, melodious playing of fast passages, and all the specific qualities that we expect to be executed by the violin were still rendered only with difficulty until the sixteenth century. They were nearly impossible quite apart from the fact that the changes of hand position required today for the domination of the tone space of string instruments were almost excluded by the type of construction. Considering the quality of the family of instruments it is not surprising that the division of the neck through frets, thus mechanical tone production, prevailed. Virdung, therefore, still calls the hand fiddle together with the more primitive string instruments useless.

In connection with the demand of court orchestras the ascension of string instruments to their perfection began in the sixteenth century. The ever-present desire for expressive sonorous beauty, for a singing tone, and elegance of the instrument itself were the driving forces in Italy of the orchestras and the instrument makers. Even before the transfer of technical supremacy in violin construction to Brescia and Cremona, one notes in the sixteenth century, gradual approximations of various parts of the instrument (especially of the form of the bridge and the sound holes) toward its final form.

What such technical development offered in possibilities, once perfection was achieved, far surpassed what had been demanded. The performance capacity of the Amati instruments was not really exploited for many decades. In the same way as the single violin, following an ineradicable conviction, first had to be "played in" and had to wait a generation before it could reach the full height of its rendition potential, so the adaptation and introduction also as compared with other instruments occurred only very slowly. Ruhlmann's supposition that modern string instruments originate in a unique, unanticipated accident goes too far. However, it remains true that the tonal potential made available by the construction of the instrument was not immediately exploited. Its availability as a special solo instrument of virtuosi could not have been guessed beforehand by the builders.

It is to be assumed that the concern of the Amati, Guarneri, and Stradivari were turned essentially toward achieving sensuous beauty and only then sturdiness in the interest of the greatest possible freedom of movement by the player. The restriction to four strings, the omission of frets, therewith mechanical tone production, and the final fixing of all single parts of the resonant body and of the systems of conducting the vibration were aesthetic consequences. Other qualities devolved upon them in the form of "secondary products" as much unwilled as the atmospheric effects of Gothic inner rooms were initially. These were involuntary consequences of purely constructive innovations.

In any case the production of the great violin builders lacked a rational foundation such as can be clearly recognized with organ, the piano, and its predecessors, as well as the wind instruments. The crwth was improved on grounds belonging to the guild. The string instruments were developed on the basis of purely empirical knowledge gained gradually in time as to the most useful shape of the top, the sound holes, the bridge and its perforation, the core, the post, the raised borders, the best qualities of wood and probably also varnish. This resulted in those achievements that today, perhaps because of the disappearance of the balsam fir, can no longer be completely imitated.

Considering their technical construction, instruments created in such manner did not as such consist of a device to promote harmonic music. On the contrary, the lack of the bridge of the older instruments facilitated their use in bringing forth chords and the bourdon strings served as the harmonic support of the melody. This was omitted in the modern instruments that, on the contrary, seemed designed as vehicles of melodic effects. Precisely this was welcome to the music of the Renaissance, governed as it was by dramatic interests.

Social Ranking of the Instruments

The new instruments were soon employed in the orchestra of the operas (according to customary suppositions, first employed in modern fashion in *Orfeo* by Monteverdi). We do not initially hear anything of their use as solo instruments. This is due to the traditional social ranking of the instruments.

Since the lute was a court instrument, the lutenist was inside the pale of society. His salary in the orchestra of Queen Elizabeth was three times as much as that of the violinist, five times as much as that of the bagpipe player. The organist was considered to be a complete artist.

Only by great efforts did the violinists first manage to gain recognition and only after this (especially through Corelli) did an extensive literature for string instruments begin to develop.

As the orchestra of the Middle Ages and Renaissance was built around the wind instruments, orchestra music today is as unthinkable without the violins. The exception is found in military music, the old natural home of wind instruments. The modern strings, precisely as used in orchestras, are indoor instruments that do not produce their full effect even in rooms surpassing a certain moderate size—to be sure, a smaller size than is ordinarily used today for chamber music.

The Keyboard Instruments: The Organ

To an even greater degree than the strings, indoor character is important for the modern keyboard instruments.

The organ consists of a combination of the panpipes with the principle of the bagpipe. It was supposedly constructed by Archimedes. It was known in any case in the second century B.C. In the time of the Romans the organ was a court, theater, and festival instrument. It was particularly important as a festival instrument in Byzantium.

The antique water organ extolled by Tertullian, to be sure without any technical comprehension, could not have penetrated into our latitudes because of the freezing of the water. Perhaps even before the use of water regulation, in any case since the fourth century (obelisk of Theodosius in Constantinople) the pneumatic organ appeared. It came to the Occident from the Byzantine empire. In Carolingian times it was still essentially a court music machine. Louis the Pious did not put the organ he received as a gift into the cathedral, but into the palace in Aachen.

Where the organ penetrated into the monasteries it became representative of all technical musical rationalization within the church. Also important, it was used for musical instruction. The regular ecclesiastical use of the organ is documented since the tenth century in connection with festivals.

In the Occident from the beginning the organ underwent continuous uninterrupted technical improvement. Around 1200 it had reached the range of three octaves. Since the thirteenth century, theoretic treatises were written about it. Since the fourteenth century its use in the large cathedrals has been universal. In the fourteenth century it became an instrument really capable of melodic performances, after the windchest had obtained its first rational form in the so-called *Springlade* for which at the end of the sixteenth century the *Schleiflade* was substituted.

In the early Middle Ages the organ was at best just able to play the *cantus firmus*. Planful mixtures were still unknown and unnecessary, for congregational singing did not exist and knowledge of the *cantus firmus* was not required. From the eleventh to the thirteenth century tones were formed by pulling out the keys, with up to forty pipes to a key in the oldest organs that are described in detail. A separation of tones as was later produced by the boards of the windchest was still impossible. For musical performance as such, compared with the pulled keys, the *Orgelschlagen,* beating with fists on the pressure keys, sometimes over a decimeter board, was an advance, though inconstancy of the wind supply even then still strongly detracted from the perfection of its temperament.

Precisely in that primitive condition, however, it was more suited than any other instrument to sustain one tone or one complex of tones above which played a figuration performed by voices or other instruments, particularly voices. Thus it functioned harmonically. With the transition to the pressure keyboard system in the twelfth century and with the increasing melodious movability achieved through special contrivances, the attempt was made to conserve the older function until the double bourdons were introduced for this purpose. Behr is right when he directs attention to the fact that (according to the Cologne *Traktat de organo*) precisely because of this function many-voiced singing accompanied by the organ was not allowed to descend beneath the lowest organ tone. As shown by the name *organizare* for the creation of many-voiced settings, the organ (and perhaps also the organistrum) played an important role in the rationalization of polyvocality.

Since the organ, in contrast to the bagpipe, was tuned diatonically, it could serve as an important support for the development of the corresponding tone feeling. On the other hand, at first it remained purely diatonic (though it early admitted the *B Moll*). What was worse, it long retained Pythagorean temperament. Thus it was unavailable for the production of thirds and sixths. But in the thirteenth and fully in the fourteenth century a highly developed coloration together with increasing development occurred. Perhaps the organ directly influenced the figurative polyphony such as prevailed at the beginning of the *ars nova.*

No instrument of older music had the same kind or amount of influence as the organ on the evolution of polyvocality. In the Occident from the beginning only ecclesiastical use offered a solid basis for the development of this instrument, which became ever more complex after invention of the pedal and led toward its perfection through the differentiation of measured musical organization, above all since the early sixteenth century. In a period without any market, the monastery organization was the only possible base on which it could prosper. Thus in the entire early period it remained an instrument particularly of the Nordic missionary territory, according to Chrodegang with its strong monasterial foundation, also in the cathedral chapters. Pope John the Eighth asked the bishop of Freising to send an organ builder who, as was then the custom, had to function as an organist.

Organ builders and organists are, at first, either monks or technicians from monasteries or from chapters instructed by monks or canons. After the end of the thirteenth century, when any sizable church obtained an organ—if not two of them—organ building and with it to a considerable degree the practical leadership in development of the tone system lay in the hands of professional secular organ builders. They not only decided the temperament of the organ, but since vibrations at an impure temperament of the organ are easily determined, they had a hand in bringing about changes far surpassing the problems of temperament in general importance. At the time, the general advance and technical elaboration of this instrument coincides with the great innovations in polyvocal singing, which in spite of initial restrictions are unthinkable without the participation of the organ.

Religious Change and the Transformed Function of the Organ

The organ was and remained the representative of ecclesiastical art music, not of the singing of laymen. It was often maintained in earlier times that it was not supposed to accompany congregational singing. Such congregational accompaniment was only very recent.

The Protestants, as in the beginning the Swiss Reformed and almost all ascetic sects, did not banish the organ (precisely because it had served art singing) from the church in the way antique Christendom did the aulos. As Rietschel, too, emphasized, even in the Lutheran church the organ preserved art music under the influence of Luther.* It remained, at first, the instrument that supported art music essentially in the old style or that substituted for it. Verses and the text, which was read by the congregation from a hymnbook arranged for the organ, alternated with the art productions of the schooled choir. After a brief period of popularity the participation of the congregation itself in the singing so much declined in

---

*Weber refers to Luther's interest in Josquin's and Senfl's music. Emphasis on art music can also be seen in Johann Walther's four- and five-part chorale settings.

some as to present hardly a recognizable contrast to the Middle Ages.

The reformed churches were more favorable to congregational singing. Particularly after the French psalm compositions had gained international diffusion, they were opposed to art music. Then, since the end of the sixteenth century the organ was introduced again step-by-step in most of the reformed churches. On the other hand, a catastrophe to old church music occurred in the Lutheran church with the advance of pietism at the end of the seventeenth century. Only the orthodox retained any considerable amount of art music. It is tragicomic that J. S. Bach's music, which corresponded to his intense religious piety and despite a strict dogmatic relationship bears an unmistakable flavor of pietism, was in his own domicile suspected by the pietists and appreciated by the orthodox.

Thus the function of the organ is relatively new as an instrument that primarily accompanies congregational singing. From olden times it preludes and fills the interludes, the entrance and recession of the congregation, the long ceremony of the communion. In the same fashion as the specifically fervent and religious cachet that organ music means for us today, above all, the sonority of the mixtures and great registers that are supposed to be considered aesthetically and that fundamentally, in spite of Helmholtz, are of barbarian emotional nature.

The organ is an instrument strongly bearing the character of a machine. The person who operates it is rigidly bound by the technical aspects of tone formation, providing him with little liberty to speak his personal language. The organ followed the machine principle in the fact that in the Middle Ages its manipulation required a number of persons, particularly bellows treaders. Machinelike contrivances increasingly substituted for this physical work. In common with the iron forge it faced the problem of creating a continuous supply of air. The twenty-four bellows of the old organ of the cathedral at Magdeburg still needed *Kalkanten*. The organ of the cathedral in Winchester in the tenth century required seventy.

The Piano

The second specifically modern keyboard instrument, the piano, had two technically different historical roots. One was the clavichord, in all probability the invention of a monk.

By increasing the number of strings the clavichord originated from the early medieval monochord, an instrument with one string and a movable bridge that was the basis for the rational tone arrangement of the entire Western civilization. Originally the clavichord had conjunct strings for several tones that, thus, could not be struck simultaneously. It had free strings for only the most important tones. The free strings were gradually increased at the expense of the conjunct strings. With the oldest clavichords, the simultaneous touching of C and E, the third, was impossible.

Its range comprised twenty-two diatonic tones in the fourteenth century (from G to E′ including B flat next to B). At Agricola's time the instrument had been brought to a chromatic scale from A to B′. Its tones, which rapidly died away, encouraged rapid, animated figuration making it an instrument adaptable to art music. The instrument was struck by tangents that limited the sounding part of the string, simultaneously silencing the latter. At the peak of its perfection, the particular sonorous effects of its expressive tone oscillations permitted it to yield before the hammer piano only when a small stratum of musicians and amateurs with delicate ears no longer decided over the fate of musical instruments, but when market situations prevailed and the production of instruments had become capitalistic.

The second source of the piano was the clavicembalo, clavecin, or cembalo, which was derived from the psalterium and English virginal. It differs in many ways. Its strings, one for each tone, were plucked by quills, therefore without capacity for modulation in volume or color, but permitting great freedom and precision of touch.

The clavecin had the same disadvantages mentioned for the organ and similar technical devices were employed in the attempt to correct them. Until the eighteenth century organists were normally the builders of keyboard instruments. Also they were the first creators of piano literature. Since the free touch was favorable to use of the instrument for the reproduction of folk tunes and dances, its specific audience was formed essentially by amateurs, particularly and quite naturally all folk circles tied to home life. In the Middle Ages it was the instrument of monks, later of women led by Queen Elizabeth. As late as 1722 as a recommendation for a new complicated keyboard type it is emphasized that even an experienced woman is able to handle the customary playing of the keyboard.

In the fifteenth and sixteenth centuries the clavecin doubtless participated in the development of music that was melodically and rhythmically transparent. It was one of the mediators for the penetration of popular simple harmonic feeling opposite the polyphonic art music. The theorists built keyboardlike instruments for themselves for experimental purposes.* In the sixteenth century, the period of general experimentation with the production of purely tempered instruments for many-voiced compositions, the clavecin was still less important than the lute for vocal accompaniment. However, the cembalo gained territory and became the characteristic instrument for the accompaniment of vocal music, then for the opera.† In the seventeenth and eighteenth centuries the conductor sat in the middle of the orchestra. As far as art music is concerned, the instrument remained strongly dependent on the organ in its musical technique until the end of the seventeenth century. Organists and pianists felt themselves to be separated but solitary artists and representatives of harmonic music in contrast, above all, to the string instruments that "could not produce any full harmony," withdrew (with this motivation) in France from the dominance of the king of the viols.

Emancipation of the Piano and Its Emergence as the Instrument of the Middle Classes

French instrumental music showed the influence of the dance, determined by the sociological structure of France. Then, following the example of violin virtuoso performance, musical emancipation of piano music from the organ style of writing was carried out. Chambonnieres may be considered the first creator of specific piano works. Domenico Scarlatti, at the beginning of the eighteenth century, is the first to exploit in virtuoso fashion the peculiar sonorous effects of the instrument. Piano virtuosity developed hand in hand with a heavy harpsichord industry that was based on the demand

---

*A famous instrument of this sort was that of the Renaissance theorist Nicolog Vincentino who defends it in his *L'antica musica ridotta alla moderna prattica* (1555).
†Weber is referring to the beginning of the seventeenth century.

of orchestras and amateurs. Continued development led on to the last great technical changes of the instrument and its typification. The first great builder of harpsichords (around 1600 the family Ruckers in Belgium) operated like a manufacturer creating individual instruments commissioned by specific consumers (orchestras and patricians) and thus in very manifold adaptation to all possible special needs quite in the manner of the organ.

The development of the hammer piano occurred by stages partly in Italy (Christoferi), partly in Germany. Inventions made in Italy remained unexploited there. Italian culture (until the threshold of the present) remained alien to the indoor culture of the Nordic Europe.

Italian ideals lacked the influence of the culture of the bourgeois-like home. They retained the ideal of a capella singing and the opera. The arias of the opera supplied the popular demand for easily comprehensible and singable tunes.

The center of gravity of the production and technical improvement of the piano lies in the musically most broadly organized country, Saxony. The bourgeois-like musical culture derived from the *Kantoreien* virtuosi and builders of instruments proceeded hand in hand with an intense interest in the orchestra of the count. Beyond this it underwent continuous improvement and popularization. In the foreground of interest was the possibility of muffling and increasing the volume of the tone, the sustaining of the tone and the beautiful perfection of the chords played in the form of arpeggios at any tone distance. In contrast to these advantages was the disadvantage (especially according to Bach) of deficient freedom, in contrast to the harpsichord and clavichord, in playing fast passages. The removal of this disadvantage was of major concern.

In place of the tapping touch of the keyboard instruments of the sixteenth century, beginning with the organ a rational fingering technique was in progress, soon extended to the harpsichord. This presented the hands working into each other, the fingers crossing over one another. To our conception this was still tortured enough. Eventually the Bachs placed fingering technique, one would like to say, on a "physiological tonal" basis by a rational use of the thumb. In antiquity the highest virtuoso achievements occurred on the aulos. Now the violin and, above all, the piano presented the most difficult tasks.

The great artists of modern piano music, Johann Sebastian and

Philipp Emanuel Bach, were still neutral toward the hammer piano. J. S. Bach in particular wrote an important part of his best work for the old types of instruments, the clavichord and harpsichord. These were weaker and more intimate than the piano and with respect to sonority calculated for more delicate ears. Only the internationally famous virtuosity of Mozart and the increasing need of music publishers and of concert managers to satisfy the large music consumption of the mass market brought the final victory of the hammer piano.

In the eighteenth century the piano builders, above all, the German, were still artisans who collaborated and experimented physically (like Silbermann). Machine-made mass production of the piano occurred first in England (Broadwood) then in America (Steinway) where first-rate iron could be pressed into construction of the frame. Moreover, iron helped overcome the numerous purely climatic difficulties that could affect adoption of the piano. Incidentally, climatic difficulties also stood in the way of adoption of the piano in the tropics. By the beginning of the nineteenth century the piano had become a standard commercial object produced for stock.

The wild competitive struggle of the factories played a role in the development of the instrument. So, too, did the virtuosi with the special modern devices of the press, exhibitions, and finally analogous to salesman techniques of breweries, of the building of concert halls, of the instrument factories of their own (with us, above all, those of the Berliner). These forces brought about that technical perfection of the instrument that alone could satisfy the ever-increasing technical demands of the composers. The older instruments were already no match for Beethoven's later creations.

Meanwhile, orchestra works were made accessible for home use only in the form of piano transcriptions. In Chopin a first-rank composer was found who restricted himself entirely to the piano. Finally in Liszt the intimate skill of the great virtuoso elicited from the instrument all that had finally been concealed of expressive possibilities.

The unshakable modern position of the piano rests upon the universality of its usefulness for domestic appropriation of almost all treasures of music literature, upon the immeasurable fullness of its own literature, and finally on its quality as a universal accompanying and schooling instrument. In its function as a school instrument, it displaced the antique kithara, the monochord, the

148 · German Essays on Music

primitive organ, and the barrel-lyre of the monastic schools. As an accompanying instrument it displaced the aulos of antiquity, the organ, and the primitive string instruments of the Middle Ages and the lute of the Renaissance. As an amateur instrument of the upper classes it displaced the kithara of antiquity, the harp, of the North, and the lute of the sixteenth century. Our exclusive education toward modern harmonic music is represented quite essentially by it.

Even the negative aspects of the piano are important. Temperament takes from our ears some of the delicacy that gave the decisive flavor to the melodious refinement of ancient music culture. Until the sixteenth century the training of singers in the Occident took place on the monochord. According to Zarline, the singers trained in this manner attempted to reintroduce perfect temperament. Today their training occurs almost exclusively on the piano. And today, at least in our latitudes, tone formation and schooling of string instruments is practiced from the beginning at the piano. It is clear that delicate hearing capacity possible with training by means of instruments in pure temperament cannot be reached. The notoriously greater imperfection in the intonation of Nordic as compared to Italian singers must be caused by it.

The idea of building pianos with twenty-four keys in the octave, as suggested by Helmholtz, is not promising for economic reasons. The building of the piano is conditioned by the mass market. It is the peculiar nature of the piano to be a middle-class home instrument. As the organ requires a giant indoor space the piano requires a moderately large indoor space to display its best enchantments. All the successes of the modern piano virtuosi cannot basically change the fact that the instrument in its independent appearances in the large concert hall is involuntarily compared with the orchestra and obviously found to be too light.

Therefore it is no accident that the representatives of pianistic culture are Nordic peoples, climatically housebound and home-centered in contrast to the South. In southern Europe the cultivation of middle-class home comforts was restricted by climatic and historical factors. The piano was invented there but did not diffuse quickly as in the North. Nor did it rise to an equivalent position as a significant piece of middle-class furniture.

Translated by Don Martindale,
Johannes Riedel, and Gertrude Neuwirth

H. H. Stuckenschmidt

The Mechanization of Music
(1925)

I.

The problems of the orchestra and the vain attempts to solve them fill the issues of contemporary music journals. Almost everything written on this subject proceeds from two perspectives:
  (1) the artistic one, and
  (2) the economic one.

There is no longer any question that the great symphony and opera orchestras are relegated either to reducing their size (which is synonymous with disbanding them) or to leading a parasitic existence, that is: to live at the expense of the state or private funding.

The great demands placed on the quantitative dimension of the orchestra by modern music since Beethoven, Berlioz, and Wagner are no longer in proportion to the public's interest and ability to pay.

General, generous patronage, like that of the petty princes of times past, can only be found sporadically anymore. One can compare the enterprising energy of a few melomaniacal Croesuses (i.e., rich people) with the proverbial drop in the bucket.

In sum: in a few years, the great symphony orchestra will have ceased to exist as a general institution. Mere mortals who do not have the good fortune to live in a metropolitan area will only have access to Wagner operas, Strauss symphonies, etc., via radio.

Examining this problem from the artistic point of view only discloses more painful perspectives.

For: the use of gigantic orchestral masses did not hinder modern composers from raising average demands on the instrumental technique of individual musicians to ever-higher levels. (One should note in this regard that the works of Wagner and Schönberg were for some time considered unperformable.) It is not only the type of technique that has been fundamentally changed; today, significantly higher performance standards are (progressively!) being demanded than ever before with regard to intonation, ensemble playing, virtuosity, etc.

Thus, it might already be considered indispensable that good orchestras consist entirely of musically and technically first-class artists, virtuosos of their instruments. The "good technician" no longer suffices.

And the intuition of the composer might well begin to exceed the bounds of humanly possible performing technique.

A solution has been proposed, which at first glance may look seductive: the chamber orchestra.

It consists of a small number of carefully chosen musicians; the basic instrumentation is: a string quintet, piano, harmonium, flute, and clarinet, whereby the harmonium is supposed to replace the missing woodwinds and brass. This circle is expanded as needed to include obligato players.

The literature for such ensembles is, of course, relatively small, in spite of the preference shown for them by some young composers. And besides, the repertoire would be completely different from that of the big orchestra.

It has therefore been suggested that orchestral works be arranged for chamber ensembles. The first such attempts on a larger scale were undertaken in Vienna by Arnold Schönberg's "Society for Private Musical Performances." This involved works by Schönberg himself as well as his pupils (Erwin Stein, Anton von Webern, and Alban Berg).

Of these arrangements, I have seen Busoni's "Berceuse élégiaque," Mahler's "Songs of a Wayfarer," and some waltzes by Johann Strauss.

All of them are masterworks, music of the most polished sound and with all of the clarity of instrumentation demanded by the material.

But the theory, that it does not matter which instrument plays a theme, is wrong.

Wrong in purely physical terms, that is, wrong as viewed from the perspective of the physics of music, because:

If we assume that Helmholtz's research on the essential nature of timbre is valid, then we know that the sound of an instrument is dependent upon the number and arrangement of its sounding overtones. Thus, every tone is accompanied by a series of other tones, which we, more or less consciously, hear clearly in the case of some instruments.

Therefore it should be evident, that the tonal mass of a chord played on the harmonium is different than if the same chord were intoned (for example) by horns, oboes, or bassoons.

If we assume further that the musical structure of a composition is dependent upon the quantity, type, and arrangement of the tones contained therein—an assumption, the validity of which even a child would realize—then the following logical conclusion results:

Through different instrumentation, a work is violated and changed in its tonal foundations. The result of such an effort may well be highly artistic; it can turn out to be masterful and perfect, but in any case (in *any* case) it will have a different nature from the original.

It will relate to the original as a reproduction relates to a picture.

In its impression, in its effect, it will deviate from the original version.

Deviate, to be sure, only through imponderables; but imponderables, trifling details (bagatelles), and latent elements are what determine the essence of any work of art.

Consequently: the crisis of the orchestra will not be resolved completely through the surrogate of the chamber orchestra. Through the latter, the listener is informed only about a portion of the qualities of an artwork, namely, its thematic, harmonic, and rhythmic elements. The timbre (the relationship of which to the other elements might be the task for future music theory) is left out of consideration.

In addition, another dilemma is not even touched by the chamber orchestra: the question of practicability by human means.

II.

The human interpreter is, like every person, subject to the limitations and shortcomings of his body and intellect.

Strength and memory are relative things. The virtuoso suffers from an advantageous or disadvantageous disposition.

The human sense for tempos is never absolute; as can be demonstrated, even the finest musician is not in a position to hold a tempo with mathematical precision; he will make a piece ten seconds shorter today than he did yesterday.

In traditional analysis, music has no tempo whatsoever. In music theory, the question of time has never yet been considered.

To us, the objection, "But it is precisely these minor deviations that represent the ingenious aspect of the conductor's or virtuoso's conception of a work" seems purely sentimental in nature. Our notion of the task of the interpreter deviates significantly from the commonly held one.

The reproducing artist should solely be a trustee of the wishes that the composer has expressed through his notation (in itself hitherto inadequate). His person, his momentary feeling, his private opinion are irrelevant to the greatest extent for the essence of the artwork. The more "objective" the interpreter, the better the interpretation. (In recent years Busoni has upset some people with the "cold objectivity" of his playing.)

The increasing need of our time for precision and clarity illuminates more and more the real inability of human beings to be considered valid interpreters of artworks.

III.

Musical notation is very rich in its indications of dynamics, phrasing, and tempo. But all of these markings are relative, are rubber concepts, and merely clues to the performer who lends them his individual gesture.

The forte of one is the fortissimo of the other; the pianissimo of this one the piano of that one.

It cannot be said that it all depends on the relation of these volume levels among each other. Dynamics are an acoustical matter, not an individual one.

Phrasing, as clear as its markings are for the interpreter, refers only to the coarsest components of the music.

The more intimate proportions are not touched by it and are left up to the "conception" of the performer.

(However, even among good musicians, there are only 5 percent who know the more intimate proportions of music by name, let alone how to give shape to them.)

IV.

Thought has been given to the means by which the tempo of a piece of music, for whose characterization terms like andante, allegro, or presto were ridiculously noncommittal, can be precisely determined.

These considerations led to the first use of a machine in music: the metronome.

The speed of a controllable pendulum outfitted with a numbered scale is an absolute standard for the timing of a tone.

Curiously, only much later did one arrive at the notion of mechanizing all other elements, that is: entrusting a machine fully with the interpretation of a piece of music. Moreover, when the first mechanical piano was constructed, it did not result from a need to play music precisely, but rather to possess an apparatus that without human labor could provide music at any time.

Only now are people beginning to grasp the value that mechanics will have for the development of music.

Two groups of mechanical instruments can be distinguished:

(1) those devices that produce the tones in a mechanical way on a real musical instrument, thus immediately replacing the hands and mouth of the interpreter; and

(2) those contrivances in which the tone itself is produced in some other way than playing on an instrument.

To the first group belong the electric pianos, the orchestrions, and the barrel organ. They operate on the same acoustical basis as the piano or the orchestra, respectively.

Among the second group we include the phonograph and the gramophone, which are in principle identical. Here, the tone is produced by a needle set in motion by sound-wave lines, which in turn brings a membrane into audible vibration.

In producing the masters, a system is preferred for both types of mechanical instruments, which has the advantage of convincing skeptics of the truly perfected possibilities of mechanical devices. For example, a good pianist was asked to play a piece and simultaneously had his playing registered automatically on a roll using a certain, extremely precise relief script, with all nuances of touch, dynamics, and pedal.

The resulting reproduction is so faithful that even the best musician cannot discern whether the pianist himself or the mechanism is playing (an assertion we proved by this experiment).

This method certainly has other advantages as well: the playing of a master will no longer cease with his death, and wreaths will be also braided posthumously for interpreters (as is the case with mime artists since the invention of cinematography).

But the essential significance of these machines lies in the possibility of authentically writing for them.

That is, after a brief period of study one can compose this relief script in them directly, as one earlier did notes; with all conceivable nuances, with mathematically precise tempos, dynamic symbols, and phrasing.

Thus, the problem of authentic notation has already been solved unobjectionably by musical machines; all that is needed is the small effort required to examine and master the script down to the smallest detail. A few composers have done it; in fifty years this knowledge will belong to elementary musical training.

Incidentally, this system is often used with the orchestrion and the barrel organ.

Of course, it is conceivable that a huge orchestrion can be built that contains all the instruments and sounds with which the orchestra operates. With that the question of orchestral music would also be taken care of, but in a most complicated and expensive manner. The construction of such a device, which would have to contain about thirty violins, twenty violas, and just as many celli, etc., would cost a fortune—a fortune, however, that would accumulate in very few years through savings in musicians' salaries.

Considerably richer perspectives are presented by the possibility of authentically composing onto the gramophone disc.

Improvements to the gramophone, on which people have been working feverishly for years, have made it into an instrument that today already produces an almost pure sound, free of extraneous noises.

In the foreseeable future it will be possible to produce devices whose sound is fully comparable to the real orchestra with respect to purity and fullness.

The script on the gramophone disc initially presents an apparently insurmountable disadvantage; it is microscopically small.

Only with the aid of magnification is it possible to study its character and the nature of its features.

Studying this is considerably more complicated than examining the relief script in the electric piano. The timbres, pitches, and volume levels are designated by endlessly small variations in the wave lines.

The issue is therefore one of making possible a significant enlargement of this wave script.

In solving this problem we are following the suggestions of painter Moholy-Nagy (of the Weimar Bauhaus).

He suggests providing a huge disc, approximately five meters in diameter, with correspondingly large lines, and then photomechanically reducing this original to the size required for the gramophone.

Upon thorough examination, this solution seems fully adequate. But, of course, others will also be found.

Compared to the mechanical piano and the orchestrion, the authentic gramophone has the great advantage of combining all conceivable timbres in an extremely simple and small apparatus.

For the composer of the future it will contain sheerly incalculable stimulation.

The number of timbres is infinite. Each instrumental sound can be given any desired range.

The differentiation of pitches is infinite. Quarter- and eighth-tones can be realized with mathematical purity.

The variety of sounds will make the old orchestra sound quite primitive.

There will be no more mistakes in ensemble playing; no late entrances; no "fracking" horn players; no broken strings; no impurely tuned timpani; no errors in interpretation.

The form of the artwork is set once and for all on the disc with mathematical precision.

V.

A few more possibilities for all types of mechanical instruments:

The tempi can be regulated beyond the limits of human technique. Sixteenth-note passages at the tempo half-note = 208 will be easy to execute.

With the electric piano, for example, all of the tones can be sounded simultaneously.

The sound power is unlimited.

The most complex rhythms can be carried on parallel to each other. These are no longer utopias. For years now musicians of consequence have been dealing with the problem of mechanization.

Arnold Schönberg favors these ideas.

Igor Stravinsky has written pieces for the electric piano.

I myself have done the basic experiments on the gramophone (simultaneously George Antheil in Paris).

The resistance of sentimentalists will not be able to impede the development of music.

The role of the interpreter belongs to the past.

Translated by Michael Gilbert

The Ivory Tower
(1955)

Worries plague composers and concert sponsors, critics and commentators, worries about the intelligibility of precisely the most important products of the art of composition in our time. For many years now efforts have been under way to bridge the gap that lies between the music producer and consumer. With emotion-stirring diligence, the probing methods of psychology and sociology have been applied in order to determine just what it is that blocks the masses from access to modern music. Attempts were made with the utilitarian music [*Gebrauchsmusik*] of the 1920s, with the school opera, laypersons' music [*Laienmusik*], the recorder cult, and even the music of Carl Orff. The results can only be labeled deficient. To be sure, the types of musical aid mentioned here have been patiently consumed and considered significant by wide circles of people—without, however, increasing the understanding of the essential works of modern music to any extent greater than that guaranteed by the passage of time itself with its reconciling and compensating power.

In the age of the social welfare state, general relief assistance, and popular theater leagues, the misguided notion that cultural goods must be capable of popularization in a fundamental, unlimited way suggested itself. Indeed, since the early nineteenth century it had become fashionable to make the artist aware of his civic responsibilities, to tell him that he must not restrict himself selfishly to the solution of problems that did not have some kind of practical, that is to say: utilitarian value for someone. The task (today one would say piously in true Heidegger fashion: "the concern") of art may be this or that, but in any case something that is profitable for mankind. And in doing so one appealed to modern social science, which of course had shown that the artist is no being unto himself, but rather a herd animal, *zoon politikon,* part of a community, a little mosaic stone in an enormous brotherhood of like beings, whose needs, inclinations, and sensual reactions he is not authorized to disavow or overlook.

The lure tossed out together with such bits of wisdom is extraordinarily attractive to artists. For one could point to the fact that their willingness to give in to the demands of "the public" would bring them considerable financial reward. One could calculate in advance the royalties a symphony or string quartet would bring in if these works were kept within the limits of a generally intelligible musical idiom.

In totalitarian political systems, this bait, also called *Pajok* (rations) in Russian, can be combined with a gentle warning. Not that the artist would be issued orders with which he had to comply strictly. No, such unpleasantries were only common quite temporarily during the Zhdanov era. But already in National Socialist Germany, the state liked to make it clear that it could only guarantee the otherwise so generously granted living assistance (welfare aid) to those who *also* showed a willingness to work in accordance with the purpose of this state. True, if one insisted on producing artworks that were accessible to only a small group of people, this wasn't forbidden. But the protective hand over the artist was then withdrawn, and how he then managed was his problem.

It soon turned out that this policy of leading artists by the hand as though they were children allowed no art to flourish that was even remotely worth discussing. The significant art produced in totalitarian states is created outside of the aesthetic square drawn by those in power. The extent to which the creative artist is able to infringe on these laws unnoticeably, yet in such a way that he cannot be caught and held liable, depends on his temperament and cleverness. But the extreme poverty of Nazi Germany with regard to the production of art of lasting value demonstrates that even this technique of sneaking-through is not particularly conducive to creativity. To be sure, Soviet Russia has brought forth musically a few significant works; but without exception they come from composers like Prokofiev and Shostakovich, who time and again had to be denounced and reprimanded for producing music that was "alien to the people" and "decadent" (i.e., not useful for the tastes of the masses).

But the history of culture provides an impressive quantity of proof that great art arose more frequently in opposition to, rather than for, its consumption by broad masses of people. It was not the worst cultures in which the artist was regarded as a sorcerer, whose trade was not understood but whom people were prepared to respect as some kind of superhuman being. The concept of the beautiful was often identical with that of the uncanny, the terrifying, or spiritually transcendent. People expected aid against death from the artist; they believed in his influence over the forces of fate, and therefore he was well cared for. In Arnold Hauser's *Social History of Art and Literature*, I find this depicted very clearly: "The artist-sorcerer thus appears to have been the first representative of specialization and the division of labor. In any case, alongside the customary magician and medicine man, he is the first to emerge from the undifferentiated masses and, as someone possessing special gifts, he is the pioneer of that actual class of priests, who, in addition to claiming extraordinary abilities and knowledge, lay claim to a kind of charisma and exempt themselves from any usual type of work." What is said here about paleolithic cultures has proven and preserved its validity to this day.

The artist is by nature "esoteric," which in German means "inwardly oriented." The work he does is familiar to only a few, the "initiates." As a result, it speaks at first only to these initiated persons. But the fruits of such activity, the great artworks, have a puzzling quality. The circle they affect enlarges itself over the course of time and their impact often outlives the creator responsible for it by generations and centuries. On the other hand, it has often turned out that those works that found great, broad resonance immediately, subsequently lost their impact after a time and in the end were as quickly forgotten as they had asserted themselves at the beginning of their existence.

It was left to our time to supply the concept "l'art pour l'art" with the stigma of the impermissible, asocial, and downright inferior. In the same measure that art was seen as a consumer good of utilitarian or nutritive value, the contempt grew for all intellectual emanations that did not prove useful or nutritious. In polemics against esoteric artists people liked to assert that such art for art's sake did not exist in earlier times; that this is a typical product of modern individualism and subjectivism, a manifestation of decline, in which the dwindling of culturally productive forces can be recognized, indeed read right off. These aestheticians of pragmatism did not know or did not want to know that the great flowering times of musical composition were introduced almost entirely by the representatives of the most hardened esoteric mind-set. Such a powerful, formal invention as the isorhythmic motet, which maintained its generative power over generations and centuries, was basically created only for connoisseurs. Those who were not familiar with or did not understand its complicated structure, consisting of two independent layers, necessarily could not appreciate this music; indeed, it could not have had any impact on them. Its creators, Philippe de Vitry and Guillaume de Machaut, were intellectuals of the highest order, and were also situated above the entire community socially. The art that they practiced in the fourteenth century has been characterized by one of the most knowledgeable experts on this era, Heinrich Besseler, as an "art of scholars and aesthetes." And it was precisely from this esoteric music that the strongest form-creating impulses for the following centuries emanated. Concerning the *ars nova,* Besseler writes (in his book *Music of the Middle Ages and Renaissance*): "At that time it was conclusively decided that the great musical art of Europe would always be supported by an elite and would therefore stand in a tension-laden and shifting relationship to the people as a whole."

The application of vulgar Marxist ideologies to cultural phenomena has led to an unsurpassable state of confusion in the realm of aesthetics. No wonder, since, in a time that has created all sorts of possibilities for the mass dissemination of music, artists resist this, not subjectively, but on an objective level. It was Herbert Read, the great English art critic, who pointed to the necessity of a double-track form of cultural thought, by showing how art at many times in history has been created on two completely separate foundations. With this it has been shown that cultures of very different kinds and orientations, one for the initiates, that is, for the intellectual elite, and another for the masses, can exist alongside each other simultaneously, occasionally without the one being even cognizant of the existence of the other. In this context *(The Grass Roots of Art)* Read cites ancient Egypt as the most striking example of a two-sided culture. "There were in the valley of the Nile for centuries two types of art existing alongside each other of a completely different character. The one, which chiefly came to the fore in public buildings and monumental sculptures, was religious; the other, consisting chiefly of paintings, small sculptures, and decorated vases of various kinds, was profane. The religious art was geometrical, rational, objective, and abstract; the other was naturalistic, lyrical, even sentimental."

The difference between the double culture of ancient Egypt and our modern double culture lies in the fact that the two sides today are well aware of each other and that the one bases itself on the claim of the masses but at the same time wishes to extend this claim to the other side. This would be the equivalent of ultimately doing without the one form of culture. And the historical record shows that with this, the essential component of our Western musical tradition: namely, its inherent power of autonomous development and socially free growth, would be lost.

In 1954, when a public discussion on music and politics took place in Rome in conjunction with the music festival of the Congress for the Freedom of Culture ("La Musica nel XX Secolo"), I represented the point of view, that art must reject every intrusion of a nonmusical type and origin. Neither politics nor religion nor philosophy nor some other type of "worldview" have anything to find in its territory or to assume a mentoring authority in the world of its forms. The well-known intervention into matters of musical style and compositional technique undertaken by the Catholic church in the sixteenth century through the Council of Trent occurred at an advantageous time. Firstly, tendencies toward a simplification of polyphony and clarification of textual declamation were present in the air as humanistic ideas. And secondly, a genius took up the task: Palestrina. But to derive from this a claim for extramusical authority, is only possible as a matter of insufficient insight into the essence of artistic affairs. In Rome I therefore recommended the ivory tower as the most suitable place for musical production. The liveliness of the discussion that my suggestion prompted even after the congress appears to demonstrate its topicality. Unfortunately, the politically leftist opponents, above all the communist musician and critic Mario Zafred, have not taken a position on this. It was only Fedele d'Amico who repeated the familiar thesis concerning the social rootedness of the artist and the intellectual, which is so inescapable that even I, for example, cannot remove myself from it. But G. Francesco Malipiero spoke out in animated fashion in favor of the ivory tower. At this point I think it necessary to define the concept itself. The image of the ivory tower is of Biblical origin; it is found in the Song of Songs (of King Solomon) where it has the function of depicting a face. The sense of this is clear: the picture has the traits of the select; ivory as a luxury material, the tower as a symbol of an edifice reaching up into higher regions. But only much later is this image transferred to the sphere of aesthetics.

By the middle of the nineteenth century the word can be found in the vocabulary of writers, for whom art becomes a beautiful end in itself. A letter of Gustave Flaubert says most clearly what is meant here: "We want to close our doors, and climb up high upon the ivory tower, to the highest step, closest to the sky. Sometimes it is cool up there, isn't it? What good does this do? One sees the flickering of the stars, and the ganders can be heard no longer" (1852). Over and above that, the image, clear enough, is Flaubert's repudiation of the marching Second Empire. He outlived it. Ivory towers are more durable than the bastions of state power.

"L'art pour l'art" has essentially the same meaning as the phrase ivory tower. France provides us with a thousand quotations; from Victor Hugo's "We only wish to consider *how* someone worked, not *about what* and *why*" to Théophile Gautier's preface to Charles Baudelaire's *Fleurs du Mal,* they all confirm the importance of isolation. Even the aging Immanuel Kant had already realized that the realms of the beautiful and the useful will forever be separate. Oscar Wilde confirms that, in spite of Tolstoy's warnings: "All art is completely useless."

It may well be that such things as the ennobling of morals happen as by-products of the impact of art. All the better for mankind, if the beautiful can have practical effects. But one must not look at such effects as a legitimation for the artist; that would mean the trivialization of his actual achievement.

Translated by Michael Gilbert

Wilhelm Furtwängler

Problems of Conducting
(1929)

The most disastrous consequence of the lack of a unified mode of feeling is the constriction and limitation of the entire improvisatory element of music making. The less the individual musician contributes by himself in a unified way, the more the agogic or dynamic nuances, etc., intended by the conductor must either be dropped entirely or achieved in a purely mechanical way—that is, through many rehearsals and endless drill. But precisely the most important and best thing, namely, that unnoticeable variability of the tempo, of the timbres, simply does not happen in a mechanical way and through rehearsal. Ultimately, the conductor is frequently faced with the either/or choice of having to exaggerate or totally omit his intentions in this regard. Either without a natural structure in his gestures, or else "prepared," intentional nuances—a situation that corresponds to present reality to a considerable degree.

The possibility of rehearsing ad infinitum, which is portrayed by some as a particular advantage, necessarily reduces the sensitivity and, with that, the quality of the conductor's technique, just as the psychic sensitivity of the orchestra then becomes accustomed to a typically noningenious, mechanical way of working. Even certain qualities that likewise can be regarded as "technical"—for example, good sight-reading ability—are forfeited to a greater or lesser degree through lack of practice. The greatest technical correctness and control one can achieve does not replace the lack of inspiration; but it does have the most fateful consequences for music making as a whole. Excessive technical control, that is, the evenly executed technical perfection of all details, which as such take on a completely different character than intended by their creators, who in their conception always proceeded from the whole, hinders the intellectual linking of these details to the whole. The naturally productive route by which the details are viewed and interpreted by way of the whole, is turned around. The improvisational element is essentially lost, indeed it loses its very concept—this improvisational quality, which does not represent some mere accident, something one can do with or without, but rather is, quite simply, the ultimate source of all great, creative, necessary music making.

The significance of the technical in art, often undervalued in earlier times, which were more inclined toward the irrational, is overvalued today. In keeping with this, one would have to expect greater insight into the determinants of the technical. But with respect to the conductor, this is not the case; at any rate, a certain scheme of conducting, an academic concept of how one should direct, has recently developed, even here, as in the case of violinists and pianists—incidentally, not to the advantage of the music. But it is conspicuously evident that it is precisely the genuine conductors—a Toscanini, a Bruno Walter—who correspond very little to this scheme. The fact is that these conductors are capable of imprinting their own sound immediately on any orchestra, whereas in the case of pedantically correct conductors, all orchestras sound the same.

The relatively young art of conducting is itself insufficently established that it could previously have been grasped to some degree in a theoretical way. What has previously been written about this is, to the extent it is not concerned with questions of interpretation (Wagner, Weingartner), is extraordinarily primitive. To be sure, these issues of interpretation cannot be separated from the problem of conducting, and here we must go back somewhat further in order to clarify at all the development of conducting or, respectively, reproductive music making in recent times. Ever since the existence of Western music as an art form, and especially since the dissociation of music from religious cult in the seventeenth century, each period was formed, shaped, and led by the productive geniuses that it brought forth. In earlier times, that revealed itself in the fact that productive and reproductive music making could hardly be distinguished from each other. Bach and Handel were famous as organists; in the case of Beethoven, indeed, even with Mendelssohn and Liszt, free fantasy was one of their essential means of expression. The creative genius formed the style of reproduction of the time, both consciously and unconsciously. The Handel oratorio, the Haydn string quartet, the Mozart opera, the Beethoven symphony—each of these represents a world unto itself; through each, the feeling and music making of one or even several generations was led and given shape. Chopin's piano pieces, Brahms's chamber music, Verdi's vocal works, Wagner's and later Strauss's orchestra—to cite only a few examples—these creators shaped the style of their time, and the army of reproducers, the pianists, instrumentalists, singers, and conductors had nothing to do but follow them, to assist in realizing their intentions and to be led by them.

However highly one might value the efforts of current musical production to arrive at an expression of itself, however necessary its often ungrateful task is in comparison with earlier times: it cannot be denied that with its style of music making, it no longer dominates and shapes the style of today. All cultivation of it by the conscience of the public cannot compensate for the elementary lack of sympathy on the part of the audience; while the past in its most significant manifestations is assuming increased power. The development of the "historical" style can be considered as much a weakness of the organically productive as a strength and expansion of the view and horizon. But the consequence of this is that the bulk of reproducing musicians is no longer led and guided by the producing ones, as was the case in earlier times. And all of this at precisely the moment when the task of the reproducing musician has grown more challenging through the greater significance of the past. The growing importance attached today to musical reproduction and especially to the conductor is thereby quite fully explained. On his shoulders lies an unprecedented burden of responsibility; for it is no longer the great creator who determines the style of the times; rather he (the conductor) must fashion the style of the individual works out of themselves, that is, out of these different works. He is no longer carried by the times; rather, to a great extent he must help carry the times. An entire chain of new problems results from this. On the basis of this situation the following are adequately explained: firstly, how important the conductor is; and secondly, how seldom the genuine conductor today is. Indeed, these two things are necessarily linked with each other. The associated abuses are likewise explained: the excessive vanity, the endless, frantic attempts to make an impact through charlatanism.

The cult of the orchestra in the American style, the whole cult of the instrument in its material essentiality corresponds to the technical attitude of the present. If the "instrument" is no longer there for the sake of the music, the music is immediately there for the sake of the instrument. Here as well the dictum applies: be either the hammer or the anvil. And with that the entire relationship is inverted. And now that ideal of a technically "dry" music making is arising, which is being presented to us by America as "exemplary." In orchestral playing this manifests itself in an even, cultivated beauty of sound, which never transgresses certain boundaries, and represents a kind of objective ideal of the sound-beauty of the instrument as such. The question is whether the intention of the composer is directed toward sounding so "beautiful"? On the contrary, it is evident that (for example) the rhythmic-motoric drive as well as the tonal chastity of Beethoven are adulterated from the ground up by such an orchestra and such conductors.

Translated by Michael Gilbert

Peter Suhrkamp

Music in the Schools
(1930)

All experiments with school music have one basic flaw: they proceed from the music and the musician. The situation can be represented this way: that musicians would like to secure a place for music in the schools without taking into consideration whether there is a need for music in the schools and what this need looks like, if such is present. The second mistake being made is that musicians continually want to explain the art of music. Even if a need for making, singing, and listening to music in the schools could be demonstrated—becoming acquainted with the art of music, let alone learning it, is something that always lies only in the interest of individual persons.

These deficiencies are not ameliorated by the fact that younger musicians today are attempting to make up for weaknesses in their own education. Experiences are hardly helpful in reforming something in the schools, even if they can point the way better than some pedagogical view, of which every teacher can have several simultaneously or consecutively. One always experiences things as an individual, even if one lives as part of a horde, and reminiscences are especially individualistic. But: the essence of the school lies in the pupils as a mass group.

If at all, music and the school can only be brought into a proper relationship on the basis of the school. The first thing is to ascertain whether a need exists for school music. That is, whether the school as a living community demands music; whether the vital interests of this community require music; and not whether the purpose for which this community comes together, that is, the school as an institute for training and education, demands music as well, simply because music belongs to the general goods of education.

At first this perspective must come as a surprise since one is hardly accustomed to thinking of the school as a community. The school is still widely viewed as an official institution in which each pupil receives his education. It is overlooked that it is the only place in which children and young people live and work most of the time, essentially among themselves. And that children and young people have their own life there, which unfolds as part of a mass group. School is the life-form of people between the ages of six and twenty. Life in the mass group and youthful life are the characteristic factors of the school. The struggle between the mind of the school and the mind of the pupils (the spirit of youth) has been going on for some time in the schools, and the style of the youthful life has been asserting itself more and more. Because school life is played out in the mass group, this life is more temperate and more vital. For now it may go too far to assert that the vital interests of the youth community are destroying the educational interests of the school; at least that is the current tendency in the development of schools. In any case it is striking that the valuation of the general goods of education is continuously declining. Among pupils, general education is treated as worthless, both among themselves, as well as to their teachers' faces. And with regard to all art forms, it looks as though the pupils are abandoning such discussion with disinterest. And that has led the teachers to fight these recurring expressions of a shift of interest, viewed as skepticism, instead of accepting them.

The fact that part of youthful life takes place outside of school as yet represents a hindrance to seeing the school as the life-form of youth. Its peculiar nature only becomes clear in those places where young people live entirely in the schools (for example, at private academies and state homes). For that reason, it is here that people have been most likely to deal with the problems of communal life. The most difficult problem of any community is discipline. Discipline, without suppressing some part of life in the community—a productive mode of discipline. And a transferrable mode of discipline that can be used in the rest of life and that doesn't merely facilitate momentarily the work of the teacher. *External* authority eliminates itself from consideration here because its approach is to restrict life. It is already a more progressive approach to direct all life in one direction with the aid of a religion or a certain worldview. But this method, too, is ultimately antithetical to life. It leads to posturing, neediness, and boredom. Moreover, it corresponds least to the constitution of people between the ages of six and twenty.

The "school district" is a form of self-governing school community. Its advantage compared to other methods lies in the fact that modes of behavior are discussed, and less in the fact that in the end a certain selection of behavioral modes is raised to the status of law. The discussion of ways of behaving is a living form, and it can yield valuable suggestions; but beyond that it can only produce opinions. But quite a distance lies between opinions and modes of behavior; opinions do not even contain a hint of behavioral modes. For modes of behaving, gesture [Gestus] is decisive. The gesture imparts itself. In doing so it is a disciplined form and at the same time a stimulator of new forms and a creator of life. It is not coincidental that the school districts invented gymnastics, theater, and *music* to complement their style of living. Yes, invented! for these things were established out of the vital needs of the school community. —And among them music occupies the premier position.

Life in large communities is governed by customs. Certain communities independent of the economy (for example, schools and military barracks) degenerate easily in their habits, forming bad habits amongst themselves. These inferior habits lead to desolation, and here the community typically declines. Therefore one must (among other things) cultivate expensive and difficult customs. And it is here that (among other things) music was put to use by school districts. One did not link up with the musical practices of the society at large where music is an article for pampering, for solemn occasions and elevated feelings. Rather, one recalled and reflected on instances in which music was cultivated less for its own sake than it was used already for certain everyday occasions. In the peoples' schools [Volksschulen] the day used to begin with a chorale, sung by the entire school. This was not a religious exercise, not an act of unanimity, but rather an exercise in a clearly set discipline. Only upon singing the chorale, which happened for the most part without thought or feeling, did one settle into the proper order. The morning chorale meant: getting oneself in order. Church music is supposed to bring the congregation together, less in terms of a feeling than with regard to the order and brightness of the spirit. Church music is therefore of a mathematical sobriety and adheres to a liturgy. This ceremonial order can be splendid and pompous in its progression and structure, but it is never a coarse, unordered agglomeration of luxurious revelries—and it can be as popularly plain as a simple barrel-organ tune.

For example, the common singing of a chorale and quiet assembly for the playing of a Bach fugue, as observed every morning by the Free School District of Wickersdorf, as a self-evident, regular exercise, are excellent and, from my experience, indispensable customs that can be done without musical training and understanding. Music itself derives no value from these exercises, but through them it becomes valuable.

In its essential nature, music is not only discipline, but, and just as much, nonreasonableness. And, "in music, if it is to remain music, the nonreasonable *and* the discipline must remain fully included" (Brecht).

It would be repeating a platitude to say that the characteristic thing about youth, its youthfulness, is its nonreasonableness; but in this context that is important. The enterprise of education has been so immensely complicated by the fact that educators have made it their task to eradicate the nonreasonableness of youth: in other words, to eradicate youth itself. How wasted is the work of such educators in the schools! It does not help. Rather, it is reasonable for the educator to acknowledge the nonreasonable. He himself can scarcely achieve this youthful nonreasonableness in something, but he must not only give it room; he must have the means at his disposal to cultivate it. In the new music movement in the schools, so much has failed simply because in selecting the music, the nonreasonable element in the music was insufficiently considered. People favored either strict or silly music. And people are still hesitant to make music in order to satisfy the nonreasonable. "Making music in order to do justice to nonreason, means acknowledging that it is reasonable to do nonreasonable things" (Brecht).

Translated by Michael Gilbert

Arnold Schering

Music and Society
(1931)

Wherever we encounter the use of music in early historic times, whether from pictorial sources or purely musical evidence, it was subservient to either religious cult, secular social life, or the need of people for aesthetic enjoyment. The development of music and its peculiar sociological reflexes have been determined by these three basic functional orientations. Of all of the arts, music has from the beginning developed the greatest society-building power: firstly, because its practice, as a rule, requires several persons of similar conviction and intention and thus leads to the formation of music-making communities; and secondly, because it has the capacity to bond together entire masses of people through its strong sensual qualities and easy combination with text, as well as the possibility of high spiritualization. For that reason music has always been a preferred instrument for the control of the spirits.

A sociology of music would first of all (I) have to deal with the historical facts associated with its appearance, in such a way that it (1) initially refers to the different functions of music in general, and then (2) looks at the social constructs themselves, and finally (3) considers the relationship of these to the overall nature of human community. A second examination (II) would then be devoted to the nature of music itself, to the extent that immediate evidence concerning sociological forms and symbols is present in its natural and stylistic dimensions.

(I.1.a) We encounter the oldest music (that of the Chinese, Babylonians, Egyptians, Israelites) as sacred cult music. Invented by the gods, according to concurring sagas, and viewed as a symbol of the cosmos on account of its mysterious connection with numbers, its power is drawn upon in the interest of the state and the common welfare, partly to conjure the gods, partly to banish demons, as is still the case today in primitive cultures. This function, as important as it was responsible, and which in ancient Greece was of a fundamental state-preserving character, required the formation of special musical castes well versed in the mysteries of this art, in whose hands (consequently) the threads of political power often converged (for example: the Levites, called upon for the Israelite temple liturgy, cf. Chronicles 1, 2). Just as often pure scholars as practicing musicians, they were entrusted with the inciting and calming effects of music, and later on, at a subsequent stage of culture, the devotional or glorifying praise of God through sound with the participation of the congregation. Of these three primary functions of music in religious cult, later eras expanded the second (mostly in a weakened sense as a means of heightening devotion and engendering a mood of atonement and repentance) and the third, creating for them the necessary performing groups in the form of ecclesiastical singers and instrumentalists who initially came from the class of priests and later from among the laity.

(b) In the meantime, alongside a "high" music, a "lower" music has existed at all times, serving the purpose of mere sociability. Where the prince and the common folk were separate, the courtly variety usually distinguishes itself sharply from the popular/middle-class type. Whereas the court procures for its entertainment its own musicians and ensembles, whose members are often treated like servants, the social construct of the street singer and minstrel arise from among the common people. To them falls the multiple task of keeping alive the body of traditional national songs, introducing new ones to the general community, and gilding the life of the citizens and peasants through their art. Known in Greece as the *rhapsode*, in Nordic countries as *bard* or *skalde*, in England as the *minstrel*, in France as the *ménétrier*, in Italy as the *strambottaio*, and in Germany as the *Fahrender* (wayfarer), the international figure of the minstrel shows new traits with each developing age and, with its history extending back thousands of years, may be considered one of the most interesting social constructs, as by itself it always had a strong need for established and even statutorily regulated organizations. Since the late Middle Ages the cities take over responsibility for social, public musical life and protect it against mediocre performances by untrained musicians by granting privileges to "city musicians" or "city-pipers" whom they themselves employed. The enormous rise of a culture of musical amateurs in the eighteenth century brings about the rapid demise of the guilds and eventually leads to the practice of social music among all classes and sectors of society. Simultaneously, the estate of "free" artists comes into being, whose existence is secured by voluntary practical and moral support of artistic amateurs and enthusiasts.

(c) With social music, the simultaneous satisfaction of aesthetic needs is not always a consideration. In light of the development of modern concert and opera music since the Renaissance, the function of music in question here must be mentioned separately. Of course, it is only high cultures that have raised themselves to the level of a purely aesthetic, disinterested contemplation of music. The initial impulse for this may have emanated from the concept of admiration (e.g., of the beautiful voice or fingering skill). But only since the later Middle Ages does a level of consciousness appear to have been reached on which the listener responds to artistic performance (both productive and reproductive) without any accompanying conceptual purpose, as evidence of some higher talent. From this intellectual attitude arise entire new forms of music (opera, oratorio, the symphony, the concerto, etc.). A new public is created, whose bonding occurs solely through a new conception of the artistic, and which now, as this conception acquires international validity, encompasses the community of all musically trained persons. Music thus appears before the forum of all cultured humanity, a state of affairs whose full magnitude is first demonstrated by the work and impact of the three Viennese classicists. At this same time, organizations develop (concert associations, academies, etc.) that in the sense of self-sacrificing service to art assist in conveying the achievements of genius to this new public.

(2) These three functions of music brought forth a host of social constructs that differ in essential ways. Also interacting to a considerable degree, they are defined by the basic relationship of the artist (as the initiate) to the layman (the nonexpert). The first gives, the

second receives. This leads to a monetary reward system that is only interrupted in instances in which the layman himself poses as artist, that is, steps forth as musical amateur (dilettante).

(a) Since cult music, like all other aspects of cult, arose from some superior (divine) commandment, the very sense of its practice is in the first instance based on the preservation and continuation of the musical legacy. To keep this tradition alive, a group of initiates forms who possess authoritative power, essentially from among the class of scholars (theoreticians). It is their task to maintain the purity of the chants, to ward off harmful influences, and to analyze the ancient music speculatively. As long as the Middle Ages viewed *ratio* (reason) as the highest power of the soul, it positioned the theoretician above the mere practicing musician and observed a strict distinction between the two in the sense of an opposition between intellectual and manual labor. A weakening of this polarity did not occur until the late Renaissance, when the sacred and secular realms penetrated each other more actively and the concept of the unity of all artistic endeavor was grasped. The propagation of tradition is carried out by schools associated with churches and dioceses. It is here that the class of church musicians arises, in some instances in splendid form (for example, the Roman schola cantorum, or the School of Cambray), or—as on Protestant ground—the German *Kantoreien* (precentor schools) develop, whose predecessors, the *Kaland*-fraternities, simultaneously performed both charitable and musical functions. Divided up according to their functions as conductors, singers, instrumentalists, or organists, and variously structured through the addition of boys' voices and voluntary auxiliary performers, these groups maintain a sharp profile within the community, and not without bringing forth special varieties, for example, the German precentor. Moreover, in Germany the close connection between school and church lent the "pupil chorus" a special cultural-historical significance, since these lay choruses produced a direct link to the community. The relationship to the church has always been one of service and regulated by more or less strict rules; but cities and communities have often granted social support in significant ways, as the church at all times has permeated the life of the citizenry.

(b) Where social music is supposed to fit into a broader framework, it will assume by itself the character of that social class that it is to serve. In accordance with this perspective, the pertinent social constructs can also be classified. The lower-class minstrel served the people in a general sense. Tramping about as a vagabond and dependent upon voluntary contributions, only modestly in command of his vocal and instrumental skills, not always free of moral defect and therefore often persecuted harshly by the law, he conquered the country in great numbers, often as a plague. The "trained" minstrel appears as his enemy. His conscious effort to perform better music drives him into guildlike organizations as a means of regulating unworthy competition. He receives privileges from the emperor or from cities that support him and make his trade honorable. As a citizen he is integrated into the municipality, which he serves with performances from the tower, at weddings, and other festive occasions and from which he receives firm wages. His significance as the foundation of middle-class musical culture cannot be assessed highly enough. Only rarely did he prefer service to high lords to this kind of secure existence. The troubadours and *Minnesänger* (medieval courtly singers), likewise the old English bards, who surrounded themselves with droves of minstrels, already had musicians in their personal service for the performance of their songs. Although these singers also possessed a sense of solidarity, they nevertheless remained in a subordinate position due to their partial training and were dependent upon the whims of their lords. Where courtly states formed and the ruler was in residence, well-funded performing ensembles *[Kapellen]* with select performers arose, which then became centers of taste for the entire province. In middle-class circles people moved toward the establishment of so-called *collegia musica,* that is: organizations of amateur musicians, whose weekly meetings (often in the form of "little circles") brought together practicing dilettantes of all classes and occupations, likewise at universities (student *collegia musica*). In both forms, the joy of making music continually and harmoniously linked together people of the most varied circumstances of life, and also linked music with the family and academic camaraderie so that it eventually permeated all classes of society like a benevolent force. The hierarchical differentiation of people into connoisseurs, amateurs, indifferent persons, and enemies of music was only of real significance at the time of the Enlightenment.

(c) Even if music in earlier eras had a predominantly "serving" character, its significance as an autonomous art was never entirely overlooked. Musical competitions documented as far back as ancient Greece, even if they were initially only for the purpose of admiring personal mastery of musical skill, demonstrate that a piece of music was also capable of captivating listeners through purely aesthetic qualities. In later eras as well, the orientation toward an aesthetic (artistic) enjoyment of music appears to have been mediated time and again through the concept of virtuosity. In the virtuosic, the artwork and its practical realization are considered in equal measure. For this reason, the "virtuoso" as such has long occupied a privileged position, either in terms of higher social status and greater compensation, or (as in the romantic era) in terms of the special veneration accorded to him. In the eighteenth century, public concert life sprang up from the contrasting relationship of artists and laypersons. Initially carried out by dilettante performers, it gradually divides both into "practitioners" and "enjoyers," or the criticized and the critics, which is the same thing. The public thus created soon becomes a force and determines the prevailing taste, especially since laypersons continue to supervise the nature and organization of musical institutions (concert clubs, vocal academies, etc.). The once resident artist is now forced to travel since he is henceforth dependent upon the ability of his listeners to pay. In all nations there arises the native "traveling virtuoso" of international reputation, whose mission consists chiefly in imparting indigenous artistic styles to foreign countries. While this is occurring, the old divisions between the nations themselves are falling, and alongside the national musical literature, a world literature emerges as the basis of general musical literacy.

(3) The extraordinary capacity of music to bond people together has not infrequently been compared to the power of religion (Luther). As cult music, for example in the form of ecclesiastical congregational hymns or musical liturgy, it indeed ties together the adherents of a certain confession just like the dogma itself (e.g., Gregorian chant or the Lutheran chorale). Since its essence is expression and every person is capable of its performance as song, music is called upon, for the most part in conjunction with text, in all places where large communities wish too lend expression to common feeling. As military and soldiers' music, as patriotic song,

as a festival or homage hymn, as the sounding motto of different groups and parties, its power affects untold masses beyond the specific framework of time and place, not seldom by heightening passion to the level of grandeur. Music also conveys other trans-temporal associations: tribal or kindred ties, national identity (e.g., German male choruses), or communities of fate. The idea of art itself or that of the creative genius has a bonding effect when people gather for the performance of masterworks, whether it be in a grand setting (as in the case of music festivals and opera) or in intimate circles (as in the case of domestic chamber music). It is well-known that on the basis of deeply felt emotion and under certain circumstances this can result in a feeling of "all people become brothers" and is uniquely symbolized by Wagner's work of Bayreuth. In connection with dance and the dancing song, music extends down into the lowest classes of the people and even in the form of "hit songs" has the impact of a ribbon enveloping great numbers of people. Recognized today among all cultured peoples as an educational factor of the highest order, transmitted to youth at an early age by primary and secondary schools and taught by masters at special institutions of all kinds, music permeates the furthest reaches of our intellectual and economic life and with the most immortal of its achievements produces lasting ties between generations and peoples. In order to make fruitful its blessings on a general basis and the impact of those called to its service, as well as to advise these persons socially and represent them effectively, societies and associations have developed in great numbers whose organization and tasks, of course, cannot be surveyed (when seen, for example, with respect to their diversity in various nations). New problems of far-reaching social significance have been created in recent decades by the development of recordings, radio, sound film, and mechanical instruments. The possibility of reaching out beyond time and place to unlimited quantities of listeners associ-ated with the industrial utilization of music has led to an as-yet-incomplete upheaval in public musical life, whose advantages (the advancement of artistic entertainment and musical literacy) and disadvantages (the exclusion of artistic manpower, the danger of self-satisfaction with surrogates) have not yet found a fully satisfac-tory balance at this time.

(II) Since music as a practically performed art requires the concept of some community, no matter how small, it must be possible to derive the reasons for its social nature from music itself. In doing so, caution is advised since the concept of what constitutes music had undergone progressive changes. From the standpoint of the artistically thinking, cultured person of the present, it seems impossible to place an Australian Negro dance without contradiction into the same category as a Beethoven string quartet. However, if one looks apart from aesthetic standards, it is precisely the sociological study of music that is suited to bridge over such heterogeneous phenomena. Just as social science as a whole assumes a certain basic relationship of the human being toward nature or to his own kind, a primary relationship of human beings to the realm of sound, a kind of primal musical experience, must be postulated, one that is approximately the same in each newly awakening individual consciousness. The ultimate aspect of this primal experience enters into the physical-physiological realm and exists as rhythm. As a principle, rhythm is as yet premusical. Impersonal and collectivist in nature, it possesses an aggressive (fascinating) power, which it exerts in the sense of a forcibly unified regulation of common external movement (as with dancing or marching) or internal movement (as in the art of the self-controlled cultured person). Rhythm creates tension, gathers together, reins in, stimulates the individual as well as the masses at the same time and thus creates the basis of an elementary communal experience. Closely associated with rhythm are dynamics (sound volume) and tempo (time measure), which, likewise of a premusical nature, function as powerful comrades of rhythm.

The sensuality of musical (i.e., measured) sound narrows this impact from the general into the artistic: the entrance into the spiritual-intellectual realm ensues. For the prerequisite of measured sounds is a tonal system, in other words, a certain scheme of musical thought, which, developed on the basis of intuition (in primitive cultures) or calculation (for example, the Pythagoreans), selects certain tones and generally expresses itself in the form of a scale with its respective intervals. Like language systems, such tonal systems are not individual creations. They encompass the boundaries of a collective musical experience of a particular cultural coloring. Regionally limited, it can, as with other tribal peculiarities, be so different (depending upon the tribe, race, or culture) that it becomes a mutually recognizable trait of those groups. And just like other tribal peculiarities, the prevailing tonal system was at all times held up in honor and at times even placed under state supervision like a kind of political or religious creed.

Melody (vocal or instrumental) appears as a practical manifestation within the tonal system. It is structured expression and therefore dependent upon race, climate, way of life, and a people's character. Melody can become a communal symbol of musical expression within nations (e.g., Russia, Scotland), a clan (gypsies), a region (Dorian, Phrygian), a cult entity (Judaism, Gregorian chant), an artistic school or movement (the *Meistersinger,* Impressionism), or partisan groups (war chants, fanfares), whereby the individual functional purposes contribute additional peculiar features. Here lie the roots of the various historical music styles, the preservation and authentic transmission of which becomes a concern of all communities, since they embody the spirit of the group. Only much later does harmony enter the picture. It differentiates itself according to the particular tonal system in question and can likewise be peculiar to a given tribe (e.g., Nordic harmony), although, in contrast to melody, which remains autochthonous longer, it generally pushes more toward leveling. As an artistic phenomenon, it is clearly associated with Western civilization, although the deeper causes of this have not yet been investigated. Similarly, studies on the origin and dispersion of the major-minor concept currently lead only into impenetrable racial/tribal connections. Out of the latent tensions that on the one hand arise between semi- and whole-tones and on the other between chords, a certain melodic character emerges in connection with rhythm, dynamics, and tempo, which ancient culture designated musical ethos and which more recent ages have simply called "expression." What is meant by this is an immediate connection to life. As *nomos,* song, or tune, it extends into the depths of the popular as well as the individual soul, and can become productive to the highest degree: on lower levels in the sense of a positive heightening of life experience (e.g., orgiastically, cathartically), and on higher levels contributing to the formation of character and disposition. For this reason, not only ethics and pedagogy, but also gymnastics and the healing arts have always welcomed music as a helper.

It is from these naturally given, supraindividual ties that the collective social construct mentioned in the first section of this article arose. But simultaneously, the various possibilities of musical practice in themselves prompt the development of art forms, whose origin is to be sought in a communal or social relation. A few of these will be highlighted here. For example, in the domain of vocal music, solo and choral song contrast with each other. If both are combined with each other, the relationship can be twofold: either the individual singer himself acts independently of the others, or he detaches himself only temporarily from the choir as a part of it and then blends in with it again. In the former instance a likeness of individual and society, in the latter an image of individual and community. In the form of strophe and counterstrophe, verse and response, lead singer and choral refrain, this musical-social double symbolism runs through the music of all eras. It appears in the (sacred) cult songs of both primitive as well as cultured peoples, in the Greek tragedy as well as the operas of the modern era, and everywhere in the social music of secular origin in which the individual appears in relation to a group. Depending upon the inner sense of the musical exercise, the mutual response can occur as confirmation, sympathy, or encouragement, or else as contradiction, admonition, opposition; and correspondingly the music can assume a similar or contrasting theme or style. The kind of deeply influential power that can emanate from this symbolism and affect the listener—one thinks for example, of the "Kyrie" of the Beethoven *Missa solemnis*—is obvious. It will grow even stronger if, as in the case of many Christian liturgies, the listeners are permitted to join in themselves in the response. But even two or more full choruses can appear opposite one another (antiphony), although as a rule the answering is supposed to express an overwhelming unity in the feeling of the groups rather than a sense of opposition. The spatial separation of the performing choirs tends to strengthen the illusion of separate communities of thought.

United choral singing has long been considered a sociological reflection of common feeling and thought, alone on the basis of the commonly expressed text. However, from a musical standpoint, four different intellectual attitudes can be distinguished here, which correspond to equally as many styles. The first instance occurs when the impulse for common singing lies outside of the aesthetic sphere, as in the mass singing of a chorale or national anthem. Here, the steadily unison (or quasi-unison) song engages itself. The singing individual is submerged in the mass, and likewise the tonal work as aesthetic object fades behind its significance as the bearer of a common will. This kind of singing is rightly a collectivist one. A second form is embodied in the literature of those motets since the thirteenth century, in which two or three different texts and melodies are coupled with each other. Each singer sings a melody and text different from that of his neighbor. This type of multivoice singing, which precedes the development of actual polyphony, fades in purity by the fifteenth century, but in principle has been preserved to this day in weakened form in canon singing and can be defined as essentially individualistic in nature. The third form appears in the vocal polyphony of the sixteenth century where the tonal work in itself displays such organicism that each individual voice is linked to the other in a common logic and is only comprehensible in this connection. Here the choir appears as a tightly cohering group with a clearly oriented group spirit: the suprapersonal nature of counterpoint with its anticipations, imitations, and common cadences links the voices firmly together. This higher manifestation of choral interaction was for a long time an ideal of cultic, chiefly catholic song. For if the church demanded of music that it express the same relationship as that existing between the church as a whole and the individual believer, there lay in this type of vocal music, where the individual in fact humbly serves the whole, a speaking symbol (e.g., the motets of Palestrina). Finally, a fourth possibility results if the singers perceive themselves not only externally (technically) as members of an art-bound tonal organism (i.e., as a mere group), but rather are responsible in equal measure for the shifting spiritual-intellectual expression of the composition as in the case of choral works by Beethoven or Brahms. In this instance, the choir represents a tool of expression in the hands of the composer; over the individual stands the idea of the artwork that demands of each participating singer the highest concentration in order to be properly realized. With this the greatest distance is reached from the first (collectivist) type of singing referred to above, and a path traversed that resembles that of societal development from the herd concept to the concept of the state.

Social symbols are reflected less in instrumental music. An orchestra is a different construct from a choir, already because its components, the instruments, are subject to differing orders of priority. Here as well the contrast between solo and tutti has produced important stylistic genres (the solo concerto, concerto grosso); but with the lack of textual associations, playing together always remains in the purely musical sphere and if need be can only be interpreted through images. But precisely because the tone-producing organism stands at the center of things in instrumental ensemble playing—unless it's of an accompanying nature, as in the case of dancing or marching—the organism moves into a special situation in relationship to listeners as well. The listener is displaced into the position of pure observation. By diverting his attention to certain externalities, for example, virtuosity, this can at times be broken through, but it can just as easily persist in grasping the aesthetic idea; and the force with which such an idea can call forth the highest experiences of community is well known. For that reason, a strong society-building power has long been a property of instrumental forms. The stylistic historian distinguishes precisely the literature of the sonata, the trio, the quartet as "chamber music" (house music) from the overture and symphony as music for large and largest assemblies and can indicate the social environment out of which and for which they respectively emerged. It is not difficult to demonstrate a stratification of listener-communities (popular, bourgeois, aristocratic, cosmopolitan) that parallels the development from the small dance and academy symphonies of the seventeenth century up to Beethoven's Ninth or Mahler's Symphony of a Thousand that are directed at the entire educated world. If a body of vocalists joins the instrumental ensemble, the field of impact can be greatly expanded. In particular, in their material, spirit, style, and execution, the oratorio and opera have always been a reflection of large, unique social bodies. The notion of a "primal artwork" [Urkunstwerk] (as entertained already by the eighteenth century) consisting of a union of poetry, music, and dance from which the individual arts subsequently broke off with the development of civilization, was taken up again by romanticism and expanded by Richard Wagner into that grand sociological utopia according to which a new human communal order can arise in the future solely on the basis of such a universal artwork that reunites all of the arts. His hypothesis, that art and the form of state, art and the form of society have always stood in a reciprocal relationship, has a certain convincing power, which of course, so decisively expressed, can only be unconditionally supported in the second instance. The increasing fragmentation of national communities into many classes separated by education, outlook, and worldview has for decades now torn apart the unity that earlier applied to music as well, and has created a gap between a popular art in the broader sense and a type of high-level art (almost in the sense of "l'art pour l'art") that for the moment appears unbridgeable. From this result problems of the most difficult sort, not only for the state and society, but for the individual as well. Their solution will be determined neither by preventive reprimands nor artificial reforms, but rather by the higher forces that will close in upon our future.

Translated by Michael Gilbert

Heinrich Schenker

Introduction to *Free Composition*
(First ed. 1935)

But those who are like the master go forth,
And beauty and sense appear in all they see.
—Hugo von Hofmannsthal:
"The Death of Titian"

To every thing there is a season, and a time to every purpose under the heaven.
—Ecclesiastes 3:1

The hearing ear, and the seeing eye,
The Lord hath made even both of them.
—Proverbs 20:12

For more than a century, a theory has been taught that claims
to provide access to the art of music, but in fact does quite the
opposite. This false theory has obscured the musical discipline of
previous centuries—that is, strict counterpoint and true thoroughbass. One might explain this break by looking to the impatience of the generation that lived during the third decade of the
nineteenth century: dazzled by the tremendous outburst of genius
that had come before them, they sought, as mediocrity usually
does, to cut the shortest possible path to genius. This shortcut, a
"practical" one, proved to be a failure, since it was essentially
contrary to the historical background and artistic development of

the great composers. It did not lead to the masters; indeed, it ultimately led away from them.

In our day it seems that this betrayal is no longer acceptable. The flight from music that characterizes our time is in truth a flight from an erroneous method of instruction, one that renders impossible an effective approach to art.

In opposition to this theory, I here present a new concept, one inherent in the works of the great masters; indeed, it is the very secret and source of their being: the concept of organic coherence. The following instructional plan provides a truly practical understanding of this concept. It is the only plan that corresponds exactly to the history and development of the masterworks, and so is the only feasible sequence: instruction in strict counterpoint (according to Fux-Schenker), in thoroughbass (according to J. S. and C. P. E. Bach), and in free composition (Schenker). Free composition, finally, combines all the others, placing them in the service of the law of organic coherence as it is revealed in the fundamental structure (fundamental line and bass arpeggiation) in the background, the voice-leading transformations in the middleground, and ultimately in the appearance of the foreground.

C. P. E. Bach wrote his treatise on thoroughbass when he realized, to his grief, that the discipline of thoroughbass might disappear both in theory and in practice, because it was not really understood. His incomparably great work was motivated by a desire to do his utmost to save and clarify that discipline. Now the time has come for me—"To every thing there is a season," says the writer of Ecclesiastes—to proclaim the new concept of organic coherence and thereby to give the fullest possible expression to what the music of the masters was and must continue to be if we wish to keep it alive.

* * *

After the publication of some of my earlier works (those that already reached toward a clearer presentation of the new concept, especially the volumes of *Der Tonwille* and the three yearbooks, *Das Meisterwerk in der Musik*), the objection was often raised, "But did the masters also know about all this?" This objection, intended to be a trap, only betrays a lack of education. Those who raised the question were unaware that the masters in fact knew nothing of that false theory that for more than a century has been taught and learned as the only practical one. Neither J. S. Bach, C. P. E. Bach, Haydn, Mozart, Beethoven, Schubert, nor Mendelssohn knew any such concepts of harmony, thoroughbass, or form. And Brahms would have none of it! The objection can be answered very simply: the great composers in their works have shown a mastery that evinces, both in preconception and in total recall, such a clear overall comprehension of the laws of art that they need say no more to us; of necessity, every artistic act—indeed any action at all—requires a preconception of inner relationships. Consequently, should the reader find that what I say about a composition is verified in the work itself, he must surely concede that the masters did have a keen awareness of such relationships.

Those who advocate the present courses of instruction explain that their teaching is an expedient, that it is designed especially to lead the young and the moderately gifted to music. Even if this were true, we would still have to ask where, in what books, in which institutions can we find a way to the true art of music, and not merely an expedient? Where does the student or the serious music lover learn what is essential to a true fugue, sonata, or symphony, what makes a true orchestration, what produces a truly great performance, true in the sense of the truth of the great masters? Expediency can give us no answer. This explanation is simply too weak. There is yet a further disgrace, for the so-called expedient could only have arisen through ignorance of the true nature of strict counterpoint and thoroughbass.

But the advocates of these erroneous teachings withhold the most important excuse: these theories have enabled many generations of teachers and musicians to earn their livelihood. Art in its truth and beauty has been ignored, but the practicalities of life have been assured, which made it easier to ascribe practicality to the teaching, whether honestly or dishonestly. These persons now fear lest my new teaching undermine their existence; they allege that its inherent difficulties make it unsuitable for large-scale exploitation in the schools. No such danger would exist, however, if teachers would devote themselves solely to one task, to training their students to hear music as the masters conceived it. The schools cannot pretend to breed composers (much less geniuses), though certain vain and arrogant young people would like them to do precisely that. Such sowing and reaping must be left to God. Only by the patient development of a truly perceptive ear can one grow to understand the meaning of what the masters learned and experienced. If a student, under firm discipline, is brought to recognize and experience the laws of music, he will also grow to love them. He will perceive that the goal toward which he strives is so meaningful and noble that it will compensate for the fact that he himself may lack a genuine talent for composition. Thus my teaching, in contrast to more rapid methods, slows the tempo of the educational process. This not only leads the student to genuine knowledge, but also improves the morale of artistic activities in general. Surely it is time to put a stop to the teaching of music in condensed courses, as languages are taught for use in commerce. It is also time that educational authorities cease to employ textbooks that are designed only for the less-capable student. In spite of all this, I would hope for a great increase in educational activity, for a multiplicity of geniuses by nature demands also a multiplicity of nongeniuses. Even though it is fundamentally only vanity that causes the average musician to compose, we must be grateful that, through vanity itself, people are brought to dedicate themselves to art.

Aphorisms

All that is organic, every relatedness belongs to God and remains His gift, even when man creates the work and perceives that it is organic.

The whole of foreground, which men call chaos, God derives from His cosmos, the background. The eternal harmony of His eternal Being is grounded in this relationship.

The astronomer knows that every system is part of a higher system; the highest system of all is God himself, God the creator.

My concepts show that the art of music is much simpler than present-day teachings would have it appear. However, the fact that the simplicity does not lie on the surface makes it no less simple. Every surface, seen for itself alone, is of necessity confusing and always complex.

Specifically, my concepts demonstrate the following:

A firmly established linear progression can withstand even the most discordant friction of voices as they move contrapuntally.

A firmly established tonality can guide even a large number of chromatic phenomena securely back into the basic triad.

A performance, in serving background, middleground, and foreground, can employ the greatest variety of color. Even the richest and most varied resources of performance can be taught—and learned—with great exactness. On the other hand, commitment to background, middleground, and foreground excludes all arbitrary personal interpretation.

The musical examples that accompany this volume are not merely practical aids; they have the same power and conviction as the visual aspect of the printed composition itself (the foreground). That is, the graphic representation is part of the actual composition, not merely an educational means. Therefore the presentation of the examples required extreme care.

There is no doubt that the great composers—in contrast to performers and listeners—experienced even their most extended works not as a sum total of measures or pages, but as entities that could be heard and perceived as a whole.

Music is always an art—in its composition, in its performance, even in its history. Under no circumstances is it a science.

Since the linear progression, as I have described it, is one of the main elements of voice leading, music is accessible to all races and creeds alike. He who masters such progressions in a creative sense, or learns to master them, produces art that is genuine and great.

In its linear progressions and other comparable tonal events, music mirrors the human soul in all its metamorphoses and moods—"alles Vergängliche ist nur ein Gleichnis" ("what is passing is only resemblance," Goethe). How different is today's idol, the machine! It simulates the organic, yet since its parts are directed toward only a partial goal, a partial achievement, its totality is only an aggregate that has nothing in common with the human soul.

Every organic being yearns for another organic being. And art, which is organic, drives toward the organic human soul. However, in these times when man himself destroys his organic nature, how is he to respond to organically developed art?

It is certain that almost half of mankind is unmusical, even incapable of singing a folk tune—a sorry ratio, one that would be unthinkable in the case of language. How then can the ear be expected to hear polyphony, which is fundamental to the linear progression? The musical person, however, is certainly capable of recognizing linear progressions and of learning to use them. Therefore, let him apply himself to this task and refrain from the "experiments" so popular today and, alas, so costly. It follows that he must also be taught the theory of organic coherence; but this does not mean that the drafting of extensive analytical sketches *[Urlinie-Tafeln]* is necessary, since this would be tantamount to a demand for creative powers.

Philosophers and aestheticians will be able to establish a general theory of music as an art only after they have absorbed my concepts. Nietzsche complains (*The Will to Power,* 838): "What we lack in music is an aesthetic that would impose laws upon musicians and give them a conscience; and as a result of this we lack a real contest concerning 'principles.' For as musicians we laugh at Herbart's velleities just as heartily as we laugh at Schopenhauer's. As a matter of fact, great difficulties present themselves here. We no longer know on what basis to found our concepts of what is 'exemplary,' 'masterly,' 'perfect.' With the instincts of old loves and old admiration we grope about in a realm of values, and we almost believe, 'that is good that pleases us.'" Ultimately it will be possible to set forth the highest principle that is common to all arts: the principle of inner tension and its corresponding outward fulfillment, a principle that manifests itself differently in different material.

Man lives his whole life in a state of tension. Rarely does he experience fulfillment; art alone bestows on him fulfillment, but only through selection and condensation.

If a differentiation is to be made between "classic" and "romantic," only the degree of tension and fulfillment should be considered. A classical work will exceed a romantic one in the height and extent of its tension and in the profundity of its fulfillment, even if it may be a short work. Thus Schubert's *Wanderers Nachtlied* [*"Der du von dem Himmel bist"*] is classical in every way by virtue of the power and tension of its few scale-degrees that unify the entire text.

The phenomenon of genius signifies a breath drawn from the unconscious, a breath that keeps the spirit ever young.

The cultivation of genius is neither romantic nor "living in the past." Rather it is the cultivation of a contemporaneity that bridges time; it is a strong belief in the absoluteness of art and its masters. If, after centuries have passed, only one person is once more capable of hearing music in the spirit of its coherence, then even in this one person music will again be resurrected in its absoluteness.

"And the Spirit of God moved upon the face of the waters." But the Creative Will has not yet been extinguished. Its fire continues in the ideas that men of genius bring to fruition for the inspiration and elevation of mankind. In the hour when an idea is born, mankind is graced with delight. That rapturous first hour in which the idea came to bless the world shall be hailed as ever young! Fortunate indeed are those who shared their young days with the birth and youth of that idea. They may justly proclaim the praise of their youth to their descendants!

Translated by Ernst Oster

Bertolt Brecht

On the Use of Music in an Epic Theater
(1935)

A s far as my own output goes, the following plays involved application of music to the epic theater: *Trommeln in der Nacht, Lebenslauf des asozialen Baal, Das Leben Eduards II. von England, Mahagonny, The Threepenny Opera, Die Mutter, Die Rundköpfe und die Spitzköpfe.*

In the first few plays music was used in a fairly conventional way; it was a matter of songs and marches, and there was usually some naturalistic pretext for each musical piece. All the same, the introduction of music meant a certain break with the dramatic conventions of the time: the drama was (as it were) lightened, made more elegant; the theater's offerings became more like virtuoso turns. The narrow stuffiness of the impressionistic drama and the manic lopsidedness of the expressionists were to some extent offset by the use of music, simply because it introduced variety. At the same time, music made possible something that we had long since ceased to take for granted, namely the "poetic theater." At first I wrote this music myself. Five years later, for the second Berlin production of the comedy *Mann ist Mann* at the Staatstheater, it was written by Kurt Weill. From now on music had the characteristics of art (could be valued for itself). The play involved a certain amount of knockabout comedy, and Weill introduced a "kleine Nachtmusik" to accompany projections by Caspar Neher, also a battle- or Schlachtmusik, and a song that was sung verse by verse during the visible changes of scene. But by then the first theories had already been put forward concerning the separation of the different elements.

The most successful demonstration of the epic theater was the production of *The Threepenny Opera* in 1928. This was the first use of theatrical music in accordance with a new point of view. Its most striking innovation lay in the strict separation of the music from all the other elements of entertainment offered. Even superficially this was evident from the fact that the small orchestra was installed visibly on the stage. For the singing of the *songs* a special change of lighting was arranged; the orchestra was lit up; the titles of the various numbers were projected on the screens at the back, for instance, "Song Concerning the Insufficiency of Human Endeavor" or "A short song allows Miss Polly Peachum to confess to her Horrified Parents that she is wedded to the Murderer Macheath"; and the actors changed their positions before the number began. There were duets, trios, solos, and final choruses. The musical items, which had the immediacy of a ballad, were of a reflective and moralizing nature. The play showed the close relationship between the emotional life of the bourgeois and that of the criminal world. The criminals showed, sometimes through the music itself, that their sensations, feelings, and prejudices were the same as those of the average citizen and theatergoer. One theme was, broadly speaking, to show that the only pleasant life is a comfortably off one, even if this involves doing without certain "higher things." A love duet was used to argue that superficial circumstances like the social origins of one's partner or her economic status should have no influence on a man's matrimonial decisions. A trio expressed concern at the fact that the uncertainties of life on this planet apparently prevent the human race from following its natural inclinations toward goodness and decent behavior. The tenderest and most moving love song in the play described the eternal, indestructible mutual attachment of a procurer and his girl. The lovers sang, not without nostalgia, of their little home, the brothel. In such ways the music, just because it took up a purely emotional attitude and spurned none of the stock narcotic attractions, became an active collaborator in the stripping bare of the middle-class corpus of ideas. It became, so to speak, a muckraker, an informer, a nark. These *songs* found a very wide public; catchwords from them cropped up in leading articles and speeches.

A lot of people sang them to piano accompaniment or from the records, as they were used to doing with musical comedy hits.

This type of *song* was created on the occasion of the Baden-Baden Music Festival of 1927, where one-act operas were to be performed, when I asked Weill simply to write new settings for half a dozen already existing *songs*. Up to that time Weill had written relatively complicated music of a mainly psychological sort, and when he agreed to set a series of more or less banal *song* texts he was making a courageous break with a prejudice that the solid bulk of serious composers stubbornly held. The success of this attempt to apply modern music to the *song* was significant. What was the real novelty of this music, other than the hitherto unaccustomed use to which it was put?

The epic theater is chiefly interested in the attitudes that people adopt toward one another, wherever they are sociohistorically significant (typical). It works out scenes where people adopt attitudes of such a sort that the social laws under which they are acting spring into sight. For that we need to find workable definitions: that is to say, such definitions of the relevant processes as can be used in order to intervene in the processes themselves. The concern of the epic theater is thus eminently practical. Human behavior is shown as alterable; man himself as dependent on certain political and economic factors and at the same time as capable of altering them. To give an example: a scene where three men are hired by a fourth for a specific illegal purpose *(Mann ist Mann)* has to be shown by the epic theater in such a way that it becomes possible to imagine the attitude of the four men other than as it is expressed there: i.e., so that one imagines either a different set of political and economic conditions under which these men would be speaking differently, or else a different approach on their part to their actual conditions, which would likewise lead them to say different things. In short, the spectator is given the chance to criticize human behavior from a social point of view, and the scene is played as a piece of history. The idea is that the spectator should be put in a position where he can make comparisons about everything that influences the way in which human beings behave. This means, from the aesthetic point of view, that the actors' social gest becomes particularly important. The arts have to begin paying attention to the gest. (Naturally this means socially significant gest, not illustrative or expressive gest.) The gestic principle takes over, as it were, from the principle of imitation.

This marks a great revolution in the art of drama. The drama of our time still follows Aristotle's recipe for achieving what he calls catharsis (the spiritual cleansing of the spectator). In Aristotelian drama the plot leads the hero into situations where he reveals his innermost being. All the incidents shown have the object of driving the hero into spiritual conflicts. It is a possibly blasphemous but quite useful comparison if one turns one's mind to the burlesque shows on Broadway, where the public, with yells of "Take it off!" forces the girls to expose their bodies more and more. The individual whose innermost being is thus driven into the open then of course comes to stand for Man with a capital *M*. Everyone (including every spectator) is then carried away by the momentum of the events portrayed, so that in a performance of *Oedipus* one has for all practical purposes an auditorium full of little Oedipuses, an auditorium full of Emperor Joneses for a performance of *The Emperor Jones*. Non-Aristotelian drama would at all costs avoid bundling together the events portrayed and presenting them as an inexorable fate, to which the human being is handed over helpless despite the beauty and significance of his reactions; on the contrary, it is precisely this fate that it would study closely, showing it up as of human contriving.

This survey, springing from the examination of a few unpretentious *songs*, might seem rather far-reaching if these *songs* did not represent the (likewise quite unpretentious) beginnings of a new, up-to-date theater, or the part that music is to play in such a theater. This music's character as a kind of gestic music can hardly be explained except by a survey to establish the social purpose of the new methods. To put it practically, gestic music is that music that allows the actor to exhibit certain basic gests on the stage. So-called cheap music, particularly that of the cabaret and the operetta, has for some time been a sort of gestic music. Serious music, however, still clings to lyricism, and cultivates expression for its own sake.

The opera *Aufstieg und Fall der Stadt Mahagonny* showed the application of the new principles on a fairly large scale. I feel I should point out that in my view Weill's music for this opera is not purely gestic; but many parts of it are, enough anyway for it to represent a serious threat to the common type of opera, which in its current manifestations we can call the purely culinary opera. The theme of the opera *Mahagonny* is the cooking process itself; I have explained the reasons for this in an essay "Anmerkungen zur Oper" in my Versuch No. 5. There you will also find an argument positing the impossibility of any renewal of the operatic medium in the capitalist countries, and explaining why. Any innovations introduced merely lead to opera's destruction. Composers aiming to renew the opera are bound, like Hindemith and Stravinsky, to come up against the opera apparatus. . . .

* * *

The dangers that the apparatus can present were shown by the New York production of *Die Mutter.* Its political standpoint puts the Theatre Union in quite a different class from the theaters that had performed the opera *Mahagonny.* Yet the apparatus behaved exactly like a machine for simulating the effects of dope. Not only the play but the music too was distorted as a result, and the didactic aim was, broadly speaking, missed. Far more deliberately than in any other play of the epic theater, the music in *Die Mutter* was designed to induce in the spectator the critical approach that has been outlined above. Eisler's music can by no means be called simple. Qua music it is relatively complicated, and I cannot think of any that is more serious. In a remarkable manner it makes possible a certain simplification of the toughest political problems, whose solution is a life-and-death matter for the working class. In the short piece that counters the accusation that Communism leads to chaos the friendly and explanatory gest of the music wins a hearing, as it were, for the voice of reason. The piece "In Praise of Learning," which links the problem of learning with that of the working class's accession to power, is infected by the music with a heroic yet naturally cheerful gest. Similarly the final chorus "In Praise of Dialectics," which might easily give the effect of a purely emotional song of triumph, has been kept in the realm of the rational by the music. (It is a frequently recurring mistake to suppose that this—epic—kind of production simply does without all emotional effects: actually, emotions are only clarified in it, steering clear of subconscious origins and carrying nobody away.)

If you imagine that the severe, yet delicate and rational gest conveyed by this music is unsuitable for a mass movement that has to face uninhibited force, oppression, and exploitation, then you have misunderstood an important aspect of this fight. It is, however, clear that the effectiveness of this kind of music largely depends on the way in which it is performed. If the actors do not start by getting hold of the right gest then there is little hope that they will be able to carry out their task of stimulating a particular approach in the spectator. Our working-class theaters need careful education and strict training if they are to master the tasks proposed here and the possibilities that are here offered to them. They in turn have to carry out a certain training of their public. It is very important to keep the productive apparatus of the working-class theater well clear of the general drug traffic conducted by bourgeois show business.

For the play *Die Rundköpfe und die Spitzköpfe,* which unlike *Die Mutter* is addressed to a "wide" public and takes more account of purely entertainment considerations, Eisler wrote *song* music. This music too is in a certain sense philosophical. It too avoids narcotic effects, chiefly by linking the solution of musical problems to the clear and intelligible underlining of the political and philosophical meaning of each poem.

All this surely goes to show what a difficult task it is for music to fulfill the demands of an epic theater.

Most "advanced" music nowadays is still written for the concert hall. A single glance at the audiences who attend concerts is enough to show how impossible it is to make any political or philosophical use of music that produces such effects. We see entire rows of human beings transported into a peculiar doped state, wholly passive, sunk without trace, seemingly in the grip of a severe poisoning attack. Their tense, congealed gaze shows that these people are the helpless and involuntary victims of the unchecked lurchings of their emotions. Trickles of sweat prove how such excesses exhaust them. The worst gangster film treats its audience more like thinking beings. Music is cast in the role of Fate. As the exceedingly complex, wholly unanalyzable fate of this period of the grisliest, most deliberate exploitation of man by man. Such music has nothing but purely culinary ambitions left. It seduces the listener into an enervating, because unproductive, act of enjoyment. No number of refinements can convince me that its social function is any different from that of the Broadway burlesques.

We should not overlook the fact that among the more serious composers a reaction against this demoralizing social function has already set in. The experiments being made within the musical field have taken on considerable proportions; the new music is doing all it can not only in the treatment of purely musical material but also in attracting new levels of consumer. And yet there is a whole series of problems that it has not yet been able to solve and whose solution it has not yet tackled. The art of setting epics to music, for instance, is wholly lost. We do not know to what sort of music the *Odyssey* and the *Nibelungenlied* were performed. The performance of narrative poems of any length is something that our composers can no longer render possible. Educational music is also in the doldrums; and yet there were times when music could be used to treat disease. . . . Our composers on the whole leave any observation of the effects of their music to the café proprietors. One of the few actual pieces of research that I have come across in the last ten years was the statement of a Paris restaurateur about the different orders that his customers placed under the influence of different types of music. He claimed to have noticed that specific drinks were always drunk to the works of specific composers. And it is perfectly true that the theater would benefit greatly if musicians were able to produce music that would have a more or less exactly foreseeable effect on the spectator. It would take a load off the actors' shoulders; it would be particularly useful, for instance, to have the actors play *against* the emotion the music called forth. (For rehearsals of works of a pretentious kind it is enough to have whatever music is available.) The silent film gave opportunities for a few experiments with music that created predetermined emotional states. I heard some interesting pieces by Hindemith and above all by Eisler. Eisler even wrote music for conventional feature films, and extremely austere music at that.

But sound films, being one of the most blooming branches of the international narcotics traffic, will hardly carry on these experiments for long.

Another opening for modern music besides the epic theater is provided in my view by the Lehrstück, or didactic cantata. Exceptionally interesting music for one or two examples of this class has been written by Weill, Hindemith, and Eisler. (Weill and Hindemith together for a radio Lehrstück for schoolchildren, *Der Lindberghflug;* Weill for the school opera *Der Jasager;* Hindemith for the *Badener Lehrstück vom Einverständnis;* Eisler for *Die Massnahme.*)

A further consideration is that the writing of meaningful and easily comprehensible music is by no means just a matter of good-will, but above all of competence and study—and study can only be undertaken in continuous contact with the masses and with other artists—not on one's own.

Translated by John Willett

Ernst Bloch

Human Expression as Inseparable from Music
(1955)

It is not the purpose of a note of music to be either vaguely emotional or merely the result of sawing a fiddle. In the first place, it is not meant to wash over the audience in a melting, effeminate way. If a violin sobs like a human breast, this is not only a bad image: the violin is playing badly or playing bad music. A note sequence whose expressiveness is lost when it is performed lucidly and objectively will never have had any expression other than a fraudulent one. But in the second place, we must not allow our repugnance against torrid music and an emotionally charged morass of sound to lead us into denying the psychically charged nature of the whole business of music. A note sequence posits spiritual contents as matters of the will to such an extent that in its archetypal forms it already announces a *striving* or a *movement*. We can sense a distinct fall between the keynote and the fifth; the seventh begs to be led downwards and the third upwards, and chords tend to associate with other chords. Not everything hinges on our empathy in this respect. On the contrary, the tonal relation itself already contains an objective factor that ineluctably determines our empathy. Even the relation of vibrating strings is heard emotionally, and this relation itself determines the first attraction of notes, as also their first friendly consonance. What started as such a physical event, independent handling and a social art that is even more independent take a stage further. Otherwise music would never go beyond descending fifths. Having started as a physical phenomenon, musical tension turns into a psychical one. And melody's most remarkable attribute—the fact that in each of its notes, the immediately following one is latently audible—lies in human anticipation and hence in expression, which is now above all a humanized expression. There might still be music if there were no listeners, but certainly there would be none without the musicians to supply the musical movement and its psychical energy, its pounding energy, in the first place. Composers turn music not only into an expression of themselves but also into an expression of the age and society in which it originates. So naturally this expression is not just romantic or quasi-freely subjective. Any number of *human tensions* are added to the tension of the fifth to create a more complicated cadence and thus the history of music. *Social trends themselves* have been reflected and expressed in the sound material, far beyond the unchanging physical facts and also far beyond a merely romantic espressivo. No other art is conditioned by social factors as much as the purportedly self-acting, even mechanically self-sufficient art of music; historical materialism, with the accent on "historical," abounds here. The dominance of the melody-carrying upper part and mobility of the other parts correspond to the rise of the entrepreneur, just as the central *cantus firmus* and terraced polyphony corresponded to the hierarchical society. Haydn and Mozart, Handel and Bach, Beethoven and Brahms all had a social mission that was very specific; it extends from the form of performance of the *ductus* of the tonal material and its composition, and to the expression, the statement, of the content. Handel's oratorios reflect, in their proud solemnity, the rise of imperialist England and her claim to be the chosen people. There would have been no Brahms without the middle-class concert society and even no musical *neue Sachlichkeit,* no purportedly expressionless music, without the enormous increase in alienation, objectification, and reification in late capitalism. It is always the consumer sector and its requirements, the feelings and aims of the ruling class that are expressed in music. Yet at the same time, thanks to its capacity for such directly human expression, music surpasses other arts in its ability to absorb the manifold griefs, wishes, and rays of hope common to the socially oppressed. And again, no art so outstrips a given age and ideology—although this, of course, is an outstripping that never abandons the human sector. It is inherent in the material of hope, even when the music is expressing sorrow at its times, society, or world, and even in death. The sound of the Bach cantata *Schlage doch, gewünschte Stunde* traverses the darkness and, by virtue of its very existence, offers a mysterious solace. *Evidently, therefore, expression of a human content is not restricted to romantic expression,* as though this were all that mattered and music would otherwise be only a sewing machine. We must not suppose that it was only Beethoven who supplied this element, in some of his slow movements, and then, in the most exorbitant way, Wagner; with the result that in stretches of Wagner, expression turns into a veritable parading of the soul, where he bares his all. As it is time to demonstrate, we find the following instead. *Preromantic music,* in connection with its social contents, actually aimed at an expression that turns out to be far more spontaneous than modern expression. For the ancient Greeks regarded even the flute as exciting, but the lyre as idyllic. The Dorian mode was considered powerful and propitious, and the Lydian mode feminine, the mode of passive emotions. Then we have the vocalises and jubilations of medieval music, which were not just decorations and melismatic excursions but went beyond words, in the interests of a wholly exalted expression. Hence St. Augustine says of the *jubilus* of the Alleluia: "When joy moves a person in the jubilation, he lets forth some sounds that do not belong to speech and have no actual meaning, and then bursts out into an exultation without words, so that it seems he is moved by joy in such song but cannot sum up in words what moves him." In the first operas around 1600, Peri's and Monteverdi's recitatives were still adopting medieval vocalises and tropes precisely because of their expressiveness. And the earlier and far more complex music, the Flemish fabric of contrapuntal movement, was by no means averse to an expression sui generis, namely, late-Gothic and Christian. What has been stigmatized as "artifice" or even "study music" in the Flemish contrapuntists, their "decadent late-Gothic formalism," may be partly accounted for simply by the fact that they have not yet been successfully revived from the purely technical viewpoint. Josquin wrote a twenty-four-part motet that contains a strict six-part canon in each of the four voices. And yet his contemporary, Luther—who was generally hostile to scholasticism—said: "Josquin is master of the notes and they have to do as he wanted; the other masters of song have to do what the notes want." This sentence can only refer to the fund of willpower and expression pervading Josquin's mammoth filigree and mammoth, multitiered structure. With the beginnings of the harmonic style in Palestrina and Orlando di Lasso, we see quite clearly the unity of the *anima christiana* and its musical framework, Raphael-like in the one instance, incipiently baroque in the other. Even Bach, who composed the most learned and at the same time most deeply inspirited music, makes nonsense of the antithesis of expression and canon. While it is absolutely wrong to romanticize Bach in the way Mendelssohn did, we do not come any closer to understanding him by merely dismissing romanticism out of hand, as though we would then be left with nothing but reified form. Bach's composing can by no means be interpreted by partisan opponents of all expressive statements as a line weaving in itself, indeed a prototype for the mechanization at which late capitalism has arrived. With an ostensibly positive slant, this so-styled *neue Sachlichkeit* is reproducing an estimation of Bach that was common fifty years after his death and virtually buried the greatest of composers. In this estimation, Bach's music was unnatural and merely for the head, a "sexton's music without spirituality" and mere periwigged arithmetic. (This view, incidentally, bears some similarity to the view of the great Flemish contrapuntists still current at the time of writing.) Such attributes are now praised in Bach as "absolute music" in a supposedly positive sense, and always with that polemical contrast to purely romantic espressivo that is totally irrelevant to the essence of Bach and *his specific espressivo*. As long ago as the 1870s, Spitta's Bach monograph was permeated and led astray by the same contrast, the same unfruitful repudiation of all emotional and expressive lines, although these make up almost the whole of Bach's music. Miserably defeated, romanticism took its revenge by reintroducing expressive interpretation nonetheless, but now not even along Mendelssohnian lines but along those of the *Gartenlaube*, allegedly pure form plus *Gartenlaube*. Take the sinfonia at the beginning of the second part of the *Christmas Oratorio*. According to Spitta, normally a great supporter of absolute music, it is "the charm of Oriental idyll and the sobriety of a clear, starry Northern winter's night" that form "the atmospheric background to this sinfonia." This, in view of the rude vitality of the flutes and violins, is untenable not only technically but even as a pictorial association. And it is instructive that Albert Schweitzer's later Bach analysis, stemming entirely from his own performing experience, demonstrated the music's specific espressivo in the greatest detail. Down to the graphic character of the score and the perceived *gestus* of the action and emotion, Schweitzer shows what Bach's espressivo involves, in the cantatas and chorales and in the instrumental music. He presents us with a catalogue of documented expression, in which the melodic-rhythmic figures actually spring up and take shape, arising from "affect" and also from its outward agitation. Thus we have figures of languor, agonized or proud grief, spontaneous or transfigured joy, horror, and triumph. We find in Bach an incomparable expressive spectrum ranging from the fear of death and longing for death to solace, assurance, peace, and victory. No form, however unified, is obstructing this, and no ground bass is thwarting the leap from one extreme to the other—extremes occurring and contrasting only in love and in the domain of religious emotion. The contrast between *O Golgatha, unsel'ges Golgatha and Der Held aus Juda siegt mit Macht* is the range covered by this baroque espressivo: baroque in its sudden peripeteia and baroque above all in its turbulent, Christian, emotional content. To this category belong not least the cantatas containing dialogues between Jesus and the soul or between solace and despair, allegorized in music. Indeed the prevalence of expression in Bach is so strong that the following verdict by Schweitzer on the chorale movements in Bach's cantatas and Passions may not appear extravagant: "From the standpoint of pure music Bach's harmonizations are wholly enigmatic, for he does not work upon a tonal succession that in itself forms an aesthetic whole, but follows the lead of the poetry and the verbal expression. How far he lets these take him from the natural principles of pure composition may be seen from his harmonization of "Solls je so sein, dass Straf und Pein," in the cantata *Ich elender Mensch, wer wird mich erlösen* (No. 48), which as pure music is indeed intolerable, Bach's purpose being to express all the wild grief for sin that is suggested in the words. . . . Before he decides simply to write beautiful music to a text, he searches the words through and through to find an emotion that, after it has been intensified, is suitable for musical representation. While statements may still be influenced by neoromantic expression rather too strongly, Schweitzer is nevertheless wholly correct on the central issue, that of the *verbal dictate that governs the music.* Indeed, in addition to the expressive power of the individual tone drawings, of which Schweitzer cites a particularly large number, there is—hardly less importantly—the expressive power of veritable tone paintings, and precisely where dissemination of the emotion in mythical terms is concerned. Key changes often occur purely in order to reflect mythical processes of rejoicing. This is seen at its plainest with the theme of the Resurrection. In the music for *Et especto resurrectionem mortuorum* in the B Minor Mass, the "exspecto" makes a hesitant, uncertain appearance, the bass sings a descending six-note scale, and a pause ensues. Then comes the transformation that confirms the expectancy: the keys undergo modulation via G minor, A major, and D minor to the D major of a Vivace allegro, at which we hear trumpets, whose timbre, with Bach, always signifies victory. And the primacy of expression is merely more latent in any music by Bach that is purely instrumental and not emotionally colored by words. Granted, the fugue does not have any lyrico-emotional expressive tension. But it does contain a dynamic expressive tension that is condensed in the theme, and the development whips up the theme to eight parts contrapuntally and resolves it triumphantly. So, even here, we never find an adherence to rules for their own sake or indeed a formalistic exclusion of man, who was heavily burdened at that time but was crying to heaven all the more ardently. Equally expressive in nature, although still unconquered in its ultimate expression, is the crystal music in the organ fugues, in all their translucence; this is the least self-sufficient of all. And the more convivial works from Bach's Cöthen period—especially the Brandenburg Concertos in their magnificent and elegantly wrought construction, the variations they work, and their heightened thematic richness—evince a supremely sociodynamic expression, which does not flower from arithmetical problems. Thus expression is part of preromantic music as well, being inherent in well-constructed music and an accretion only where the music is badly constructed. In well-constructed music it is never introduced through an emotional delivery. The performance—however much it must allow the "mind" of the lines and forms to be heard—discovers expression in the lines and forms themselves, and within these alone. Expression is realized in forms regarded not as reifications and an end in themselves but as means to a word-surpassing or wordless statement and always, ultimately, to the *utterance of a—call [Ruf]*.

On Biedermeier soil the emotionally charged voice often interposes, of course. This produces a great stir or much superfluous heat, yields soulfulness without expense, and is an effect without a cause. It is found in romantic music and romantic music only, but never, significantly, in its well-wrought passages. And the demand not for lack of expression but for genuine, musically founded expression revolts against an accretion that makes Syrinx the nymph slimy and cheapens music's inherent sense of loss. Of course false emotion did have better origins, probably connected with the heartfelt popular style at the start of the folk song's demise. The damage begins with the Count's accents in the last act of *The Marriage of Figaro* ("Contessa, perdono!"); it continues with Florestan's "In des Lebens Frühlingstagen." It culminates in such pieces as the Prize Song of *The Mastersingers,* otherwise an opera of such solid power, and it makes itself felt in the "Recordare Jesu pie" of the otherwise thoroughly genuine Verdi Requiem. Finally, Strauss presents this emotion, if not cynically, then with all the fervor that cellos can muster in the caressing tone of the Dyer's "Mir anvertraut, dass ich dich hege" in *Die Frau ohne Schatten.* These are all merely episodic examples, but there would have been no room for their pastoso at all before romanticism, and within the latter it constitutes a peril. For all Wagner's genius, this applies to many passages in his music, especially in *The Ring* where we have shrillness or the unctuous Wotan. The unique expressive gains, the Sleep motif, Erda's motif in *The Ring,* the motif of midsummer madness in *The Mastersingers* and so many musical gems and insights, the powerful unrest and nostalgia in this music and its pronouncements were not infrequently paid for with lengthy wallowing in self-sufficient lyrical rhetoric. Of the great poets, only Schiller was haunted by the spell of a distortedly expressive monstrousness, a spell that is by no means synonymous with pathos or even false pathos. The virus takes different forms: it inhabits the senseless fervor of romantic violin tone and the bloated imprecations of Wagnerian heroines, and it is always effect composed of affects or affect composed of effects. Archromantic music, then, was without doubt peculiarly threatened by this, and no doubt there were causes behind it that were at least recognized and no longer approved in more advanced regions. Its social cause was the broad urban bourgeoisie with its need for vague titillation and above all the lower middle class with its retailing of emotions at bargain prices. Technically speaking the psychical, all too psychical virus was carried by middle parts inserted for the sake of color instead of plasticity, by thick instrumentation and by basically torrid or overexcited rhythms. Tchaikovsky's music often constitutes a whole monument to this kind of espressivo (not forgetting the first act of *The Valkyrie*). But such extreme cases, needless to say, are not the *real* expression of romantic music. Nor is its *real* expression divorced from, or added on to, the *great technical construction*. Expression is always music's *terminus a quo* and *terminus ad quem* to such a degree that good music will shape it as inevitably as bad music will counterfeit it and turn espressivo into its opposite: meaninglessness. So we are not concerned with any of this unformed, illicit, expression from the romantic period, which discredited the term "expression." It was mere bodily warmth, or a herd-warmth *[Kuhwärme]*, as Thomas Mann put it, and it lacked strict control and a pleasure in orderliness. This was the garbage of the romantic movement, not that classical face that *is* portrayed in its music. The quartet in *Fidelio* and the quintet in the *Mastersingers* provide expressive music that is both canonic and romantic; for this reason the two pieces are also the most finely constructed. We cannot miss the part writing on account of the soul-searching, any more than we can miss the pathos inherent in a very great contrapuntal marvel like the *Crucifixus* of Bach's B Minor Mass. True, romantic music did sometimes also endow its expression with *literary* signposts that are redundant (Beethoven's headings to the *Pastoral* Symphony) or not in fact conducive to the best results (the out-and-out program symphony from Berlioz to Strauss). But even this was a means of pursuing intrinsically musical interests: the object was to instil in music an ever-greater expressive precision by means of the series of ideas provided. Admittedly, another danger was that music would be comprehended as a mere illustration of literary imaginative devices, contrary to its latent power of expression far beyond all the words in the dictionary. Even here, however, as in all more exalted use of a text, the charm of the verbal expression is wholly subservient to music's deepest concern: to be, discover, or become a language sui generis. Since, indeed, its power of expression lies beyond anything we can put a name to, the final issue at stake is no longer expression in music at all but *music itself as expression.* That is to say, the *sum total of its meaning, significant, and representation, and of that which it represents so mistily and yet, in both senses of the word, so grippingly.* And it is with this sole purpose that music—such a recent art in its polyphonic form—is approaching the hour of its own special language and its poesis *a se*, prefigured in powerful expression but still unknown all the same. This language, of course, comes solely from absolute music, not from some fixed text that is superimposed. To borrow a comparison from Wagner, any literature that is set to great music bears the same relation to music's ineffable expressive power as a commentary by Gervinus bears to a Shakespeare play. In the last analysis, then, musical expression as a whole *is the viceroy for an articulate utterance that goes much farther than is currently understood.* This has occurred, in different contexts, in all great music. But it will only be fully perceived when the hour of eloquence has come, in the form of a revelatory music. What Isolde hears as a fountain, in the nocturnal silence, still sounds like a fanfare of horns to Brangäne. That is to say, should visionary hearing of that kind be attained through successful musical poesis *a se*, then all music we already know will *later sound and give forth other expressive contents besides those it has had so far.* Then the musical expression perceived up to now could seem like a child's stammering by comparison, a language of an ultimate kind that is seeking to take shape but has come close to doing so only in a few, very exalted places. Nobody can understand it yet, although it is occasionally possible to surmise its meaning. *But nobody has as yet heard Mozart, Beethoven, or Bach as they are really calling, designating, and teaching;* this will only happen much later, with the fullest maturation of these and all great works. It will happen, therefore, with the earmuff removed that intensively besets music, an earmuff that stems from the fact that the note does not yet have, or give forth, the full eloquent light of its understanding. Among the arts, music contains a very special ingredient lending itself to the quotation of that still-wordless element that achieves expression instrumentally and can penetrate within the sung word to both its undertone and overtones. Thus the utopian art of music, which as polyphony is so recent, is itself still making for a special, utopian course, that of full-fledged *exprimatio* (within and instead of emotional or descriptive espressivo). The *utopikum* of this expression is the *hour of eloquence through music, understood as visionary hearing.* It is a poesis *a se* with passwords affording entry into the material tonal nature of everything that flows, before, while, and indeed after, it becomes more or less adequately manifest. This something that is adequate to our own and to all core has not yet emerged; its conscience, throbbing affectively and yet not just affectively, its rhythmic-melodic summons, produced by great masters: this is finally music. "If we could name ourselves our Chief would come, and music is the one subjective theurgy," i.e., one whose purpose is to sing and invoke the essentiality most in the likeness of men. This song and its expression are subjective, far more so than in any other art save for lyric poetry. To this extent, the experience of musicians provides the best access to the hermeneutics of affects and in particular the affects of expectancy. But music is also subjective in a significantly different sense, in that its *expression* not only mirrors the *affective looking glass* reflecting *a given society and the world as it occurs* in *affective correlates*. Music also comes close to the subject-based *hearth and driving force* of events, as a subject-based exterior. This *agens* is still in a state of ferment beneath everything already determined and has not itself emerged yet in an objectively stated form. Hence musical expression, too, is still fermenting and has not emerged yet in a finished, definable form. This objective-indeterminate element in the expressed, represented, musical content is the (temporary) defect of its qualities. Accordingly it is the art of presemblance [*des Vor-Scheins*] that is related to the flowing existential core (instant) of that-which-is-in-being most intensively, and to the horizon of the latter most expansively. *Cantus essentiam fontis vocat*—music names the essence of the fountainhead.

Translated by Peter Palmer

Bruno Walter

Thoughts on the Essential Nature of Music
(1957)

From my early days on, I have felt that music is more than a purely artistic concern. As a young man, I was already disinclined to see in it an art like any other. Man's gift for the *visual* arts finds models of colors and patterns in nature that through the eye work on his soul; from the wealth of visible objects rises the spark that incites the creative talent to depiction. Nothing comparable is given by Nature to the sense of hearing: whatever audible phenomena there are cannot—in a way analogous to the process in the realm of the visible—spark off the urge to their artistic representation in a talented listener. Thus—granting such exceptions as the birdcalls and thunderstorm in Beethoven's *Pastoral* Symphony—it could never happen that the physically audible should become the subject matter of musical creation. For it is not the sensuous ear—albeit an organ closer to the soul than the eye—that perceives that "intrinsic essence of the world" that, according to a profound philosophical definition, is demonstrated by music; it is an organ of the soul, which we can with justification call "the *inner ear*," that receives the powerful stimulus toward musical representation that emanates from the *intrinsic* essence of creation.

It was thus borne in on me by my daily contact with and growing appreciation of our art that music is a world in its own right, removed from the other arts, and that the mighty river of our music as we see it before us, springs from, and is replenished by, a hidden source that lies outside the world of reality. Music ever spoke to me of a mysterious world beyond, which moved my heart deeply and eloquently intimated its transcendental nature.

I refer here, of course, to music in general, that is, absolute music that is nothing but itself, as well as vocal music that is influenced by the word. It may appear that the latter is an objective, representative art taking for its aim, perhaps, the descriptive rendering of the text; in actual fact, however, it is able to deploy, while doing justice to the word, its full, autonomous musical power beyond the limits of language. Shouldering, as it were, the word on its flight through its limitless domain, transmuting its meaning into a musical one, dissolving it in music, vocal composition remains, at least in the works of the great masters, true to the spirit of absolute music. The art of music, born of cosmic origin, acquired in the course of its development through the creative genius of man an intensification of its expressive powers that now embraces the most humanly personal statement; well could Schopenhauer say of music that its exclusive concern was with "our weal and woe." But this, in its widest sense, is a fundamental theme of every man's life. Thus, the incomparably intimate relation that exists between a sentient human being and music is explained by the fact that within the mighty universal flow of sound man recognizes the beating of his own heart.

If, for the moment, we disregard what is *expressed* by music, and turn our attention to its essential character, to the sublime order of its sounding, moving universe in which a creative spirit unmistakably reveals itself, we shall be inclined to consider music a parable of creation itself, ruled by the logos. I am of the belief that there is no more immediate access to an understanding of the logos granted to man than by way of music, which bears resounding witness to the latter's divinely creative and ruling character.

Yet it is not only the unmusical who might refuse to place the notion of music, its composition and interpretation, in so exalted a context. It is quite possible to be musical in the ordinary sense of the word, to love music and even exercise it with talent, and yet consider any not strictly intra-artistic view of music as high-flown. These skeptics should ask themselves, however, why it is that music has attended almost every sort of communal ceremony in the life of the nations, and in particular those solemn rites that draw our minds to the supernatural. The use of music in religious cults is well known, dating back, with the Greeks, to Homeric times. This function of music as a contribution to worship can only be *explained* by its transcendental nature; its consolatory impact on suffering humanity may result from the fact that the frequently meaningless and painful *text* of life (to quote Schopenhauer's bold metaphor) is rendered meaningful to the groping mind in its interpretation by the *melody*. Thus, the setting of sacred words as we find it in the musical part of divine service has always been considered a legitimate employment of music; even those who reject any but the aesthetic view of music will feel that the setting of sacred texts is natural and germane to the nature of music. The combination of music and religion has always seemed pertinent to both the religious and the aesthetic mind. The universal significance of such works as Bach's *St. Matthew Passion* and B Minor *Mass*, Mozart's *Requiem*, Beethoven's *Missa Solemnis*, Handel's *Messiah*, Bruckner's *Te Deum*, etc., springs not only from admiration for their supreme artistic standards, but also from a general conviction that the essence of music is commensurate with religion.

It does not, of course, follow from this proximity to religion that music's transcendental message can only reach our soul by attaching itself to words or images of the religious sphere. On the contrary, music is immeasurably more powerful for being uncommitted, deploying, as it does, its most impressive eloquence in absolute and, above all, symphonic music. It is in the highest form of absolute music that the workings of the logos find their clearest reflection, and can thus be symbolically grasped by us. In view of the multiformity and boundless extent of the realm of music, however, we are faced with the following questions: is transcendental significance an essential attribute of music, or does it only pertain to its highest manifestations? And how can it happen that music may descend from its lofty place, stooping to banality and vulgarity; how can one call by the same name of music what spills out from dance halls and bars, or assaults us, with yowls and screeches, in the grotesquely distorted melodies, harmonies, and rhythms of jazz and allied forms of dance music?

The answer would seem to be that there is no such thing as "music in itself," and that music, having its existence only in the written works of composers, is dependent, in regard to the value and character of each work, on the talent and skill, inspiration and intention, and spiritual and ethical qualities of every composer. The character of music, as that of every other art, can be superlatively ennobled by chosen individuals, or debased beyond recognition by the inept, inferior, or perverse.

And yet, as I have pointed out above, music is not mere *material*, helplessly delivered into the hands of the composer for any and every use, as is the amorphous, dead clay in the hands of a sculptor. The elements music consists of, the cells, as it were, from which musical organisms are made, have their own life; they can only be combined in compliance with the innate laws by which musical language is ruled as verbal language is by grammar. In the first place, there are the twelve notes from which the composer has to construct his piece, joining them to simultaneous and successive sounds, grouping them into patterns, and establishing time relations between them. In their boldest as well as in their simplest combinations there are active those elemental laws, the elucidation and systematization of which are the task of the theory of music. The composer who were to sin, intentionally or unintentionally, against these fundamental laws would only produce "nonmusic."

I am strictly referring to tonal music here, for any musical consecution without a tonal center, in an imaginary atonal field, seems amusical to me. To every musical mind these fundamental laws have always seemed natural, that is, founded in the nature of music, and the atonal composer's revolt against them is as senseless as would be a rebellion against the laws of physics.

Familiarity with these laws immanent in the function of the elements of music was inborn to me as to every musician, and theoretical studies only went to confirm what we knew instinctively and experienced in the daily round of making music. As I have pointed out in my essay *Von den moralischen Kräften in der Musik*, what seems to me the most significant trait of that autonomy of the elements of music is the striving of the dissonance toward resolution in the consonance. A conflict demands solution, unrest yearns for rest. I think I am right in finding here an allegory for an inner law of the world; I would even submit that a sharper eye than mine might find in this elemental sequence, in this striving for peace and conciliation, the quality that enables music to be the carrier of the exalted message I mentioned before.

Seeing that every composition consists of a combination of elements in which these immanent laws reside, one should assume that even the most ordinary piece of music would evince, by virtue of the strength of those self-sufficient elemental forces, some ves-

tiges of the altitude at which the spirit of music dwells. I have often
asked myself whether this is not so; whether, that is, the heavenly
drop of nectar contained in it does not give to even the most trivial
musical concoction that contrasting flavor that makes it so deplor-
ably attractive.

While the elementary laws of verbal language, which we call
grammar, are of a rational kind, I recognize in those of musical
language an emotional quality. The drive from movement, unrest,
conflict to peace and rest, although it renews itself with every dissonance, always comes to rest eventually in the final consonance of
a piece, and thus is invested with the optimistic significance of a
promise. This may explain why even the most somber piece of
music does not plunge us into hopelessness. Amidst the negation
of a tragic composition we perceive the positiveness of the very
element in which it expresses itself; music confirms to us the insight
that came to Nietzsche when, at dead of night, he looked at the
world: "Joy is deeper than grief."

In Grillparzer's masterly story, *Der arme Spielmann,* we read of
the author overhearing this most humble devotee of music as he
played his violin in entranced solitude; it was a single note that he
bowed again and again; swelling and fading, he delighted in sustaining it, then alternating it with the fourth, the fifth, and the
third—it was obvious that this simple production of notes with an
occasional change gave him great happiness.

And must we not agree with the "poor minstrel" that a mere
sound of definite pitch—unlike the spoken word with its indefinite
pitch—has the power to stir our feelings? Even a single note, this
most humble messenger from the exalted sphere of music, contains
a little of the emotional quality we find in its elements and that,
heightened to a spiritual revelation in the stupendous works of the
great masters, floods over us and shakes our hearts.

Translated by Paul Hamburger

Theodor W. Adorno

Classes and Strata
(1962)

I f music really is ideology, not a phenomenon of truth—in other
words, if the form in which it is experienced by a population
befuddles their perception of social reality—one question that will
necessarily arise concerns the relation of music to the social classes.
Today the existence of classes is concealed by ideological appearances. We need not even think of vested interests calling for, and
launching, ideologies. There is no shortage of such interests. But
their subjective initiative, although it may be added, is secondary
in comparison with the objectively benighting context. That context also creates the ideological appearance of music. In the exchange relationship, any adjustment to that which the World Spirit
has made of men defrauds them at the same time. As a source of
socially false consciousness, functioning music is entwined in social
conflict, without the planners' intent or the consumers' knowledge.

Yet this is the cause of the central difficulties under which insights
in musical sociology are laboring to this day. As long as it fails to
encompass the concrete structure of society, that sociology remains
mere social psychology and noncommittal. But the nonobjective
and nonconceptual character of music balks at tangible classifications and identifications between its various dimensions, on the
one hand, and classes or strata on the other. This is just what
the East's dogmatically frozen social theory profited by. The more
puzzling the relation of music and specific classes, the more conve-
nient its dispatch by labeling. All we need do is take the music

consumed by the masses, willy-nilly, and equate it on the basis of its alleged closeness to the people with true music—regardless of the similarity between the alleged Socialist Realism of official Communist music and the dregs of the late romanticist music from the capitalist countries of the fin de siècle. An equally simple measure is to seize the authority of famous music from the past for one's own authoritarian requirements. A stroke of the dictatorial pen coordinates it with the People's Democracy, and the same mindlessness governs the treatment of avant-garde musical art. From outside, heedless of its immanent composition, this is excoriated as decadent because of failure to serve as a social cement, and any recalcitrant individualists among composers are shown the knout with a mien of comradely solicitude.

Inquiries into the social distributions and preferences of musical consumption tell us little about the class aspect. The musical sociologist is faced with a choice between flat statements that apply the class concept to music—without any justification other than the current political aims of the powers that be—and a body of research that equates pure science with knowing whether middle-income urban housewives between the ages of thirty-five and forty would rather hear Mozart or Tchaikovsky, and how they differ in this point from a statistically comparable group of peasant women. If anything at all has been surveyed here it is strata defined as subjectively characterized units. They must not be confused with the class as a theoretical-objective concept.

Nor would the origin, the social background of composers let us infer anything cogent about the class import of music. Such elements may play a part in music—can anyone perceive the sort of beery coziness that Richard Strauss exudes at the wrong moments, in Mycenae or in eighteenth-century nobility, without thinking of rich philistines?—but their definition tends to evaporate and to grow vague. In attempting a social interpretation of Strauss's effect in the era of his fame one would surely have a better right to associate him with words like *heavy industry, imperialism, grand bourgeoisie.* Conversely, there is not much modern music with more of a haut monde habitus than Ravel's, and he came out of the most cramped lower-middle-class circumstances. A differential analysis of family backgrounds is unproductive. Those of Mozart and Beethoven were similar; so, probably, were their milieus once Beethoven had moved to Vienna, rather better off than the materially insecure Austrian native; the age difference between them was no more than fourteen years. And yet Beethoven's social climate with its touch of Rousseau, Kant, Fichte, Hegel, is altogether incompatible with Mozart's.

We might cite cases that work better, but the chances are that the idea itself, the search for correspondences between class membership and a composer's social origin, involves an error in principle. The strongest argument against it is not even that in music the so-called social standpoint that an individual occupies is not directly translated into the tone language. To be considered first of all is whether, from the viewpoint of the producers' class membership, there has ever been anything other than bourgeois music—a problem, by the way, that affects the sociology of art far beyond music. In feudal and absolutist times mental labor was not too highly esteemed, and the ruling classes generally used to delegate such labor rather than perform it themselves. Even the products of medieval courts and chivalry would have to be further investigated to establish in what measure those poets and musicians really were representative of the classes to which, as knights, they formally belonged. On the other hand, the social status of the proletariat within bourgeois society served largely to impede artistic production by workers and workers' children. The realism taught by want is not as one with the free unfoldment of consciousness. Determining how all this stands in Russia would presuppose submitting the stratification over there to an analysis that would scarcely be tolerated.

The social odium that for thousands of years weighed especially on the arts that involve an artist's personal appearance, arts such as the theater, the dance, and music, has greatly limited the circle of persons from which those artists were recruited. Nor was the grand bourgeoisie apt to supply a great many musicians. Mendelssohn was a banker's son, but as a Jew, at least, an outsider in his own stratum; the slickness of his compositions has some of the excessive zeal of one who is not quite accepted. Except for Mendelssohn, Richard Strauss was probably the only famed composer born to wealth. Prince Gesualdo da Venosa, an outsider in every sense, defies modern sociological categories. Composers mostly arose from the petty bourgeois middle class or from their own guild: Bach, Mozart, Beethoven, Brahms grew up as musicians' children in modest circumstances, sometimes in stark poverty; even Strauss was the son of a hornist. Wagner came from the half-amateurish Bohemia to which his stepfather belonged.

Exaggerating a bit, all these might be called secularizations of the sphere of "wandering minstrels." For the most part the production of music was evidently handled by men who even before starting to compose belonged to the so-called third persons,* assigned the practice of all art by bourgeois society. Handel would be a typical case; for all his fame in wealthy England he was denied bourgeois security and had "ups and downs" like Mozart. If we do in fact want to construe a link between the subjective origin of music and its social import, it is the concept of the third person, down to the dependency of servants, which may help to explain why music as a "service" to gentlefolk had so long unprotestingly complied with socially ordained ends. The brand of shame that once attached to vagabonds has turned into obedience to the purveyors of one's livelihood; in literature this held no such naked sway, at least. A marginal existence of protracted waiting for crumbs from the seignorial table, with no place in the regular bourgeois labor process—this was the specific social destiny of music under the aspect of its producers.

Until far into the nineteenth century—in other words, in a fully developed capitalist society—composers were anachronistically kept in this situation. Their work had long been marketed as a commodity, but under backward copyright laws it did not provide them with an adequate living even if the theaters got rich on it. This, above all, was Wagner's fate during his years in exile. Ernest Newman rightly points out the mendacity of the hue and cry at Wagner's extravagance and constant scrounging: for decades, bourgeois society rooked him out of the bourgeois profit that German opera houses were not ashamed to pocket from *Tannhäuser, Lohengrin,* and *The Flying Dutchman.* Among famed composers of the official musical culture, the first to make full capitalist use of their production were probably Puccini and Richard Strauss; of their predecessors, Rossini, Brahms, and Verdi became well-to-do, at least—Rossini thanks to the protection of the Rothschilds. Society controlled music by holding its composers on a tight and not

---

*A neologism referring to those who in seventeenth- or eighteenth-century German usage were addressed in the third person singular.—Transl.

so very golden leash; potential petitioner status never favors social opposition. That's why there is so much merry music.

Now let us turn to the sphere in which a social differentiation of music should most likely be notable, to the sphere of reception. Even there, a stringent link between the thing and its ideological function is hard to make out. Considering the unconscious and preconscious nature of musical effects upon most people, and the difficulty of accounting for those effects in words, their empirical study is hazardous. A few conclusions might be drawn if a random sample of listeners were asked to choose between crude statements ranging from "Like it very much" to "Don't like it at all," and even more if the listening habits of different social strata in regard to different radio programs were examined. Presumably we still lack data that would justify conclusive assertions, but a plausible hypothesis seems to be that the relation between types of music and social stratification corresponds more or less to the prevailing evaluation, the accumulated prestige of musical types and levels in the cultural climate. The result of standardized surveying mechanisms will inevitably be a rougher posing of this sort of problem, and such hypotheses too would therefore have to be simplified to the limit of their truth content—on the order of highbrow music for the upper classes, middlebrow music for the middle class, and lowbrow music for those at the bottom of the social pyramid.

It is to be feared that empirical results would not much differ from this simplification. We would need only to have a blue-ribbon panel work out a kind of hierarchy of musical values—which, by the way, coincides not at all with authentic quality—to reencounter the experts' division in that of the listeners. Exclusively culture-conscious representatives of education and property would revel in the Ninth Symphony's appeal to mankind or wallow in the amorous plights of the highborn, as in *Der Rosenkavalier*, or else they would flock to Bayreuth. People from more modest income groups—who do, however, pride themselves on their bourgeois status and incline to what they consider culture—would respond to elevated entertainment, rather, to nineteenth-century operas and standard favorites such as the Arlésienne suites and the minuet from Mozart's Symphony No. 24 in E Flat Major, to Schubert's arrangements, to the intermezzo from *Cavalleria Rusticana,* and the like. Downward this would go on to a wretched infinity, via synthetic folk music complete with *lederhosen,* down to the hell of humor. In this schema, the few individuals not looking for entertainment would probably be distributed according to the ratio one might expect from their typological description.

For sociological cognition of music's relation to social classes such results would not be of much use—because of their superficiality, for one thing. They already are more reflective of the supply planned according to strata and offered for sale by the culture industry than they are indicative of any class significance of musical phenomena. It is even conceivable that the subjective leveling tendencies in the consumer sphere may by now have gone too far for that tripartition to come into drastic view. The gradations one might see in it are apt to resemble the high and low price ranges so carefully weighed by the automobile industry. There is probably no primary differentiation at all, only a secondary one according to "lines" offered to a consciousness that has been leveled in principle. The task of confirming or refuting this would oblige empirical researchers to go in for many complicated reflections and methodical inquiries.

The very simplest of these reflections shows how little an inventory of the stratification of consuming habits would contribute to insights into the context of music, ideology, and classes. Any assumption of a special affinity for ideologically kindred music in the conservatively class-conscious upper stratum, for instance, would in all likelihood be contradicted by the findings. Actually great music is apt to be preferred there, and that, as Hegel said, implies a sense of needs; what that music receives into its own formal constitution is the problematics, however sublimated, of realities which that stratum prefers to dodge. In this sense the music they appreciate upstairs is less ideological, not more, than the one they like downstairs. The ideological role which that music plays in privileged households is the role of their privilege and altogether different from its own truth content.

Empirical sociology has projected another, equally crude dichotomy: that today's upper stratum likes to interpret itself as idealistic while the lower boasts of its realism. Yet the purely hedonistic music consumed below stairs is surely not more realistic than the one valid above; it does even more to veil reality. If it occurred to an East German sociologist to speak of the extra-aesthetic leaning that the uneducated feel to music as to something unintellectual, a mere sensual stimulus, and to describe this leaning as materialistic in nature and therefore compatible with Marxism, such a description would be a demagogic swindle. Even if we accepted the philistine hypothesis, it would remain true that such stimuli, even in entertainment music, are more apt to occur in the expensive product of skilled arrangers than in the cheap domain of mouth organ and zither clubs. Above all, music is indelibly a matter of the mind since even on its lowest level the sensual element cannot be literally savored like a leg of veal. It is precisely where the way of serving it is culinary that its preparation has been ideological from the start.

We can infer from this why a recourse to listening habits remains so fruitless for the relation of music and classes. The reception of music can turn it into something altogether different; indeed, it will presumably and regularly become different from what is currently believed to be its inalienable content. The musical effect comes to diverge from, if not to conflict with, the character of what has been consumed: this is what makes the analysis of effects so unfit to yield insights into the specific social sense of music.

An instructive model is Chopin. If a social bearing can without arbitrariness be attributed to any music at all, Chopin's music is aristocratic—in a pathos disdaining all prosaic sobriety, in a kind of luxury in suffering, also in the self-evident assumption of a homogeneous audience committed to good manners. Chopin's differentiated eroticism is conceivable only in turning one's back upon material practice, and so is his eclectic dread of banality amidst a traditionalism he does not sensationally violate anywhere. Seignorial, finally, is the habitus of an exuberance squandered. Corresponding to all this in Chopin's day was the social locus of his effect, and indeed, even as a pianist he would not so much appear on public concert stages as at the soirées of high society.

Yet this music, exclusive in both origin and attitude, has within a hundred years become exceedingly popular and ultimately, by way of one or two Hollywood hits, a mass item. Chopin's aristocratic side was the very one to invite socialization. Countless millions hum the melody of the Polonaise in A Flat Major, and when they strike that pose of a chosen one at the piano to tinkle out some of the less-demanding Préludes or Nocturnes, we may assume that they are vaguely counting themselves with the elite. The role that Chopin, an important composer of great originality and an unmistakable tone, came to play in the musical household of the masses resembled the role Van Dyck or Gainsborough played in their visual household—if indeed his ill-suited function was not that of a writer who acquaints his millions of customers with the alleged morals and mores of countesses. This is how much, and with respect to class relations in particular, a music's social function may diverge from the social meaning it embodies, even when the embodiment is as obvious as Chopin.

Without any extraneous attribution to an origin or an effective context, Chopin's music marks its social horizon. But the same applies less obviously, perhaps, to a great deal of music that can still be spontaneously grasped at all. If we listen to Beethoven and do not hear anything of the revolutionary bourgeoisie—not the echo of its slogans, the need to realize them, the cry for that totality in which reason and freedom are to have their warrant—we understand Beethoven no better than does one who cannot follow the purely musical content of his pieces, the inner history that happens to their themes. If so many dismiss that specifically social element as a mere additive of sociological interpretation, if they see the thing itself in the actual notes alone, this is not due to the music but to a neutralized consciousness. The musical experience has been insulated from the experience of the reality in which it finds itself—however polemically—and to which it responds. While compositorial analysis was learning to trace the most delicate ramifications of the facture, and while musicology was accounting at length for the biographical circumstances of composer and work, the method of deciphering the specific social characteristics of music has lagged pitifully and must be largely content with improvisations.

If we wished to catch up, to release the cognition of music from its inane isolation, it would be necessary to develop a physiognomics of the types of musical expression. Beethoven would have to remind us of the compositorial gestures of restiveness and refractoriness, of a handwriting in which good manners, conventions respected even in differentiation, are knocked aside, so to speak, by sforzati and dynamic jammings and abrupt piano continuations of crescendi. All this and far more deeply hidden things could be obtained from something I have occasionally called "Mahler's material theory of musical forms"; of these, however, we see hardly any rudiments. The scientific consciousness of music breaks asunder into blind technology and such poeticizing, childishly noncommittal exegeses as the ones of Beethoven by Schering. The rest is a matter of taste.

In thetical form a vast amount of music can be called by its social name; but until now such experiences have failed completely to be linked with the musically immanent facts, and that failure even serves as a pretext for arguing the most evident things out of existence. To hear the petty bourgeois in Lortzing, we do not need to know the texts; a medley from *Zar und Zimmermann* ringing from the bandstand at a summer resort will do. That Wagner has brought a decisive change in the pathos of bourgeois emancipation strikes us in his music, whether or not we reflect on Schopenhauer's pessimism. The leitmotif champion's abandonment of properly motive-thematic work, the triumph of compulsive repetition over the productive imagination of unfolding variations—these things tell us something about the resignation of a collective consciousness that can see nothing ahead anymore. Wagner's tone denotes the social tendency of men to disavow the toil and stress of their own reason in favor of brutal and persuasive force, and to return from freedom to the disconsolate monotony of the cycle of nature. His is the very music in which expressive characters, technical procedures, and social significance are so fused that each one is legible in the other. The point of my own book on Wagner—if I may state it here in so many words—was to replace the sterile juxtaposition of music and social exegesis with at least a draft of models for the concrete unity of both.

Music is not ideology pure and simple, it is ideological only insofar as it is a false consciousness. Accordingly, a sociology of music would have to set in at the fissures and fractures of what happens in it, unless those are attributable merely to the subjective inadequacy of an individual composer. Musical sociology is social critique accomplished through that of art. Where music is intrinsically brittle, antinomical, but with the antinomies covered under a vocal facade rather than fought out, it is always ideological, itself imprisoned in the false consciousness. In interpretations moving within this horizon, sensibility of reaction must make up for any temporary, though perhaps not accidental, lack in methods capable of being handed down.

That Brahms—like the entire evolution since Schumann, even since Schubert—bears the mark of bourgeois society's individualistic phase is indisputable enough to have become a platitude. In

Beethoven the category of totality still preserves a picture of the right society; in Brahms it fades increasingly into a self-sufficiently aesthetic principle for the organization of private feelings. This is the academic side of Brahms. His music beats a mournful retreat to the individual, but as the individual is falsely absolutized over society Brahms's work too is surely part of a false consciousness—of one from which no modern art can escape without sacrificing itself. It would be barbarian and pedantic to elaborate that fatality into a verdict on the private person's music, and ultimately into one on all allegedly merely subjective music. In Brahms's case the private sphere as the substrate of expression does displace what might be called the substantial public character of music. But in his phase that public character itself was no longer substantial socially, no longer anything but ideology, and it retained a touch of this throughout bourgeois history. The artistic withdrawal from it is not only that flight that the dauntless progressives are so quick and pharisaical to damn. If music, and art as a whole, is resigned to its own social possibilities, if it fully develops them within itself, it ranks primarily—even in social truth content—above an art that out of an extraneous social will tries to exceed its dictated bounds and miscarries.

Music may also turn ideological when its social reflections make it take the standpoint of a consciousness that looks correct from without but conflicts with its own inner composition and its necessities, and thus with the things it can express. The social critique of class relations is not all the same with musical critique. Brahms's or Wagner's social topology devalues neither man. Brahms, in pensively and somehow worriedly taking the standpoint of the isolated, alienated, self-submerging private individual, negates negation. The great, encompassing problems of form are not simply cut off; Brahms transforms them, rather, preserving them in the question of whether there can be a binding suprapersonal formulation of the personal. Unconsciously posited in this is the moment of that privacy's social mediation. The objectification by form manifests the universal even in the private. Socially, in music, adequate presentation is everything; mere conviction is nothing. The higher critique, which must eventually name the element of untruth in the content of both Brahms and Wagner, extends to social bounds of artistic objectification, but it does not dictate norms of what music must be.

Nietzsche, who had more flair than anyone for the social aspects of music, forfeited his main chance when he let the wishful image of Antiquity induce him to equate critique of content too directly with aesthetic critique. There is, of course, no separating the two. The ideological side of Brahms also turns musically wrong when the standpoint of the subject's pure being-for-itself keeps compromising with the traditional collective formal language of music, which is not that subject's language anymore. The fiber and the form of Brahms's music already point in different directions. But music, in the unchanged split society, is not therefore allowed to wave conviction's magic wand so as to surrogate a supraindividual position. It must be incomparably less reserved than Brahms in yielding to that individualization of the lyrical subject if, without lying, it wants to perceive there something that is more than individual. The manner in which art corrects a socially false consciousness is not collective adjustment; rather, it is an act of carrying that consciousness so far that it will shed all appearance. Another way to put it would be that the question whether or not music is ideology is settled at the centers of its technical complexion.

In our time, with music directly involved in social struggles by partisan propaganda and totalitarian measures, judgments about the class significance of musical phenomena are doubly precarious. The stamp that political movements put upon musical ones has often nothing to do with the music and its content. We know what music the Nazis denounced as "cultural bolshevism" and—with the cheapest equivocations between a fissured-looking score and alleged social implications—christened "subversive"; it was the same music that the Eastern bloc ideology indicts for bourgeois decadence. The former found it politically too far left; the latter rails at "rightest deviationism." Conversely, actual difference in social content do slip through the meshes of political frames of reference, sociological as much as compositorial.

Stravinsky and Hindemith are equally undesirable to the totalitarian regimes. My first major piece of writing about musical sociology was an essay "*Zur gesellschaftlichen Lage der Musik*" (On the Social Position of Music) that appeared in the periodical *Zeitschrift für Sozialforschung* in 1932, just before the outbreak of fascism. There I called Stravinsky's music "grand bourgeois," and Hindemith's, "petty bourgeois." But this distinction was not merely based upon unweighable and uncontrollable impressions.

Stravinsky's neoclassicism—whose explication, by the way, would require an exegesis of the whole neoclassicist movement about 1920—was not meant literally; rather, the turns from the so-called preclassic past were handled with a self-pointing, self-estranging license. Underscoring this license were fractures and intentional trespasses against the traditional tonal idiom and the familiar appearance of its rationality. No respecter of the sanctity of the individual, Stravinsky stood above himself, so to speak. His irrational objectivism recalls games of chance or the posture of men whose power lets them ignore rules of the game. He paid no more attention to the tonal rules than to those of the marketplace, though the facade was left standing in both places. His sovereignty and his freedom combined with cynicism in regard to his own self-decreed order. All this is as grand bourgeois as the supremacy of taste, which in the end, simultaneously blind and selective, decides alone what is or is not to be done.

By Hindemith, on the other hand, who for decades aped Stravinsky with conscientious craftsmanship, the great gambler is deprived of his savor. The classicistic formulas are taken literally, sought to be fused with the traditional language—with Reger's, little by little—and trimmed into a system of humbly serious bustle. It finally converges not only with musical academicism but with the dauntless positivity of quiet souls. Having found himself, Hindemith follows some tried and true models in ruing the excesses of his youth. "Systems are for little people," says Henrich Regius in his *Dämmerung.* "The great have intuition; they bet on whatever numbers come to mind. The larger a man's capital, the better the chance of new intuitions making up for those that failed. It cannot happen to the rich that they stop playing because their money runs out, or that as they walk out of the door they hear the very number coming up that they could no longer bet on. The intuitions of the rich are more trustworthy than the laborious calculations of the poor—calculations that always fail because they cannot be thoroughly tested." This physiognomics fits the difference between Stravinsky and Hindemith; with such categories the class significance of contemporary music might perhaps be handled. Confirmation comes, moreover, from the intellectual ambience of the two composers, from their choice of texts, from their slogans. Stravinsky, heading an elegant *cénacle,* would issue the latest watchwords and be non-committally aware of his top position, like the haute couture. Hindemith plied an archaiezing guildsman's humility, composing "to measure" halfway through the twentieth century.

But things are not always so plausible in musical sociology. The literary and theoretical self-comprehension of the Schönberg school lags far behind the thoroughly critical content of its music. It would not only be easy to uncover petty bourgeois elements in its treasury of associative conceptions; the very ideal of that music, its *terminus ad quem*, was traditionalist and tied to the bourgeois faith in authority and culture. For all its expressionism, the dramaturgy of the stage composer Schönberg was Wagnerian all the way to *Moses und Aron*. Even Webern was still guided by a traditional, affirmative concept of music: there are radical departures from bourgeois culture in his oeuvre, but he himself was as unaware of them as Schönberg could not understand why his merry opera *Von heute auf morgen* did not score a hit with the public. I take it that all this is not entirely irrelevant to the social content of the matter either. But the truth about it, like any truth, is fragile. There can be no inquiring after it whatsoever until the sociology of contemporary music has been emancipated from all outwardly disposing classifications.

There have been very few attempts to imbue music itself, the compositorial habitus, with something like class significance. Aside from a couple of Russian composers soon after the Revolution, men whose names have long been buried under battle and victory symphonies, those attempts include some of Hanns Eisler's works, mainly workers' choruses from the late twenties and early thirties. There a genuine compositorial imagination and considerable technical skill entered the service of expressive characters, of purely musical phrasings that in themselves, prior to any extramusical program and content, show a distinct kind of sharp and pointed aggressiveness. This music achieved an exceedingly close union with the agitational texts; at times it rang directly, concretely polemical. It was art seeking to occupy its class position by its behavior, a procedure analogous to that of George Grosz, who placed his graphic artistry at the service of unmerciful social critique. Today, of course, such music is no longer written in the East. Finding out whether those workers' choruses can still be performed there at all might be worth one's while. The musical handwriting of Weill, in any case—once brought into the same force field by his collaboration with Brecht—no longer had anything in common with that acuity; this music could effortlessly turn away from the goals it had used to excite itself for a time.

Even in such cases there remains an element of undefinability. If music can harangue, it is nonetheless doubtful what for, and what against. Kurt Weill's music made him seem a leftist social critic in the prefascist years; in the Third Reich he found apocryphal successors who would at least rearrange his musical dramaturgy and much of Brecht's epic theater so as to fit the collectivism of Hitler's dictatorship. As a matter of principle, instead of searching for the musical expression of class standpoints one will do better so to conceive the relation of music to the classes that any music will present the picture of antagonistic society as a whole—and will do it less in the language it speaks than in its inner structural composition. One criterion of the truth of music is whether greasepaint is found to cover up the antagonism that extends to its relations with the audience—thus involving it in the more hopeless aesthetic contradictions—or whether the antagonistic experience is faced in the music's own structure.

Intramusical tensions are the unconscious phenomena of social tensions. Ever since the industrial revolution all of music has been suffering from the unreconciled state of the universal and the particular, from the chasm between their traditional, encompassing forms and the specific musical occurrences within those forms. It was this that eventually compelled the cancellation of the schemata—in other words, the new music. In that music the social tendency itself turns into sound. The divergence of general and individual interests is musically admitted, whereas the official ideology teaches the harmony of both. Authentic music, like probably any authentic art, is as much a cryptogram of the unreconciled antithesis between individual fate and human destiny as it is a presentation of the bonds, however questionable, that tie the antagonistic individual interests into a whole, and as it is finally a presentation of the hope for real reconcilement. The elements of stratification touching the several musics are secondary in comparison.

Music has something to do with classes insofar as it reflects the class relationship in toto. The standpoints that the musical idiom occupies in the process remain epiphenomena as opposed to that phenomenon of the essence. The purer and more unalloyed its grasp of the antagonism and the more profound its representation, the less ideological the music and the more correct its posture as objective consciousness. An objection to the effect that representation itself is reconcilement already, and is thus ideological, would touch upon the wound of art in general. Yet representation does justice to reality insofar as the organized and differentiated totality, the totality from which representation derives its idea, attests that through all sacrifice and all distress the life of mankind goes on.

In the exuberance of the nascent bourgeois era this was expressed in the humor of Haydn, who smiled at the world's course as an estranged bustle while affirming it with that same smile. It is by the anti-ideological resolution of conflicts, by a cognitive behavior without an inkling of the object of its cognition, that great music takes a stand in social struggles: by enlightenment, not by aligning itself, as one likes to call that, with an ideology. The very content of its manifest ideological positions is historically vulnerable; Beethoven's pathos of humanity, meant critically on the spot, can be debased into a ritual celebration of the status quo. This change of functions gave Beethoven his position as a classic, from which he ought to be rescued.

He who would socially decipher the central content of music cannot use too delicate a touch. It is by force or on occasion only that antagonistic moments will be musically identifiable in Mozart, whose music so clearly echoes the passage from enlightened late absolutism to the bourgeoisie, a transition deeply akin to Goethe. Rather, his social aspect is the force with which his music returns to itself, the detachment from empiricism. The menacingly looming power of unleashed economics is sedimented in his form as follows: as though afraid of getting lost at any touch, the form keeps the degraded life at arm's length, yet without feigning a content other than the one it can humanely fulfill by its own means, i.e., without romanticism.

Of all the tasks awaiting us in the social interpretation of music, that of Mozart would be the most difficult and the most urgent. But if one finds the social complexion of music in its own interior, not simply in its effective links with society, he will not rely on any social adjustment, of whichever kind, to take him past whatever is false consciousness in music. Such adjustments merely add to the general fungibility, and thus to the social ills. What is unattainable for music of the utmost integrity might solely be hoped for from a better-organized society, not from customer service. The end of music as an ideology will have to await the end of antagonistic society.

Although in 1962 I would no longer phrase the constellation of music and classes in the same terms as thirty years ago, I would still stand by a few lines I wrote then, in that essay for *Zeitschrift für Sozialforschung*. They read as follows:

> Here and now, music can do nothing else but represent, in its own structure, the social antinomies that also bear the guilt of its isolation. It will be the better, the more deeply it can make its forms lend shape to the power of those contradictions, and to the need to overcome them socially—the more purely the antinomies of its own formal language will express the calamities of the social condition and call for change in the cipher script of suffering. It does not behoove music to stare at society in helpless horror; its social function will be more exactly fulfilled if the social problems contained in it, in the inmost cells of its technique, are presented in its own material and according to its own formal laws. The task of music as an art comes thus to be a kind of analogue to that of social theory.

Translated by E. B. Ashton

Georg Knepler

Music Historiography in Eastern Europe
(1972)

What we call Eastern Europe is composed of some ten countries in which a score of languages is spoken, ranging from branches of the Slavonic family to Hungarian, Romanian, and German. In some of these countries, after World War II, musicology had to begin practically from the start and did so with the impetus characteristic of new starts. In other countries, such as the Soviet Union, the Polish and the Czechoslovak People's Republics and the German Democratic Republic, there already existed a tradition of musicology upon which scholars could, and did, build and enlarge. Thus the material for my lecture this afternoon is taken from a great number of books, periodical articles, music editions, and discs in more than a dozen languages. It will, therefore, be clear that I cannot possibly aim at completeness. Instead, I propose to concentrate on the methods of music historiography employed in Eastern Europe. In doing so I will refer to certain works that seem noteworthy to me, with the understanding that I may have omitted others of equal importance.

Turning to methods of historical research used in Eastern Europe, I should first point out that they are not uniform. The Marxist method, about which I will have more to say in a moment, is not accepted by several musicologists, some of them of high repute. Let me name Max Schneider, Heinrich Besseler, and Walther Vetter in the German Democratic Republic, similarly Bence Szabolcsi in Hungary, Hieronim Feicht in Poland, and so on. A few of these scholars have expressed interest in, and respect for, the Marxist approach, and said that they owe something to it; but they come from different schools of thought and traditions and cannot accept it as a whole—some not at all. Others, among them some young scholars, feel that they have to reject the philosophically materialistic approach of Marxism although they find its methodology indispensable. This is, in my view, inconsistent, yet it must be recorded as fact.

Marxist philosophy is taught in schools and universities in most socialist countries. Its application to the method of various branches of knowledge, including historiography, has produced arguments, hypotheses, and working methods that, while continuously being developed, have grown into a system. I will try to expound some of its implications for the writing of music history.

Discussing the scholar's motives for investigating the history of music, Professor Arthur Mendel has said that we should, according to a common explanation, "maintain that we study music history in order to understand history in general, which, in turn, we study in order to learn from the past what to do about the future." He added: "But in actual fact those who inquire into the past are in general not those who do a great deal about the future." And he came to the conclusion: "No—our primary reason for studying history is not utilitarian." Without fear of being contradicted by most of my colleagues in Eastern Europe I can say that our aim is utilitarian. Our aim is the improvement of our musical culture.

As soon as one has made such a statement one finds oneself involved, I know, in a number of philosophical problems. Can one apply standards of value to musical culture? Even if one can, is it possible to influence the course of music history, or general history? And if the answer be in the affirmative, what is the relation between one's activity and the laws of development? Obviously, if one cannot design a model for a better musical culture because there is no way of deciding whether one is better than another; if there are no laws discernible in the development of music; if music history moves in cycles, the course of which we cannot influence any more than the ebb and flow of oceans; if it develops according to laws the depths of which we cannot ever hope to fathom or else according to no laws at all—what use would there be in a "utilitarian" history of music, to quote Professor Mendel's expression once more?

I will not try to answer all these questions fully, but rather outline the way in which we think answers can be found. Marxist music historians regard their subject as part of general history. One could say, to formulate it in a radical way, that there is no such thing as "music history." When we deal with our subject we are, whether we know it or not, concerned with the history of man. Our subject, though of special interest to us, is but one of several aspects of mankind's history. While one cannot and should not necessarily inflict the economic, juridical, cultural, and other ramifications of history on a person interested in, say, the history of the sonata, one should keep in mind that all these ramifications are, to a lesser or greater degree, relevant to the sonata. This thesis is probably not controversial in itself. But how are the links between general history and music to be viewed? Curt Sachs must have thought about this a great deal. In his *Commonwealth of Art,* he makes short shrift of those who, "in establishing a self-sufficient, autonomous music history in which some symphony stems from some other symphony in virgin birth . . . lead the catastrophic way to severing music from man and music history from the evolution of the human mind. This should not happen." Sachs himself gives examples of the way in which he sees music tethered to society. "It has almost become a truism," he says, for instance, "to connect the political currents in later Greece with her subjective art; medieval universalism with Gothic art; the new society in the cities of the Renaissance with their vocal chamber music; the enlightenment of the eighteenth century with its *style bourgeois.* Such connections are perfectly legitimate and even indispensable. . . ." But at this point, as if he had gone too far, Sachs qualifies his statement and warns that no "priority of politics," as he puts it, must be implied. And a few pages earlier he gives examples of how "art is able to ignore the trends of outer life." Philip II of Spain had "plunged his country into misery and moral disintegration; whole quarters were deserted, crafts died out and the treasurer's collecting box rattled from house to house. . . . And this was the Spain of Cervantes and Lope de Vega, of Greco and Victoria." Another one of Sach's examples refers to Beethoven: "Napoléon won a crushing victory over Austrians at Austerlitz, not too far from the gates of Vienna, where the master was busy with *Fidelio* and the three Leonoras, with the gay Fourth Symphony, the Concerto for Violin," and so on. "Was this," asks Sachs, "his anguish, dejection, defeat?"

I should perhaps make it clear, before I go on, that we think of

Curt Sachs and his work with great respect. I single out this, to my mind, less-successful book of his because it is typical of a certain tradition in music historiography. This tradition goes back to a group of German philosophers of the late nineteenth century, of whom Wilhelm Dilthey was the most influential in the historiography of the arts. The tradition of this philosophy lives on in countless publications on music history and general history to this very day. It is characterized by the attempt to sever the laws of nature from those of society, and to draw a dividing line between man's artistic and philosophical production on the one hand, and his economic, social, and political activities on the other. This is of particular interest in our connection because ideas of this sort developed in more or less conscious opposition to Marxist philosophy, which began to influence thinking as early as the forties of the last century. Nobody would wish to overlook the differences between a natural law and a social law. Nature works without consciousness, while in society human beings, each with his or her own psychology, are at work. Nevertheless, as Marxist philosophers point out, laws of an objective, general, essential nature are detectable in society, no less than in nature. We spend a great deal of thought on the difficult interrelationships between subjective human activity and objective social forces. The term *dialectical determinism* has been coined to denote this relationship. Take the musical style of a given period. Obviously, it is the work of a great number of individual musicians. But one would not speak of style if the products of these countless individuals had not a certain minimum of characteristics in common. Now how does this come about? Certainly not only through learning from and imitating one another. One is forced to conclude that, while general trends are carried along by individuals, in a certain manner individuals are carried along by general trends. There must be detectable laws that link general trends and individual effort.

To come back to Curt Sach's problem, one may assume that he had come across writings, perhaps professed Marxist writings, which postulated a "priority of politics" over the production of art or drew what we would call mechanical parallels between social events and artistic production. Not so Marx and Engels: not so the more recent Marxist philosophy and theory of culture. Curt Sachs simply overlooked the fact that what goes on in the artist's mind—or in anybody else's, for that matter—is not directly dependent on what he experiences and cannot, therefore, be judged along the lines of behaviorism. Nobody is mechanically conditioned by his surroundings. He sifts, interprets, evaluates his experience. Sach's alternative—either an impoverished Spain could not have produced great art and Beethoven had to write bellicose music in times of war, or else outer events can play no role in the production of music—cannot be accepted. A highly complex network of cultural and ideological phenomena has to be taken into account. And our insight into the mechanism of the human mind is as yet small, as we all know. But nothing prevents us from analyzing the class structure of the society in which a piece of music is produced and consumed, this society's sociological and cultural structure and the different sets of ideas at work in the various social layers of that society and in the artist's mind, in such detail as our knowledge of history, sociology, and psychology will permit.

We think that one must allow for a certain independence of the various branches of human knowledge. It would be just as wrong to claim that a man who philosophizes or writes a mathematical treatise or paints moves along paths that are outside society, as it would be to ignore the very specialized set of ideas, rules, and methods that he uses. These are not independent of general conditions of society either, but their relationships to society are of a complex nature. While this in no way deflects from the fact that, in the last analysis, the workings of economy determine the general laws that are responsible for social phenomena, including the production of music with all its rules and methods, one must take into account the ways in which the special ideas, rules, and methods work. Neither the common chord nor the prohibition of parallel fifths can be directly deduced from the social conditions of the society in which they originated; nor can they be separated from that society and reduced, say, to the workings of eternal laws of nature. To denote this general truth the term *relative autonomy* has been coined.

Relative autonomy—to turn toward music sociology is not the worst way of finding out how relative this autonomy is. In view of the abundant definitions of, and ideas about, music sociology, it will not be superfluous to explain what I understand the term to mean. In accordance with a recent book on the subject, I would say that music history concentrates on genetic and music sociology on structural matters. Music sociology has the task of presenting a cross section of a musical culture at a given historical moment, never forgetting that all the facts, relationships, and artifacts it reveals are the result of historical change and are subject to change again as soon as one's momentary picture is mapped and even while it is being mapped. History, on the other hand, while it is per se directed toward change, cannot but work on the assumption that it deals with quasi-stable configurations. In other words, music history and music sociology complement one another—only the stress is different. The use of empirical methods is not a necessary criterion of sociology; sociological methods can be used in the analysis of musical cultures of the past to whatever extent available material allows. And, as a rule, it allows for far more than the majority of music histories would lead one to assume.

Let us try to examine the emergence of composition from the sociological point of view. Unless one is aware of the fact that within one and the same society and at one and the same historical moment various social layers were engaged in very different ways of making music—music different in structure, in function, in effect—the emergence of composition from age-old traditions of making music by improvisation cannot be accounted for. For a start, composition may be defined by the fact that three phases must be detectable: conceptual thinking and working; notation in writing; performance in which the composer himself need not take part. A further definition of composition—the decisive definition, I think—can be gained from a description of the oldest pieces of music that can without any doubt be regarded as compositions. These seem to me to be the organa of the twelfth and thirteenth centuries; no criteria applicable to even the most highly developed forms of improvisation apply to these. When analyzing these pieces the term that springs to mind is *synthesis*. Heinrich Besseler, for example, speaks of a turning point that was reached in the Notre Dame art and sees in this "the final separation of European musical language from the Gregorian. The force on which the historical effect of the Notre Dame organa rests does not stem from the church but from the region of song and dance. The organum emerges as a daring synthesis." Heinrich Husmann also points out what was "completely new" about the compositions for Notre Dame and speaks in this connection of the "abandonment of Gregorian rhythm" and of the linking-up of the two opposed types of melody: "Gregorian church music and secular lyric."

About 1,500 years earlier the great conservative, Plato, had raised a warning voice in his *Laws* against those people who, although gifted, had placed themselves above all law. "They mingled elegies with hymns, paeans with dithyrambs, imitated aulos music with string instruments, mixed everything with everything," and had also committed the irregularity of judging music by the pleasure and happiness that it gave. Does it not appear that what Plato meant was an activity that approaches composition? Is not in fact the linking together of musical elements stemming from different social spheres an important characteristic of composition? So the sociological point of view has produced a thesis that could not have come to life had one regarded the musical culture of a given period as a monolithic block. The compositional synthesis of various elements emerges clearly when compared with ancient types of improvisation. Nothing is synthesized there. Before the improviser has opened his mouth or enticed the first sound from his instrument, one knows—so long as one knows his traditions—within what bounds the expected music will lie. This is not so in the case of the composer. The worst composer is that much ahead of the best improviser in that he has far greater possibilities to surprise. Where the musical traditions of a social sphere were unbroken, no composition occurred; where they were questioned, codifications were laid down to which the improvisers were bound; where social traditions became unstable and people with other ways of life, thought, and music making could no longer be banned from the orbit of the learned music makers, composition was born.

Let us turn to the problem of value criteria in music. When it comes to comparing musical cultures of various epochs or countries, accepted artistic standards are not helpful. In every single culture you can expect to find many men of talent and a few of genius. But such attention to individuals does not help us either to discern trends in the development of music or to find a yardstick by which to measure one music culture against another. Yet this, certainly, is a prerequisite for improving musical culture. The picture changes when one examines not only the individual composer and his work, but the listener as well; not only those of whom we know, or have reason to assume, listen to masterpieces, but also those who, for whatever reason, do not listen to masterpieces at all. We use the terms *objective* and *subjective* culture to denote what is, at any given historical moment, objectively available and to what an extent a social class, a group, an individual makes use of this availability. All known cultures, from the time when social classes originated in primeval society, show a gap between objective and subjective culture. To narrow and finally to overcome this gap is one of our aims in improving musical culture, and this provides a useful, although not the only, criterion for the value of a musical culture. In this way social progress comes into the picture, progress being measured by the degree to which the forces of material and intellectual production are released and the results made available.

But can working for progress be reconciled with objectivity? Professor Grout, in his essay "Current Historiography and Music History" enumerates what he calls "certain rough but generally satisfactory criteria of objectivity . . .: criteria such as respect for truth, no blinking at awkward facts, no gratuitous moralizing, no ulterior interest (as in propaganda)." When I examine these four criteria I have no quarrel at all with the first three. If the historian has no respect for truth, if he has not learned to look facts in the face, including facts that do not seem to square with his ideas, if he engages in moralizing, gratuitous or otherwise, he had better give up writing history. Professor Mendel, in the address to which I previously referred, quotes Isaiah Berlin, who formulates the historian's wish to come as near the facts as possible ". . . seen from as many points of view and at as many levels as possible, including as many components, factors, aspects, as the widest and deepest knowledge, the greatest analytic power, insight, imagination, can present." One can subscribe fully to these words. It was, if I am not mistaken, Charles Darwin who said that he was equally interested in facts that seemed to contradict his theory as in those that seemed to bear it out—indeed, more interested in them.

But the Marxist historian would part company with Professor Grout on his fourth point: "no ulterior interest." In the Marxist view it is unavoidable for this historian to have an ulterior motive. I do not refer to personal interests, of course. The historian is a product of history himself, and of his situation. However hard he may try, he cannot escape the molding of his mind by his experience and his surroundings. Professor Grout also quotes E. H. Carr as saying that a historian "is the less likely to be at the mercy of his own particular situation the more he is aware of it." This is very true. As soon as he becomes aware of his own particular situation, and as soon as he realizes that there is such a thing as progress in society, he will find it difficult to be persuaded that objectivity should prevent him from taking sides with progress. Nor can the philosophical arguments underlying this interdiction be easily defended. Progress, as we see it, is the course of history, although this course is anything but straightforward or secure. Our own individual ideology cannot be independent of the course of history; the freedom given to us is only the margin between seeing, accepting, and throwing in our lot with what we have recognized as the course of history on the one hand, and being indifferent to or working against it on the other. Nor does experience teach us that objectivity is the key to understanding history. The great advances of the French in the eighteenth century in writing the general history of mankind were inspired by the passionate desire to bring to an end the very conditions into whose history they had developed so assiduously. *Ulterior* means "lying beyond what is immediate or present." If you want a change for the better, you have to find out, and if you want to find out, you have to go beyond, both in the direction of the past and of the future.

It is in this light that historical research in the Eastern European countries must be seen. In the fall of 1966 a remarkable congress was held in the Polish town of Bydgoszcz. Several visitors from the United States were present. It was called Musica Antiqua Europae Orientalis. It lasted a full week and consisted of a congress proper, at which papers were read and discussed, and a festival of music, which offered performances of old music of some ten different countries, all in Eastern Europe. Professor Zofia Lissa, of the University of Warsaw, planned and organized it. In her opening address, she stated that its aim was to draw attention to the fact that, not only since the nineteenth century but all through the ages, Eastern Europe had played its part in the world history of music, and the time had come for this fact to be recognized. The Bydgoszcz congress came at the right historical moment. From several sides it had been recognized that the time when Western Europe was *considered* the center of music making, and *was*, actually, the center of thinking and writing about music had irrevocably come to an end. (Parenthetically, I have sometimes wondered why musicology in the United States, on the whole, was not quicker to see this.) As we now know, the modern musicologist must take into consideration the whole world, not as peripheral regions

(*Randgebiete*, as the music cultures of several countries used to be called by German writers not so long ago), but as regions demanding, and gradually receiving, full attention.

In the socialist countries considerable research is devoted to the documentation of their individual musical pasts. A wealth of new material, part of which could be heard in performance at the Bydgoszcz congress, has come to light. Romania and Bulgaria had to begin their investigations virtually from the start; but colleagues from Poland, Czechoslovakia, Yugoslavia, and Hungary had already achieved much in the rewriting of their history. The list of publications is growing fast.

But the main significance of our work lies in the interpenetration of historical and theoretical research. We see many unsolved problems. But the question of whether or not objective laws of history can be uncovered is not one of them. This problem was solved by Marx and subsequent philosophers. What is on our research agenda is a further development of these laws and their application to the special problems of our field. It is impossible for us to accept a skeptical philosophy of history that tends to reduce theory to a matter of personal opinion, which can neither be proved wrong or right. The various aspects of Marxist historiography—those I have mentioned and others I have not—have been worked out to such a degree that they tend to form a system in the cybernetic sense of the term. This is well in keeping with Marxist tradition.

More than a hundred years ago Marx spoke of society as an "organic system." Marxist philosophy and theory of history have applied the findings of cybernetics and have thus broken many a traditional pattern of historiography. One has to imagine society as a hierarchical system. The class structure of a given society, which, in turn, rests on its economic structure, determines its workings in the last analysis. But, as I have pointed out before, we see the action of men not as mechanically tied to the system of society to which they belong, but as relatively autonomous, dialectically determined. This theory has been specially worked out by philosophers, theoreticians of historiography, and general historians. While I am better informed about what has been done in this field in the German Democratic Republic, particularly in the pages of the *Deutsche Zeitschrift für Philosophie,* I know that writers in the Soviet Union, in Poland, and in Czechoslovakia have made contributions to this philosophy of history. Moreover, a comparatively large number of musicologists are well grounded in a modern approach to music history. In the universities of the German Democratic Republic, groups have been formed to bring into closer contact historians of fields related to historiography of the arts. There is also a growing tendency toward integrating various branches of the sciences, both within and without the compass of traditional musicology. Important spade work has been done in the field of music sociology, first, by Czechoslovak colleagues, later also in the DDR. Professor Antonín Sychra of Prague has worked on problems of phonetics, psychology, semantics, and theory of information to deepen the understanding of Marxist aesthetics. Professor Zofia Lissa must be mentioned again as having contributed to various theoretical areas of aesthetics and music historiography. Professor Harry Goldschmidt of the DDR is working on a new theory that sees vocal and instrumental music as an aesthetic entity. Young scholars in the DDR have worked in sociology and analysis of music with the help of a computer.

In short, the stage is set for writing of music history that incorporates not only the results of other branches of musicology, especially of aesthetics, analysis, psychology, and sociology, but the knowledge, the hypotheses, the methods of our philosophers and theoreticians as well. So far, it is true, the most significant contributions of Marxists to music historiography have been monographs and biographies. One of the best is still E. H. Meyer's *English Chamber Music*. It was, as far as I know, the first Marxist essay to deal with a lengthy period of music history. I think that some Soviet authors have produced remarkable contributions in similar fields. János Maróthy's books should be mentioned—and the list could be prolonged.

It seems to me that the way of further progress lies in the direction of tackling ever more complex and comprehensive tasks, such as a world history of music into which all available knowledge can be integrated. Many lacunae will become apparent in the progress of such work. It is obvious, for instance, how little we know about the effect of music on people. But without such knowledge how can a history of music be complete? No single discipline can hope to find the missing links by itself. But history and sociology could do a great deal more in providing us with detailed charts of the respective historical fields in which man makes, and listens to, music. Experimental psychology, while it cannot answer all questions of music aesthetics, could certainly help to pose and answer some of them more precisely. Music analysis, if presented with results of music psychology, would find it easier to escape the ruts of traditional analysis. In short, if history, sociology, psychology, analysis, aesthetics of music (and other disciplines) were made to ask one another more exact questions, the resulting cross-fertilization could contribute a good deal toward filling many lacunae.

Finally, I would suggest that the manner of presenting music history is undergoing revision. It is traditional to write music histories as narratives and somehow to smuggle in the unavoidable explanations. But if it is true that so many factors must be integrated into music history this will have to be reflected in the presentation. In my opinion the subject should be looked at from various angles, one at a time, and the various findings be presented in such a way that jointly they form the whole story. Hard and fast rules cannot be laid down—I can only say that I have found it advantageous to use four such avenues of approach.

The first consideration would be general, including economic and social history, history of philosophy, literature, and the other arts. Generally speaking, the music historian will not, at this point, be concerned with formulating matters for himself. He will not, as a rule, develop his own theories of history, but will be content to point out relationships that are important to investigate further. For example, it would be superfluous in a presentation of the music history of the First World War and the twenties to discuss military events. But it would be important to show how, with the crumbling of states at the end of the war, old traditions also crumbled and events like the revolution in Russia and other countries opened up new ways of looking at things.

The second consideration is the first of the specifically musical approaches. Among these we give precedence to the most general, to the genetic before the structural, to the historical before the sociological. Here the broad trends of musical development within the given period should be outlined. The emphasis should be on music making in its historical development. The more clearly each approach is worked out in its separateness, the better the chance of making its interaction with the others clear. Furthermore, trends in compositional methods must also be dealt with. They must be reviewed in their relation to newly emerging subject matters and tasks, and to the changing demands and needs of the potential audience. Musical theories and their consequences should be viewed in relation to objective needs and possibilities. *The achievements of individual artists and thinkers,* however, can be only incompletely shown by this approach. We are more concerned here with general trends. At best only a minor composer may be completely characterized by a general tendency. But the greater the composer, the more he will elude such classification. With our approach one would examine trends and schools of composition and thought, and exemplify them by what seems to represent them most clearly. In this way one would do justice to the trends without pretending to have dealt adequately with the individual artists.

A third approach would be more specific than the above, more structural than genetic, more sociological than historical. It would be devoted more to the musical genres than to the predilection for this or that type of music. Especially when confronted with the social spheres of music making, the genres allow one an insight into the fabric of music life. It is highly significant that opera is completely missing in peasant and bourgeois strata of the seventeenth century, while in the nineteenth century it penetrates various spheres of many European countries. To take another example, in seventeenth-century Germany the song can be found practically everywhere, but in very different types and qualities. These are facts that tend to be overlooked unless dealt with specifically.

Finally, when we have adequately examined the general conditions under which a composer works and a "noncomposer" listens, we may concentrate, in our last approach, on what all too often used to be the only subject matter for music historians: the creative achievement of the individual. Carried by trends and schools, participating in them, helping to create, modifying and overcoming, renewing and learning, integrating what seems irreconcilable, the composer can now be viewed as a creative individual in a network of social conditions. His life and work will be better understood, the more clearly the fabric of social relationships is spread out and examined from the several points of view outlined above. Musicologists in the United States have expressed concern that research in their country is "too positivistic, too preoccupied with the collection of data and the determination of detail." It is my impression that music research in Eastern Europe, while not neglecting data and detail, is well equipped to escape their snares. It is the cornerstone of our views that mankind today possesses all the prerequisites for overcoming our age's fundamental ill—privilege—and, thereby, for bringing out creative potentialities in all human beings. This belief determines the climate in which we work. Thus it is no accident that our quest for the understanding of the past focuses on points of view, concentrates on connections that have never been fully investigated. Nor is it accidental that in so doing we synthesize findings of various branches of knowledge. The Marxist method of music historical research, emerging from dogmatic deformation of the recent past, demands such a synthesis. Since we aim at guiding historical change, we have to understand the past, for our own guidance, as thoroughly as advanced methods will allow.

Eastern European music history offers several points of great interest. Wide stretches of that part of Europe, over long periods of its history, offered very limited opportunities for the emergence of rich musical cultures. It is, therefore, all the more illuminating to investigate conditions in those eminent musical cultures of Eastern Europe that did emerge. Also, the origins of composition, after age-old traditions of music making without notation, can be observed in certain parts of Eastern Europe even today; it is everywhere in this part of the world a more recent phenomenon than in Western Europe. But perhaps the most important claim to universal interest lies in the fact that Eastern Europe offers one of the rare chances of observing something like a gigantic social experiment. The social and political conditions have been created for the development of a socialist music culture. I believe that it is worthwhile to study our experiences and achievements in the theoretical and practical fields, our plans for the future, as well as our shortcomings and what we do to overcome them.

Translated by Barry S. Brooks et al.

Dietrich Fischer-Dieskau

The Composer
(c. 1978)

Franz Schubert transformed a world of poetry into music. He raised the art song [*Kunstlied*] to hitherto unknown heights and laid bare the essence of all art: intensity, concentration, a distillation into the purest of forms. "Nature and Art seem to shun one another, but before one realizes it, they have found each other again." Schubert's works confirm Goethe's wise aperçu.

We live in an age that rejoices in paradoxes. This is particularly obvious to those of us who perform Schubert's Lieder, either professionally or as amateurs. No matter how great our admiration for Schubert may be, we only realize later in life what it is that raises him so far above the level of other composers: Schubert is *authentic*. His "style" should not really be called style, since his successors have accustomed us to think of "style" as something affected, something attained by "art," in a studio. Schubert writes as he thinks, feels, and speaks, and his thoughts, feelings, and words are faithfully reflected in the notes of his music. This must be called a "natural style," although we should not wish to claim that such a natural style is the hallmark of the great composer. There are far too many important exceptions. But we would repeat: the musician whose style is "natural" is one of the miracles of music. That the public and the critics ever managed to consider Schubert as an intuitive creative artist *only* surely proves that they do not believe in miracles?

Almost all of his contemporaries, even the musicians, underestimated Schubert's greatness. It is true that, in his continual hungering after knowledge, he preferred the company of literary men and painters, and that, in his circle of friends, only a few composers are to be found—and they too had little enough to say about him later. Apart from Beethoven (whom he probably did not want to meet) and Hummel, whose sporadic praises pleased him, there was first and foremost Anselm Hüttenbrenner (1794-1868) who, however, even in Schubert's lifetime, lived mostly in Graz, as a landowner, composer, and director of music. (The songs that he began to write in 1850, to poems already set by Schubert, betray a Schubertian influence.) Another friend from his student days under Antonio Salieri, and a fellow choirboy from the years in the *Konvikt*— the Imperial and Royal City Seminary—was the composer and conductor Benedikt Randhartinger (1802-1893). Franz Lachner (1803-1890), who was far and away the best musician in the Schubert circle, was his closest friend. Like all the children of the Lachner family (the sisters included), this son of an unknown Bavarian village organist was an organist, too. Lachner came to Vienna in 1822 when he was twenty. A brilliant success in a music competition rescued the young man from penury and provided him with the position of organist in the Protestant church. Schubert and Lachner did not become closer friends until 1826, when Lachner, then deputy conductor at the Kärntnertor Theater, began to hold musical evenings at his home at which some of Schubert's works were performed. Along with an extraordinary amount of chamber music, Franz Lachner, an extremely prolific composer, also wrote songs that betray a strong Schubertian influence and often set, quite independently, the same poems as Schubert. One might count Lachner and Randhartinger among the first to help the *Lied* on its triumphal progress round the world. After Schubert's death, however, both men held exaggerated opinions of their own importance and were therefore in some part responsible for those misleading judgments that damaged Schubert's reputation for so long. Randhartinger, for example, could write: "I am truly sorry that he remained something of a dilettante to the end," and Lachner, speaking to the Schubert scholar, Max Friedländer, in 1884, said: "It is a pity that Schubert didn't learn as much as I did, since, with his extraordinary talents, he could have become a master too."

Yet it was only Schubert's work that survived. We should not forget nevertheless how shamefully few of his songs have actually become part and parcel of the general music consciousness. His enormous output seems to have militated against this, and it is certainly to the credit of our much-maligned commercial music industry that it has managed to rescue hitherto unknown treasures from oblivion.

The speed of Schubert's way of working, the ease with which he composed, has led critics time and again to overstress the "intuitive" side of his character and the "unconscious" element in his composing. Yet this "intuition" is always only a beginning, the raw material, as it were, nothing more. The anecdote that Schubert is supposed not to have recognized one of his own early songs is grist to the mill of those who claim that the creator of more than six hundred songs could not have achieved this as part of a conscious process. Such a point of view fails to recognize a fortiori an undeniable factor in Schubert's instrumental music—namely, the proof of his wrestling with structural and contextual problems.

Nor is the often-heard assertion that Schubert simply "threw off" his compositions and was content to abide by his first version anywhere near the truth. Schubert's way of working was different from Haydn's, Mozart's, or Beethoven's. It is strange that he rarely made sketches, a fact that contributed substantially to the "throwing off" legend. It is true that the musical "polishing," which makes Beethoven's sketchbooks look like battlefields, was not Schubert's method. Since the work was already clearly conceived in his head, he was able to write down a composition from beginning to end and corrections were only rarely necessary. If, after the last revision, the work did not satisfy his intentions, it would be begun again after three days, a few weeks, six months, or even several years. Thus, he frequently made different versions of the same texts after varying periods of time—which led to confusion, since it was not always the final version that found its way into the printed editions.

Because Schubert often composed a series of songs in one day—five on August 19, 1815, six on the twenty-fifth of the same month and as many as eight on October 19, 1815—many people have felt able to deduce that such productivity could only be the result of instinctive inspiration. One glance at the concise accuracy with which he put his intentions down on paper should give the lie to such fantasies. It is true that Schubert supplied only a few indications of dynamics in his songs, yet, where they do exist, the surest way to the best interpretation is to follow them to the letter. If the strophic songs, in particular, lack detailed notations, it is clear that the treatment of words and emotions varies from stanza to stanza.

In all of Schubert's works, in the largely instrumental as well as in the vocal works, *piano* and *pianissimo* play a very important role in the resolution of contrasts as well as in the introduction of the main themes. The additional dynamic significance of the *crescendo*—and *diminuendo*—signs should also be noted. These dynamics are never merely externals—they obey an internal logic.

Can genius, the most sublime manifestation of intellectuality, *really* work passively to the dictates of hypnosis? Shortly before his death, Schubert considered resuming the study of counterpoint with Simon Sechter, a leading exponent of the theory of music, a proof, surely, of his awareness of the need for ordering and structuring his first inspirations?

In his *Kulturgeschichte der Neuzeit* (A Cultural History of Modern Times), Egon Friedell describes the gauche, bespectacled, obstinate suburban schoolmaster whose private world and greatest joy were the conversations at the *Heurigen*—the Viennese festival of the new wine—and who was the first to show mankind what a *Lied* really was: "Just as the German *Märchen* was created by the Grimm Brothers, not invented but raised to a work of art," wrote Friedell, "so Schubert ennobled the folksong and gave it a place alongside the highest forms of art." But this remark should not lead us to believe that Schubert was a "folksy" artist. This was made abundantly clear when, in his later years, Schubert gradually abandoned the strophic form.

He was torn between two worlds. Music as a tonal, dynamic form, the beautiful illusion of aesthetics, the dominating element in many of his early songs, found its essence endangered. Schubert's love of the ingenuous clashes with his love of expression. Nowhere more than in music does the ingenuous seem to be nurtured and developed by technical ability. But its very marriage to verse compels music to reassert itself.

To achieve this, Franz Schubert orientated himself on Goethe. The titanic lyrics of *Prometheus* or *An Schwager Kronos* became the medium (and, at that time, certainly not the obvious medium) for plumbing the unknown depths of the soul. Schubert, the lieder composer, a child of the new age in his surprising major-minor modulations, fertilizes Schubert, the instrumental composer, even beyond the five actual cases in which lieder were the direct models for instrumental works.

These authentic song variations offer to the miniature art form an inexhaustible supply of new material. Probably heading the list are the variations on the theme of *Der Tod und das Mädchen* from the D Minor String Quartet, probably one of Schubert's most impressive movements; then the use of the C-sharp Minor cantilena from *Der Wanderer* in the C Major Fantasia for piano as a basis for ingenious variations that illuminate the musical idea from all sides. The difficult but joyous Variations for flute and piano on *Trockene Blumen* should also be mentioned here, as well as the very demanding A-flat Major Variations on *Sei mir gegrüßt* that form the slow movement of the C Major Fantasia for violin and piano. Finally, the timeless charm of the *Trout* theme with its metamorphoses in the Pianoforte Quintet in A Major. Schubert's creative sensibility has colored the tone, and color and tone acknowledge their relationship in a musician from whom flow neverending riches. The art of transition, which was to become the glory of modern music, is hinted at early in Schubert's works.

The narrow view of Schubert based on the falsely sentimental picture of a "Schwammerl" ("Tubby"—Schubert's nickname) has been replaced for a large section of the public by an appreciation of the true radiant force of his work—particularly for the most recent generations, unencumbered by old-fashioned notions. It has taken long enough for the general public to accord him the independent position that is his by right—and not to place him in the shadow of Haydn, Mozart, and Beethoven. Those who deny him the role of innovator must be deaf to the futuristic chords that can be heard in the piano sonatas, the quartets, the String Quintet, and in *Die Winterreise;* one is astonished at every turn. Perhaps the pedants have seen him in such a light because he is so difficult to categorize? Nomenclatures such as "classical predecessor of Romanticism," "the Romantic outsider of Classicism," mean little to those truly bewitched by him.

Our concentration on the relationship of the songs to Schubert's life is justified not only by his acknowledged reputation as the "Prince of Song," a title granted to him during his lifetime and enjoyed by none more than he. The first truly comprehensive publication of his lieder on LP records gave me the stimulus to collect material, and the idea of offering my own contribution to the truly vast literature on Schubert. Much to my surprise, and in much greater compass than intended, my work on the lieder produced a literary portrait that, in broad outlines and with the help of typical examples, covered a century of German lyric poetry, from the German anacreontics by way of the classics to the romantics. Poems set to music by Schubert from the older world literatures, those of Aeschylus, Anacreon, Petrarch, Shakespeare, Ossian, and Scott, for example, without exception exercised a considerable influence on Schubert's century; he knew them through the translations of his friends or of distinguished poets of his age.

There is really little to tell about Schubert's life; he lived it from within, under the compulsion of composition that was his attempt to impose a form on his life. He needed to imagine what he could not experience. That is why he loved poets above all others. They gave him inspiration and stimulus, they offered him pictures and shapes, a reality that he would otherwise never have known. Led by them, he could enter the realm of the word, and could enjoy such an intimate relationship with them because he so rarely thought of himself.

The literature on Schubert, now swollen to about four thousand titles, is based on a very limited number of documents mostly unearthed by the Austrian scholar, Professor Otto Erich Deutsch. All who write on Schubert are indebted to his labors. Faced with these documents, we must in many cases resort to vague speculation; in others, we must strive to reach the median of probability in the reminiscences of Schubert's friends, culled from their fading memories after Schubert's death and which are therefore often contradictory. Fortunately, Schubert's letters and sketches offer a more reliable gloss on these events. But the enormous gaps in our knowledge are made visible when one thinks of Beethoven's fifteen hundred or so letters and Mozart's three hundred. The few Schubert documents that we do possess are all the more important because not many of his actual conversations have been handed down. I have not hesitated to make use of certain works and song texts—even when they are of dubious literary value—to fill in some of these gaps. Above all, they fill in *psychological* gaps. The fact that Schubert's creativity is uniquely related to his life is of great value.

Schubert's music was truly his life's work. His life is a mere shadow and it is not surprising that the world around him was of little significance. The texts of his songs hint at the bitterness within him, and these texts can perhaps explain how complete a representation of and for his age he was, without presenting us simply with sentimental pictures of the romantic *Biedermeier*.* Perhaps he was interpreting in music the daydreams of his friends.

It is typical of our age that it has no such protoartist—not among musicians at least. The food for the intellect that Schubert offered his contemporaries and their grandchildren is still enjoyed by young people today because the power of his art transcends the mediocrity or evanescence of many of the poems that he chose. Sorrow and happiness, humility and arrogance, modesty and pride, contemplation and passion speak to us out of Schubert's music, now as then. We know that Schubert did not command such immediacy of musical language at all times in his short career. If we examine his songs from the first to the last, we can see how he developed into a musical poet. At the beginning, he simply supplied a background to the poem. As he developed, his work took on the character of a translation into the language of music, and, in that process, the music frequently defines the poetic thought more precisely—or develops it further.

There are three basic lied-types: in the *strophic* song, the melody and the accompaniment do not change from stanza to stanza. In the *scenic* song, several contrasting sections are combined in different keys and tempos. In the *"through-composed"* [*durchkomponiert*] song, a single accompaniment unites thoughts and moods that are independent of the stanzas of the poem. There is also the *modified strophic* song where the original melody is slightly altered in the reprise. When we examine the songs, we see that Schubert did not develop from the "elementary" strophic song to the "advanced" through-composed song, as it were. He remains faithful to the strophic song to the end, as *Am Meer* or *Die Taubenpost* (D 957, nos. 12 and 14) prove.

When we think of the high regard and the love that Schubert's lieder evoked from his friends and his first listeners, then we can scarcely doubt that, despite all the faith he had in himself and in the sureness of his technique, he did not abide rigidly by his principles of composition in all cases. Popular taste was certainly the

---

*The name given to an art style in Germany between 1815 and 1848. A sober domesticity.—Ed.

deciding factor in many of his light pieces, without however damaging the song in question. It is evident from his songs that Schubert was well aware that his music was expressing something that no one before him had been able to convey.

Schubert always manages to surprise us. Within a relatively narrow technical compass lie inexhaustible riches. And always, when he leaves a beloved poetical territory, such as "birds" or "wandering" or "childhood" or "death" to turn to another, *he* changes too. His material reveals itself to him through the love he brings to it. Art is no different from other spheres of life; without love, the secrets remain hidden forever.

Translated by Kenneth S. Whitton

Carl Dahlhaus

Absolute Music as an Aesthetic Paradigm
(1978)

The aesthetics of music is not popular. Musicians suspect it of being abstract talk far removed from musical reality; the musical public fears philosophical reflections of the kind one ought to leave to the initiated, rather than plaguing one's own mind with unnecessary philosophical difficulties. Understandable as this mistrustful irritation with the sundry chatter of self-proclaimed music aesthetics might be, it would be erroneous to imagine that aesthetic problems in music are located in the hazy distance beyond everyday musical matters. In fact, when viewed dispassionately, they are thoroughly tangible and immediate.

Anyone who finds it burdensome to have to read the literary program of a symphonic poem by Franz Liszt or Richard Strauss before a concert; who asks for dimmed lights at a lieder recital, making the lyrics printed in the program illegible; who finds it superfluous to familiarize himself with the plot summary before attending an opera sung in Italian—in other words, whoever treats the verbal component of the music at a concert or opera with casual disdain is making a music-aesthetic decision. He may consider his decision to be based on his own taste, when in fact it is the expression of a general, dominant tendency that has spread ever further in the last 150 years without sufficient recognition of its importance to musical culture. Above and beyond the individual and his coincidental preferences, nothing less than a profound change in the very concept of music is taking place: no mere style change among forms and techniques, but a fundamental transformation of what music is, what it means, and how it is understood.

Listeners who react in the manner described above are aligning themselves to a music-aesthetic "paradigm" (to use the term that Thomas Kuhn applied to the history of science): that of "absolute music." Paradigms, basic concepts that guide musical perception and musical thought, form one of the central themes of one kind of music aesthetics that does not lose itself in speculation, but instead explains assumptions that stand inconspicuously and little considered behind everyday musical custom.

Hanns Eisler, who made a serious attempt to apply Marxism to music and music aesthetics, described the concept of absolute music as a figment of the "bourgeois period": an era he looked down on, but to which he also considered himself an heir. "Concert music, along with its social form, the concert, represents a historical epoch in the evolution of music. Its specific development is intertwined with the rise of modern bourgeois society. The predominance of music without words, popularly called 'absolute music,' the division between music and work, between serious and light music, between professionals and dilettantes, is typical of music in capitalist society." However vague the term *modern bourgeois society* might be, Eisler seems to have felt certain that "absolute music" was not simply a "timeless" synonym for textless, independent instrumental music not bound to "extramusical" functions or programs. Instead, the term denoted a concept around which a specific historical epoch grouped its ideas concerning the nature of music. Eisler, surprisingly enough, calls the expression "absolute music" a "popular" one; this is doubtless hidden rancor against a coinage whose lofty claim—the connotation of absolute music allowing a premonition of the absolute—could hardly have escaped the son of a philosopher.

In the central European musical culture of the nineteenth century—as opposed to the Italian-French opera culture of the time—the concept of absolute music was so deep-rooted that, as we shall see, even Richard Wagner, though he polemicized against it on the surface, was convinced of its fundamental validity. In fact, it would hardly be an exaggeration to claim that the concept of absolute music was the leading idea of the classical and romantic era in music aesthetics. As we have already suggested, the principle was surely restricted geographically, but it would be premature at the very least to call it a provincialism, given the aesthetic significance of autonomous instrumental music in the late eighteenth and early nineteenth centuries. On the other hand, the omnipresence of absolute music in the twentieth century must not be allowed to obscure the historical fact that—according to sociological, not aesthetic, criteria—symphony and chamber music in the nineteenth century represented mere enclaves in a "serious" musical culture characterized by opera, romance, virtuoso display, and salon pieces (not to mention the lower depths of "trivial music").

That the concept of absolute music originated in German romanticism (despite the importance of its meaning within a music-historical context in the nineteenth century, a meaning that has taken on external, sociohistorical importance in the twentieth century), that it owed its pathos—the association of music "detached" from text, program, or function with the expression or notion of the absolute—to German poetry and philosophy around 1800, was clearly recognized in France, oddly enough, as an 1895 essay by Jules Combarieu shows. He writes that it was through "the German fugues and symphonies" that "thinking in music, thinking with sounds, the way a writer thinks with words" first entered the French consciousness, which had always clung to the connection between music and language to derive a "meaning" from music.

Thus, despite its fundamental aesthetic importance due to the artistic caliber and historical influence of the works that realized it, the geographical and social range of the idea of absolute music was quite limited at first. Likewise, the historical description in Eisler's rough sketch is too broad rather than too constricted. One can hardly speak of a music-aesthetic paradigm for the "entire" bourgeois period. The idea of absolute music, which has a social character that cannot be reduced to any simple formula, stands in direct opposition to the music aesthetics original to the "modern bourgeois society" of eighteenth-century Germany. Johann Georg Sulzer, in the article on "Music" in his *General Theory of the Fine Arts,* bases his verdict about autonomous instrumental music on moral philosophy—i.e., on the eighteenth century's authentically bourgeois mode of thought. His bluntness forms a curious contrast to Burney's generous term *innocent luxury*; this may be explained by the moral fervor of an upwardly mobile bourgeoisie as opposed to the laxity of an established one. Sulzer writes: "In the last position we place the application of music to concerts, which are presented merely as entertainments, and perhaps for practice in playing. To this category belong concertos, symphonies, sonatas, and solos, which generally present a lively and not unpleasant noise, or a civil and entertaining chatter, but not one that engages the heart." The bourgeois moral philosopher's animus toward the musical diversions he found arcane and idle is unmistakable. If Haydn, in contrast, attempted to represent "moral characters" in his symphonies, as Georg August Griesinger reports, then this aesthetic intention meant nothing less than a vindication of the symphony's honor in an age whose bourgeoisie viewed art as a means of discourse about problems of morality, i.e, the social coexistence of human beings. Insofar as art withdrew from its purpose, it was scorned as a superfluous game of suspicious character, either above or below the bourgeoisie. This view applied primarily to literature, but, in a secondary sense, to music as well.

Only in opposition to the aesthetic, of bourgeois origin and generated by moral philosophy, that Sulzer represented, was a philosophy of art formed that proceeded from the concept of the self-sufficient, autonomous work. In essays written between 1785 and 1788, Karl Philipp Moritz (whose ideas were accepted unreservedly by Goethe, hesitantly by Schiller) proclaimed the principle of *l'art pour l'art* with a bluntness attributable to his disgust with moral philosophy's rationalizations about art, and to the urge to escape into aesthetic contemplation from the world of bourgeois work and life that he found oppressive. "The merely useful object is thus not something whole or perfect in itself, but attains that state only in fulfilling its purpose through me, or being completed within me. In observing the beautiful, however, I return the purpose from myself to the object: I observe the object as something not within me, but perfect in itself; that is, it constitutes a whole in itself, and gives me pleasure for the sake of itself, in that I do not so much impart to the beautiful object a relationship to myself, but rather impart to myself a relationship to it." However, not only the Horatian *prodesse* but also *delectare* is judged foreign to art; the recognition art demands, not the pleasure it provides, is decisive. "We do not need the beautiful in order that we may be delighted by it, as much as the beautiful requires us so that it may be recognized." The one attitude that Moritz finds appropriate to the work of art is that of aesthetic contemplation in which self and world are forgotten; his fervor in describing it betrays his pietistic origins.

"As long as the beautiful draws our attention completely to itself, it shifts it away from ourselves for a while, and makes us seem to lose ourselves in the beautiful object; just this losing, this forgetting of the self, is the highest degree of the pure and unselfish pleasure that beauty grants us. At that moment we give up our individual, limited existence in favor of a kind of higher existence."

When the idea of aesthetic autonomy, formerly limited to the general artistic theory that applied primarily to poetry, painting, or sculpture, was extended to musical culture, it found an adequate expression in the "absolute" music that was disassociated from "extramusical" functions and programs. Though this seems natural and almost self-evident in hindsight, it was rather surprising at the time. As Jean-Jacques Rousseau's invective and Sulzer's contemptuous comments show, bourgeois thought held instrumental music without purpose, concrete concept, or object to be insignificant and empty—despite the Mannheim orchestra's success in Paris and Haydn's growing fame. Furthermore, the beginnings of a theory of instrumental music were distinguished by apologetics trapped in the opposition's terminology. When in 1739 Johann Mattheson characterized "instrumental music" as "sound oratory or tone speech," he was attempting to justify it by arguing that instrumental music is essentially the same as vocal music. It too should—and can—move the heart, or usefully engage the listener's imagination by being an image of a comprehensible discourse. "In that case, it is a pleasure, and one needs much more skill and a stronger imagination to succeed without words than with their aid."

Such early defenses of instrumental music, dependent on the model of vocal music, were based on the formulas and arguments of the doctrine of affections and the aesthetics of sentiment. As we shall show in a later chapter, when an independent theory of instrumental music developed, there was a tendency to contradict the sentimental characterization of music as the "language of the heart," or at least to reinterpret the tangible affects as ephemeral, abstract feelings divorced from the world. Novalis and Friedrich Schlegel combined this tendency with an aristocratic attitude of polemical irritation with the eighteenth-century culture of sentiment and social life, a culture they found narrow-minded. Like the moral-philosophical theory of art to which it was closely connected, the sentimental aesthetic was truly of the bourgeoisie; it was only in contradiction to that aesthetic, its social character, and the doctrine of utility that the principle of autonomy originated. Now instrumental music, previously viewed as a deficient form of vocal music, a mere shadow of the real thing, was exalted as a music-aesthetic paradigm in the name of autonomy—made into the epitome of music, its essence. The lack of a concept or a concrete topic, hitherto seen as a deficiency of instrumental music, was now deemed an advantage.

One may without exaggeration call this a music-aesthetic "paradigm shift," a reversal of aesthetic premises. A bourgeois gentleman like Sulzer must have thought the elevation of instrumental music above and beyond any moral valuation (already heralded in Johann Abraham Peter Schulz's article "Symphony" in Sulzer's own *General Theory of the Fine Arts*) an annoying paradox. The idea of "absolute music"—as we may henceforth call independent instrumental music, even though the term did not arise for another half-century—consists of the conviction that instrumental music purely and clearly expresses the true nature of music by its very lack of concept, object, and purpose. Not its existence, but what it stands for, is decisive. Instrumental music, as pure "structure," represents itself. Detached from the affections and feelings of the real world, it forms a "separate world for itself." It is no coincidence that E. T. A. Hoffmann, who was the first to speak emphatically of music as "structure," proclaimed that instrumental music was the true music: that, in a sense, language in music therefore represented an addition "from without." "When speaking of music as an independent art, one should always mean instrumental music alone, which, disdaining any aid or admixture of another art, expresses the characteristic nature of art that is only recognizable within music itself."

The idea that instrumental music devoid of function or program is the "true" music has since been eroded to a commonplace that determines the day-to-day use of music without our being aware of it, let alone doubting it. But when it was new it must have seemed a challenging paradox, for it bluntly contradicted an older idea of music established in a tradition that spanned millennia. What may seem obvious today, as though indicated in the nature of the thing—that music is a sounding phenomenon and nothing more, that a text is therefore considered an "extramusical" impetus—proves to be a historically molded theorem no more than two centuries old. Understanding the historical character of the idea serves two purposes: first, to prepare for the insight that what has come about historically can also be changed again; second, to understand more precisely the nature of today's predominant conception of music by becoming aware of its origins, i.e., the assumptions that underlie it, and of the background against which it sets itself off.

The older idea of music, against which the idea of absolute music had to prevail, was the concept, originating in antiquity and never doubted until the seventeenth century, that music, as Plato put it, consisted of *harmonia, rhythmos,* and *logos. Harmonia* meant regular, rationally systematized relationships among tones; *rhythmos,* the system of musical time, which in ancient times included dance and organized motion; and *logos,* language as the expression of human reason. Music without language was therefore reduced, its nature constricted: a deficient type of mere shadow of what music actually is. (Using a concept of music that includes language, one can justify not only vocal but even program music: it does not appear as a secondary application of literature to "absolute" music, nor is the program an addition "from without," but a reminder of the logos that music should always include in order to be its whole self.)

According to Arnold Schering (who still adhered even in the twentieth century to the older concept of music, which explains his tendency to discover "hidden programs" in Beethoven's symphonies), not until around 1800 "does the pernicious specter of dualism between 'applied' (dependent) and 'absolute' music enter European musical awareness, leading to serious conflicts. Thereafter there is no longer a *single* concept of music, as previous generations knew it, but *two,* about whose rank and historical priority one soon begins to quarrel, just as one disputes the question of the boundaries between them and their definition." One cannot speak of an unbroken dominance of the idea of absolute music. Despite Haydn and Beethoven, mistrust of absolute instrumental music independent of language had not yet receded among nineteenth-century aestheticians such as Hegel and, later, Gervinus, Heinrich Bellerman, and Eduard Grell. They suspected the "artificiality" of instrumental music of being a deviation from the "natural," or its "conceptlessness" a renunciation of "reason." The traditional prejudice was deep-rooted: that music had to depend on words to avoid either degeneration into pleasant noise that neither touched the heart nor employed the mind, or becoming an impenetrable spirit language. And insofar as one did not reject "absolute music"—i.e., instrumental music that both disdained tone painting and was not to be perceived as the "language of the heart"—one sought refuge in a hermeneutics that forced upon "pure, absolute music" just what it sought to avoid: programs and characterizations. If instrumental music had been a "pleasant noise" *beneath* language to the commonsense aestheticians of the eighteenth century, then the romantic metaphysics of art declared it a language *above* language. The urge to include it in the central sphere of language could not be suppressed.

And yet the idea of absolute music—gradually and against resistance—became the aesthetic paradigm of German musical culture in the nineteenth century. Whereas a glance at repertoires and catalogues of works would deny any superficial predominance of instrumental music in the romantic and postromantic periods, it is just as undeniable that the concept of music in that era was ever more decidedly molded by the aesthetic of absolute music. (Except for opera and some oratorios and songs, instrumental music predominates today, but this reflection of historical impact should not obscure the former prevalence of vocal music.) When even Hanslick's opponents called the text in vocal music an "extramusical" influence, the battle against "formalism" was lost even before it began, for Hanslick had already prevailed in the vocabulary with which they opposed him. (At first, the rise to predominance of "pure, absolute music" as a paradigm of musical thought was not at all correlated with the decay of literary culture the way it was in the twentieth century. In fact, as we shall demonstrate, the idea of absolute music in the first half of the nineteenth century was entwined with an aesthetic driven by the concept of the "poetic"— the epitome not of the "literary," but of a substance common to the various arts. In the aesthetics of Schopenhauer, Wagner, and Nietzsche, i.e., the reigning theory of art in the second half of the century, music was considered to be an expression of the "essence" of things, as opposed to the language of concepts that cleaved to mere "appearances." Although this was a triumph of the idea of absolute music within the doctrine of music drama, it by no means signified that poetry, as the mere vehicle of music, deserved neglect.)

The symphony was used as a prototype for the development of the theory of absolute music around 1800, viz. Wackenroder's "Psychology of Modern Instrumental Music," Tieck's essay "Symphonies," or E. T. A. Hoffmann's sketch of a romantic metaphysics of music that forms the introduction to a review of Beethoven's Fifth Symphony. And when Daniel Schubart, as early as 1791, praised a piece of instrumental music with words that remind one of E. T. A. Hoffmann's dithyrambs for Beethoven, it was likewise a symphony that kindled his enthusiasm, albeit one by Christian Cannabich: "It is not the mere din of voices . . . it is a musical whole whose parts, like emanations of spirit, form a whole again." The discussion of that time does not include chamber music. As Gottfried Wilhelm Fink wrote as late as 1838 in Gustav Schilling's *Encyclopedia of All Musical Sciences,* the "acknowledged apex of instrumental music" was the symphony.

On the other hand, those writers' interpretations of the symphony as "language of a spirit world," "mysterious Sanskrit," or hieroglyphics were not the only attempt to understand the nature of absolute, object- and concept-free instrumental music. When Paul Bekker, writing during the German republican fervor of 1918, explained the symphony by the composer's intention "to speak, through instrumental music, to a multitude," he was, presumably without knowing it, reverting to an exegesis that stems from the classical period. Heinrich Christoph Koch's *Musical Lexicon* of 1802 (i.e., even before the *Eroica*) stated: "Because instrumental music is nothing but the imitation of song, the symphony especially represents the choir, and thus, like the choir, has the purpose of expressing the sentiment of a multitude." Contrary to the romantics, who discovered the "true" music in instrumental music, Koch, a music theorist of the classical period, upheld the older interpretation that instrumental music was an "abstraction" of vocal music, and not the reverse, that vocal music was "applied" instrumental music. (The *Allgemeine Musikalische Zeitung* wrote in 1801 that Carl Philip Emanuel Bach had demonstrated that "pure music was not merely a shell for applied music, nor an abstraction of it.")

E. T. A. Hoffmann's famous remark that the symphony had become, "so to speak, the opera of the instruments" (which Fink still quoted in 1838) seems at first glance to express something similar to Koch's characterization. However, one would misinterpret Hoffmann by maintaining that in 1809, a year before the review of Beethoven's Fifth Symphony, he was still convinced that vocal models were required for the aesthetic comprehension of instrumental forms. Hoffmann is actually saying that the symphony's rank within instrumental music compares to that of the opera within vocal music; furthermore, he suggests that the symphony is like a "musical drama." This concept of a drama of the instruments points to Wackenroder and Tieck, whose *Fantasies on Art* Hoffmann seems to follow. It means nothing but the variety (or, as Tieck put it, the "beautiful confusion") of musical characters in a symphonic movement. However, the chaos of affections, which Christian Gottfried Körner opposed with a demand for unity of character, is only a superficial phenomenon. Although a hasty glance creates the impression of an "utter lack of true unity and inner coherence, . . . a deeper vision is rewarded by the growth of a beautiful tree, buds and leaves, blossoms and fruit springing from its seed." To Hoffmann, this is the common trait of the Beethovenian symphony and the Shakespearean drama, the latter being the romantic paradigm of the drama. The remark about "drama of the instruments" is thus an aesthetic analogy meant to indicate, by reference to Shakespeare, the "high thoughtfulness" behind the seeming disorder of the symphony.

Fink, in 1838, hesitantly accepted the description of the symphony as "opera of the instruments," but he transformed—or, as thought, distilled—it into a characterization: that "the grand symphony [was] comparable to a dramatized sentimental novella." "It is a dramatically expressed story, developed in a psychological context, told in tones, of some sentimental state of a community that, stimulated by a central impetus, expresses its essential feeling in every kind of popular representation individually through each instrument taken into the whole." Fink's prototype for his description, eclectic in its mixture of lyric, epic, and dramatic elements, is obviously Beethoven's *Eroica*. The same work inspired Adolph Bernhard Marx in 1859 to his theory of "ideal music." (One could assert, with a certain amount of exaggeration, that the romantic- "poetic" exegesis referred to the Fifth Symphony, the Young Hegelian "characterizing" exegesis to the Third, and the New German School's "programmatic" exegesis to the Ninth.) According to Marx, the *Eroica* is "that piece in which musical art first steps independently—without connection to the poet's word or the dramatist's action—out of the play of form and uncertain impulses and feelings and into the sphere of brighter, more certain consciousness, in which it comes of age and takes its place as a peer in the circle of its sisters." (Music's "equality of rank" with poetry and painting was also a central theme in Liszt's apologia for program music.) This construction, a matter of aesthetics and philosophy of history, that supports Marx's interpretation of Beethoven, is based on the threefold scheme of faculty psychology, a division of mental powers into senses, feelings, and mind. Thus Marx sees the mere "play of tones" as a first, primitive stage of development, and the "uncertain impulses and feelings" as a second and higher one that nevertheless must be surpassed. Only by transition from the "sphere of feelings" to that of the "idea" does music reach its predestined goal. "This was Beethoven's accomplishment." Music history is consummated in the *Eroica*. However, an "idea"—of which a symphony must be the "material manifestation" in order to elevate itself to art in the emphatic sense—is none other than a "portrait progressing in psychological, inexorable development." Marx, in the spirit of Young Hegelianism, brings romantic metaphysics down to earth.

Portrait—a term recurring in Friedrich Theodor Vischer's *Aesthetics* as a characteristic of the symphony—appears as the key word in a theory of the symphony that represents a counterproject to the "poetics" of absolute music. First, Marx trivialized the concept of "absolute" music "dissolved" from functions, texts, and finally even affections—a concept that both the Young Hegelians and the New German School found useless for Beethoven interpretation—into the idea of a "merely formal" music reduced to its sensual force, in which—by a strange projection of faculty psychology onto history—he claimed to perceive a first stage in the development of music. Second, the musically spiritual, which romantic metaphysics found expressed in the "pure, absolute musical art" (as an "intimation of the infinite," the absolute), was claimed by Marx for "characteristic" music, and by Brendel even for "program" music, in which one perceived "progress" from the expression of "indefinite" feelings to the representation of "definite" ideas. (Marx's aesthetics undeniably attached itself to an authentic tradition: the tendency toward "characterization" in Körner's sense, which belonged to the principal features of the classical symphony, Beethoven's as well as Haydn's.) Rather than in the ethereal "poetic," Marx sought the nature of the symphony in the firmly outlined "characteristic" mode, Brendel even in the detailed "programmatic" one. (The metaphysics of instrumental music, which seemed dead and buried in 1850, soon celebrated its resurrection in the Schopenhauer renaissance brought about by Wagner and later by Nietzsche.)

That the symphony and not the string quartet (as the epitome of chamber music) represented the intuitive model for the development of the idea of absolute music stems less from the nature of the music than from the nature of the aesthetic writings in question. As publicity, they were oriented to the symphony as a form of public concert; the string quartet, which belonged to a private musical culture, was overshadowed. Beethoven, albeit hesitantly, had already sought the transition to a public style of quartet at the beginning of the century: in Opus 59 the change in social character is part of the composition, as it were; on the other hand, the *Quartetto Serioso,* Opus 95 was originally intended to remain withheld from the public. Even so, Robert Schumann, in his "Second Matinée of Quartets" (1838), could still call a piece by Karl Gottlieb Reissiger "a quartet to be heard by bright candlelight, among beautiful women,"—i.e., a salon piece—"whereas real Beethovenians lock the door, imbibing and reveling in every single measure." In the 1830s, "Beethovenians" were not simply adherents of Beethoven, but those who also, and above all, venerated the late works. However, abstruseness characterized the string quartet just when it completely expressed the nature of "pure, absolute musical art" instead of tending toward salon music, as Reissiger's piece did. Thus public awareness was inhibited in connecting the idea of absolute music, which was more current among literati than among musicians, to a genre that, by internal criteria, must have seemed predestined for such a connection. Carl Maria von Weber's comment on quartets by Friedrich Ernst Fesca is also typical: just by choosing the genre, the composer demonstrated that one could "count him among the few who, in these times that often tend toward shallowness in art, is still serious about studying the innermost essence of art." On the other hand, he describes the "quartet style" as "belonging more to the social, domestically serious sphere." In other words: the "innermost essence of art" reveals itself where one secludes oneself from the world, from the public.

Ferdinand Hand's *Aesthetics of Art* is historically significant insofar as, lacking the prejudice of philosophical demands or unusual musical judgments, it represents the "normal awareness," so to speak, of educated people around 1840. Although he still saw the "culmination" of instrumental music in the symphony, he praised the string quartet as "the flower of the new music: for it erects the purest result of harmony. . . . Whoever has penetrated the nature and effect of harmony will on the one hand consider Weber's calling it the cerebral element of music completely justified, and on the other hand recognize the totality of mental activity with which such a work is both created by the artist and received by the listener." (*Harmony* is to be understood as a synonym for "strict composition," the artificial part of music.) For a time, the symphony, the "drama of the instruments," still appears as the highest genre of instrumental music (analogous to the drama in the poetics of the nineteenth century). But if the string quartet represents the "cerebral in music," then it must gradually become the epitome of absolute music, growing in proportion to the decline of metaphysical import (the intimation of the absolute) in favor of the specifically aesthetic component of the idea (the thought that form in music is spirit and spirit in music is form).

According to Karl Köstlin, who wrote the specifically music-theoretical sections of Friedrich Theodor Vischer's *Aesthetics,* the string quartet is "a thought-music of pure art": "both sides, the formal and the material"—i.e., the artificial, artistic one and the "shadowy" one of sound—"are finally united in one and the same result, namely, in that this music"—the string quartet—"is the most intellectual kind; it leads us out of the din of life and into the still, shadowy realm of the ideal"—the accepted metaphysics of the beginning of the century has paled to a comforting fiction—"into the nonmaterial world of the mind that has withdrawn into itself, into its most secret affective life, and that internally confronts that affective life. It realizes just this ideal side of instrumental music; it is a thought-music of pure art, from which, to be sure, we soon desire to return to the full reality of forms more naturalistically rich in sound." In the term *pure art,* as Köstlin uses it, an older meaning—"art" as the epitome of the technical, artificial, and learned, of strict composition—flows into a new one: "art" as artistic character in the sense of the aesthetic nature of music. The history of the word reflects an intellectual and social change: in the 1850s—Hanslick published his treatise *The Beautiful in Music* in 1854—"pure art" in the formal sense, which had always been conceded to the string quartet, was accepted also as "pure art" in the aesthetic sense, as a pure realization of the "material appearance of the idea" (Hegel).

Although Hanslick's muting of the romantic metaphysics of instrumental music to an aesthetics of the "specifically musical," combined with the axiom that form in music was spirit, gave the "purely formal" string quartet the chance to appear as the paradigm of "pure, absolute music," this does not mean that the metaphysical side of the idea of absolute music had been extinguished: it reappeared in the Schopenhauerian renaissance, brought about by Wagner, starting in the 1860s. Moreover, in Beethoven's late quartets, which—not least due to the efforts of the Müller brothers—were entering the public's musical consciousness around that time, the artificial, esoteric motive is inseparable from the motive of metaphysical intimation. To Nietzsche, they therefore represent the purest expression of absolute music: "The highest revelations of music make us perceive, even involuntarily, the crudity of all imagery, and of every affect chosen for analogy; e.g., as the last Beethoven quartets put every perception, and for that matter, the entire realm of empirical reality, to shame. In the presence of the highest god, truly revealing himself,"—i.e, Dionysus—"the symbol has no meaning anymore: truly, it now seems to be an offensive triviality." Around 1870, Beethoven's quartets became the paradigm of the idea of absolute music that had been created around 1800 as a theory of the symphony: the idea that music is a revelation of the absolute, specifically because it "dissolves" itself from the sensual, and finally even from the affective sphere.

Translated by Roger Lustig

Günter Mayer

From *On the Relationship of the Political and Musical Avant-garde* (1989)

Thesis 1: Revolution in Music

In the historical time span between 1200 and c. 2000 two revolutions in music can be discerned:

The first one occurred with the process of the *visualization* of music in the eleventh and twelfth centuries: with the introduction and establishment of notation as a new technical quality of trans-memorial storage and the evolution of musical composition in and with notational script made possible by this (the elementarization of tones, the new complexity and flexibility of musical structures, both tonally and melodically). At the same time, this revolution also involved the development of polyphony; it brought about the distinction between composition and interpretation as a division of labor; and led as well to an interaction of hitherto strictly separated music-making spheres in an "intersocial-synthetic stylistics" (the intrusion of secular music into the sacred realm, the enrichment of the liturgical canon with folk language and elements of folk music). All of this constituted a profound, qualitative change in the deep structures of musical thought and experience, in the understanding and shaping of tradition, in the expansion of creative potential (both expressively and in terms of productive technique), in the social functions of music, and in the organizational forms of the historically new "intersocial appropriation." What was occurring here as a revolution in music was both reflex and cause, a moment of far-reaching social upheaval, which, to mention a few key points, was marked by changes in the agrarian mode of production, the crisis of the classic feudal system, the blossoming of the trades and commerce, the ascendant social force of the city-dwelling bourgeoisie as a new social class, and urbanization (through increased founding of cities). This social revolutionizing, marking a new era and affecting all forms of production and life, of thinking and opinion, was fought out only much later in political revolutions: as the overturning of the obsolete political order of feudalism in favor of the by now economically dominant bourgeoisie, the unfolding of the capitalist system of social relations—mediated through various types of political organization (states, parties). In the eleventh and twelfth centuries, the contradiction between feudal aristocracy and bourgeoisie began to leave its mark on social structure and determined, as we know today, the further logic of development of society.

The second revolution in music took and continues to take place with the electrification of music in the twentieth century: with the introduction and establishment of the electroacoustical recording as a new quality of technically mediated, transmemorial storage, technical reproducibility and producibility of sounds. This means a far-reaching transformation of the act of composing per electroacoustical equipment in the recording studio. With this, a revolutionary change is occurring that is comparable to that which proceeded from the advent of musical notation and its impact on musical production and composing. This second upheaval could be conceived of as the negation of negation. The elementarization of sounds takes on a new quality, one dissolving the appearance of the natural, likewise the complexity and flexibility of musical structures—transcending the traditional parameters of melody, harmony, and rhythm—and without the technical distance inherent to writing. The production detour by way of the eye is no longer needed; it is dialectically suspended with the electrification of sounds. That applies as well to the suspension of the differentiation of composition and interpretation as a division of labor. Musical production now proceeds again (as in the early forms of memory-based tradition prior to the eleventh and twelfth centuries) via the ear, through listening and subsequent decision making. The gathering and/or synthesizing of sounds and noises, their construction and combination through mixing, can be accomplished concretely and empirically. The potential for storing preexistent sounds (music and nonmusic of all kinds, including "acoustical photography" in the sense of a documentary authenticity and directness of auditory world experience) as well as the creation of the previously "unheard-of" is sheerly limitless: in the form of immediately reviewable and usable variants (as well as those to be rejected) offered increasingly by such apparatus. The new medium also encourages collective creativity. Improvisatory modes of music making (also those that have arisen in jazz) are now, on a higher level, once again essential as a moment of the compositional process. Improvisation and composition can flow into each other.

Since the equipment for electroacoustical sound production and fabrication is becoming increasingly smaller and cheaper, and therefore individually accessible and operable, as a consequence of both rapid technological development and the profit-oriented practice of the electronics and music industries, an enormous, immanently political potential is forming here, not only in terms of the "democratization" of reception processes, but also with regard to musical production, relatively independent of the studios of large institutions—which has been quite apparent now for years in the broad domain of popular music.

"Intersocial-synthetic stylistics" now affect music of all types from both the past and present: "The coexistence of very different and very noncontemporaneously originating acoustical phenomena is the musically new factor and a pregnant peculiarity of this century." Through its electrification, through technically mediated storage and reproducibility, the entire domain of music, in other words, all that which has evolved since the eleventh and twelfth centuries in the form of notated, composed, and interpreted music, is now becoming available on a global scale, likewise the broad domain of memory-based tradition and transmission, to the extent it can still be retrieved or reconstructed. Just as in the eleventh and twelfth centuries secular music (folk music)—at that time quite limited territorially—penetrated into the sacred realm, in the twentieth century, everyday music (popular music)—now a global phenomenon—is invading the quasi-sacred realm of "art music." With these developments, the distinction between "serious" and "entertaining" music is at first sharpened, but then, with the electrification of the latter, increasingly effaced.

All of this is once again a profound qualitative change in the deep structures of musical thought and experience, in the understanding of tradition and transmission, in the expansion of creative potential (both in terms of productive technique and expression), in the social functions of music, in the organizational forms of its "intersocial appropriation." The de-privileging of musical experience and creativity has become a determining factor beyond all social and national boundaries, including those imposed by opposing social systems.

What is happening here as a revolution in music is just as much reflex as cause, a moment of far-reaching social upheaval, which since the beginning of the twentieth century, to mention a few key points, has been marked by involved changes in the industrial mode of production, the crisis of classic capitalist social systems in the age of imperialism, the ascendant social power of the proletariat as a new, politically organized, future-determining force, the October Revolution and the building of a socialist-oriented type of society after the First and Second World Wars, the tumultuous unfolding of the scientific-technical revolution (on up to the more recent, phenomenal changes in information and communications technologies in the 1970s), in short: progressive, capitalist- or socialist-oriented processes of social transformation. . . .

Thesis 2: The Musical Avant-garde

The innovative thrust causing this revolution in music eminates from extraordinary individual achievements that suspend the traditional value structure of music—and not from musical avant-gardes: "Whether the concept avant-garde, commonly used to circumscribe a conglomerate of individual 'material revolutions' in the area of so-called serious, new, or contemporary music, can remain viable as a historiographic category with a centering claim, is already called into question by a fleeting glance at present-day musical realities." This concept was taken from the realm of politics and the military, chiefly after the mid–nineteenth century, and uncritically applied to the arts, including music. The musical "revolutionaries" shaped what has historically proven to be "out in front" (often without wanting to be or knowing themselves to be), without the "guard." Indeed, its progressive character, its advancement away from the conventional musical value structure—typically seen as historical progress but vehemently rejected from the position of the hitherto prevailing musical ideology of the vast majority of traditionalists, the epigones among musicians, by musical functionaries in state bureaucracies and by the majority of music lovers as an "overthrow," as the "desecration of music"— by no means makes "avant-gardists" out of these revolutionaries. What is entirely lacking in these significant and heterogeneously creative achievements (also in the case of a phenomenon such as the Second Viennese School, from which Eisler is always omitted) is precisely what defines the avant-garde in the military and politics: organization, discipline, an orientation toward guiding masses of people (soldiers, members, nonorganized persons of a certain class, the nation) to victorious actions—mediated by the assembling and functioning of leadership groups, institutions, and bureaucracies.

To be certain, in the other arts there were tendencies toward revolt and a new beginning, a radical critique and questioning of bourgeois cultural and artistic relations, in the circles congregating around cubism, dadaism, Russian futurism, surrealism, and constructivism during the first three decades of our century. These were characterized by "the attack on autonomy-aesthetics," by "the mission of linking art with life," by "a forced association with technology and attempt to gain social content as well as new structural character from this relationship, thus, generally: by a high degree of innovation in the realm of artistic means," and ultimately by "a high degree of organization, group formation, and internationalization," as well as an implicitly or explicitly progressive orientation toward the social interests and needs of the masses (one thinks of the *Bauhaus,* for example). However, in the new, modern, progressive music, whether expressionism or new objectivity (as its antithesis) or some other common designation, comparable characteristics cannot be discerned, in spite of many points of contact with such "avant-garde" phenomena in the other arts. And the agents of musical change themselves were not inclined to designate themselves as revolutionaries, as "avant-gardists," or to allow themselves to be so designated. In the eleventh and twelfth centuries, such a constellation simply did not exist. What took place at that time in terms of revolutionary upheaval must be conceived in some other category than what has been linked together with the concept of the historical avant-garde in relation to the first three decades of the twentieth century, or, respectively, with the very general, common concept of the musical avant-garde and an inner logic of musical development after World War II, from serialism to aleatoric music and electronic music.

The statements made above in Thesis 1 concerning the second musical revolution, in which we as yet find ourselves, lead to consequences on the basis of which the concept "musical avant-garde" was and is genuinely problematic—long before the nostalgic critique of the "avant-garde" by the so-called neoromantic or new simplicity, long before the turn toward so-called postmodernism. In terms of both the people and things involved, these revolutionary achievements must be far more broadly conceived than is commonly the case:

(a) This revolution cannot be understood solely on the basis of high musical culture, looking (for example) at the famous electronic studios in Cologne, Milan, etc., the new, modern, progressive electronic music and its performance in concerts, festivals or special forums such as Karlheinz Stockhausen's spherical auditorium in Osaka. This revolution is likewise taking place in the realm of popular music (in progressive jazz, progressive rock, in the productions of performance artists), and in contrast to "mainstream," benchmark-setting models of "avant-garde" and electroacoustical composition in the "serious" realm, it is reaching—even in its progressive "popular" forms—an incomparably larger circle of above all younger listeners, and, in the case of the "mainstream," conventionalized innovations of rock music exploited by the music industry (for example, in disco music), it is reaching a mass public that experiences electroacoustic music for hours every day.

(b) This revolution cannot be understood solely in relation to professional producers of music who have absolved years of preprofessional training. If these professionals are viewed from a much wider angle, taking popular music into account, and considering the much stronger elements of collectivity in contrast to the great bourgeois- or socialist-oriented individualists in their "serious" electronic studios, it is clear that many innovations in the electroacoustical revolution are produced by a broad stream of "amateurs," by "ingenious dilettantes," who increasingly make use of "professional" techniques, who are part of the mass public (above all its younger ranks), and who as a rule do not lose the close association with the youthful reality of life even with their professionalization and ascendance into big-time music business.

(c) This revolution cannot be understood solely on the basis of compositional technique or from a work-centered perspective. It is being staged not only by composers, but rather by many innovators, without whose creative achievements the new products, the revolutionary transformation of musical relations, indeed the musical culture as a whole, cannot be grasped. The nature of musical production alone extends here beyond the traditional composition process. Taking part in it, and simultaneously influencing it, are conductors, studio technicians, producers, music functionaries in the broadest sense of the term, as well as scientists, inventers, and electronics engineers.

(d) This revolution is leading to the effacement of the boundaries between "serious" and "entertaining" music, and between the genres of music themselves: to a new combination and synthesis, to collage, to montage, and since the 1980s, to the "bricolage" of the performance artists. And it is leading to an effacement of the boundaries between music and the other arts in the sense of multimedia forms. With regard to the postmodern or trans-avant-garde tendencies marking recorded music, in which the electrification of music is now also playing a role, one could assume that it is hardly appropriate to inquire about progressive achievements let alone respond to such questions. One simply can't speak here about avant-*gardes*. On the other hand, there are certainly revolts going on, but they are now directed against the avant, against modernism, against the *avant*-garde. And the previous orientation of musical revolutionaries toward modernity, toward newness in the sense of musical and social progress, is now being called into question, its possibility denied, the continuity and mutual obligation of values, indeed, of a sensible shift in values ironicized or disavowed. It appears that all values are being sold off cheaply or gambled away in the sounding supermarkets and luxury hotels located at the edge of the abyss.

We should not abandon the simple question: whom does it serve? and, at the same time, we should protect ourselves from sweeping judgments. What is actually at stake in this "postmodern," multilingual situation in terms of deep disappointments, self-irony, fears and presentiments, and perhaps insights and possibilities for development (and thus connecting pieces to modernism); what is really involved in its balance of extreme complexity and utmost simplicity, in its demonstrative eclecticism and contrived banality: all of this needs to be seriously examined first. And this is more likely to lead to useful results if the inquiry and analysis are carried out with a certain specific interest in mind, namely: the basic question concerning the sense and perspective of human existence, and with this, at the same time, concerning a sensible and sovereign handling of musical possibilities, implying as well a centering and consequent limitation thereof, in other words: the question concerning sensible social functions of music in societies that are not interested in "amusing themselves to death" or sinking "helplessly and in a good mood" into barbarism. And this is more likely to lead to useful results, if, with this basic interest in mind, one asks in a differentiated way which fundamental philosophical positions— including those in opposition to what is desired or not desired—can be distinguished in the multitude of sound events, in the invariables apparent in them, and just where these stand objectively in relation to the needs and interests of politically and economically powerful minorities without a future, respectively, the vast majority of all living persons on this threatened earth. In turn, this requires thorough analysis, real conceptual, rational exertion in relation to philosophy and social, personality and cultural theory, in order to grasp the causes of this end-of-time crisis in the developed capitalist countries, but also the causes of the crisis of the international communistic and workers' movement, as well as the hitherto prevailing concept of progress in the socialist countries; in order to gain realistic insights into present reality and to conceive of possibilities for the future in such a way that sensible, competent, and cooperative action—"knowing and unfortunate"—becomes possible and brings about genuine change.

Thesis 3: The Political Avant-garde

The concept of the political avant-garde requires historicizing. There have been political avant-gardes, there are now, and, if the future is to be made possible, there will have to be avant-gardes in a different form from before—for without organization, without the programmatic generalization of progressive political experience, without coordinated mass action, the necessary alternatives of further social development will not be found and able to assert themselves.

Political avant-gardes represent a certain category of political parties—neither the conservative, nor the liberal, to say nothing of the fascistic. Rather, the concept of political avant-garde has applied (since the mid–nineteenth century and above all in the twentieth) to those types of communist and workers' parties that view themselves as a "fighting league of partisans," as "a party of cadres," as the political "vanguard," whose goal consists of leading the masses of the working class and people as a whole toward socialist revolution, of overcoming the rule of capital and the associated antagonisms of alienation, of constructing a new, initially socialist society, and gradually transforming it into a communistic one, in which there are no more classes, no politics, and no more political avant-gardes. The following things are essential for these political avant-gardes: revolutionary discipline through consciousness, democratic centralism, mass propaganda and agitation, coordinated collective action, national as well as international solidarity, criticism, and self-criticism.

These avant-gardes were politically "out in front" as long as they understood how to question radically, to analyze the existing social contradictions more deeply than other parties, and to work out general platforms in strategy and tactics as well as concrete plans of action that were on the level of the historically necessary and possible. They were politically "out in front" as long as they understood how to reach the masses of the working class and the people, to stimulate and generalize initiatives, to make the necessary alliances, and to promote, through real actions against exploitation and oppression, the difficult process of real mass emancipation in the sense of the growth of sovereignty vis-à-vis the natural and social conditions of life. With its central connection to the interests of the working class, this avant-garde was and is at the same time essentially concerned with the interests of all humankind (consistent with its goal of instituting a classless society); thus its consequent role in actions against imperialist warfare, against all forms of fascism and racism, against the armaments race, and for a turnaround in global politics.

That applies—generally—for its political functions under the prevailing capitalist conditions and, respectively, after the victorious revolution, with the assumption of total responsibility for a socialist transformation of all aspects of social development.

It is well-known that in the course of the twentieth century this "ideal type" of political avant-garde has realized itself in a non-

"ideal" manner in a both nationally and internationally very complicated process—under variously challenging conditions (economically and culturally underdeveloped regions, poorly developed political experience of the popular masses, the strength and flexibility of the as-yet-prevailing national bourgeoisie or the strong self-interested influence of the international bourgeoisie on the conflict between capitalism and socialism). It is well-known that there have been great successes, periods of great change, times of enthusiasm and upward movement, and mass-scale experiences of real upheaval: the victorious October Revolution and the famous twenties in the young Soviet Union (which politically, artistically, and culturally—at least in its urban centers—was a "progressive society" at that time in spite of economic backwardness); the influence of this on the political practice of the German Communist party until the end of the Weimar Republic (with the victory of the fascist counterrevolution); in the 1930s in Spain (once again defeated by fascism); after World War II in the now-European socialist countries (following the victory of the Soviet Union in its struggle against German fascism and largely without indigenous, national, victorious revolutions); in China, Korea, Vietnam, Cuba, and some African countries (through victorious revolutions); in the 1960s and 1970s in France and Italy (without victorious revolutions); and to some extent in Portugal, Chile, Nicaragua, and elsewhere. Thus, in the struggle with fascism there were great defeats (which affected not only the political avant-gardes but also the vast majority of the people). And it is well-known that there have also been great defeats within the political avant-gardes and the political practice controlled by it: the disastrous consequences of Stalinism in the Soviet Union, with its effects on the socialist countries and the international communist movement—i.e., political deformations that could not be overcome on the first try after 1956, whose effects were actually felt on into the 1980s, and that are now being fought energetically by the new leadership of the Soviet Communist party. In their defeats at the hands of fascism, the communists, whose *garde* was widely struck down, maintained the *avant* position. But through the defeats in their own ranks, through the inability to overcome deformations in a consequent manner and implement realistic political thought and action, these political avant-gardes at times largely forfeited the historically progressive function that they claimed for themselves. And presently they also find themselves in a complicated and contradictory situation: the development of capitalism possesses a "far greater stability than previously assumed": "For the masses in the Western nations, socialism has not yet delivered a convincing example of a far-reaching democratization of society and a radical and quicker solution for economic problems. On top of that, there are the negative developmental processes at work in a series of socialist countries . . ." that have led to stagnation and symptoms of crisis. Finally: "In terms of international cooperation," the communists are distinctly behind, "considering the activities of internationalists from other political orientations and parties—social democrats, the 'Greens,' Christians, conservatives, and liberals." They have "clearly defaulted" into the position of "*arrière*-gardes" by virtue of their failure to come to grips with the new realities of the late twentieth century." In the meantime this has all been recognized and has found expression in the many initiatives of the Soviet Communist party, in its new *avant* position in international and national politics. And this leads to, as both prerequisite and consequence, a reconstruction of the "guards" and a thoroughgoing reform of the totality of political circumstances, which, if this is to be successful, must take on the quality of renewed revolution. This "revolutionary" turn of events has manifested itself internationally in a new politics of reason and dialogue, which is oriented toward coexistence, cooperation, and the coevolution of both the existing and quite oppositely oriented social systems; toward a new breadth of alliances possessing the necessary tolerance toward those who think differently; and nationally, toward a consequent socialist democratization in a political course corresponding to current conditions. All of this presently amounts to a complicated process of disputation and discussion with reactionary or conservative forces among the bourgeoisie as well as with conservative elements in the communist movement and the socialist countries.

Thesis 4: Political Avant-garde—Musical Avant-garde?

From these cursory thoughts on a historicizing of the concept of the political avant-garde, consequences result for the examination of its relationship to modern, new, progressive music (and for the revolution in music occurring through electrification), as well as the other way around: for the relationship of the musicians involved in this music or confronted with it to the political avant-garde. The problem area "political avant-garde—musical avant-garde" has only existed since the October Revolution.

(a) In those periods in which the political avant-gardes were in a position not only to trigger but also to lead processes of broad societal renewal in close association with the masses of the working class and people as a whole, they had an inspiring, supportive impact on the development of progressive music. For example, in the young Soviet Union the political avant-garde and progressive music were objectively, in their essential nature, on one and the same level; the political engagement of the (few) progressive musicians was almost self-evident; the orientation toward the politicized part of the working masses was no hindrance to innovation and experimentation, indeed, it served as an occasion to try new things on one's own initiative, both in content and form, and in new forms of public practice extending beyond academic conceptions of art.

The policy-making people in the leadership were, in spite of their basically classicistic attitude, relatively tolerant in musical matters. And it is well-known that in the developed capitalist countries, for example, in Germany, these processes led to the fact that in the 1920s, for the first time in the history of the working class and workers' music movement, professional musicians also—or better: precisely—on the basis of their progressive musical practice, moved closer to the political avant-garde and movement, allied themselves with its revolutionary aims, and brought their high qualifications into the political, cultural, and musical practice of the workers' movement, as well as into a new collectivity of like-minded persons from the other arts, in order to help qualify them (Scherchen, the November-Group, Eisler, "Struggle Music," the League of Proletarian-Revolutionary Writers, etc.). At that time there was relatively great leeway for experimenting, for discovering new social content, for pursuing a new, original synthesis of artistic *niveau* and simplicity, for connecting the revolution in musical material with the political and technical revolution, for example, in Eisler's concept of "applied music." And, of course, this did not occur without contradictions. But, at the same time, there was no regimentation. Similar things could be said for the comparable periods after World War II, for instance, the 1960s and 1970s in Italy, in which the Italian Communist party was a potent political force with great tradition and authority, with considerable, broad impact, and which, in critically defining itself in opposition to Zhdanovist vulgarisms, had a musical policy open to everything new, in which not all forms of musical creativity were measured against the criteria of their ties to tradition and mass impact. In those years, the Italian Communist party also had the musically progressive composers on its side politically, in their very own ranks (Nono, Manzoni, Gentilucci, Liberovici, Lombardi; also the movement and journal *Musica/Realtà*).

(b) But there were also periods marked by the musical-political effects of Stalinism and its long-lasting consequences for the musical cultures: in the early 1930s in the Soviet Union, after 1948 even more sharply there; and on into the 1960s and early 1970s in the other socialist countries. The sociologically vulgar, classicistic interpretation of ties to tradition and mass orientation (the overemphasis on the classical heritage and folk music), the exaggerated opposition to the "enemy" ideological influences of "bourgeois," "decadent" music, whose internal contradictions were not understood: these policies were inspired and administratively carried out by a paternalistic dictatorship acting in the name of the people (musically little qualified or spoiled), by poorly qualified functionaries who were musically half- or noneducated. The well-known campaigns against "formalism," against "modernism" in music affected not only the musicians of the historical "avant-garde" in the narrower sense: in 1948, works by Shostakovich, Prokofiev, or Bartók and Hindemith, and even Eisler were involved. And this policy, damaging to the entirety of musical relations, was actively represented and "realized" by socialist-oriented musicians and music ideologues, who simply did not know where to begin with the new, progressive music and who, in their vulgar argumentation, directly or indirectly, relied upon the vulgar critique of conservative bourgeois ideologues (and in doing so wound up in disastrously close proximity to fascist musical ideology). Since these people were considered "experts" by the political functionaries, who confirmed the latter's rejection of the "avant-garde" and uncritically seized upon the distaste of the mass public for all types of modern music as an essential criterion, that which the progressive musicians had actually accomplished and were accomplishing (in terms of historically new and forward-leading music) had no chance of becoming socially accepted, understood, and influential. Even the progressive musicians with socialist convictions were not understood in those years by others in their own ranks and at times had to endure great difficulties and conflicts. This disastrous situation was not able to suppress the interest in "progressive music" among truly interested specialists, but overall, it had very negative consequences for musical culture, since the moderate "modernists" of a conservative or epigonal persuasion were able to set the tone undisturbed for a long time. Nevertheless, there were great achievements in the appropriation of the classical heritage as well as democratic musical traditions. But although the political "avant-gardes" generally brought about downright great things, even in those times, in terms of reconstruction, the economy, and social programs, with regard to "progressive music," they were downright conservative to reactionary—and illusionary in their populist goals.

* * *

Since the 1970s this adversarial attitude toward the avant-garde is no longer a factor in official music policy. The mechanistic demands for a realistic and socialistically oriented music have been relativized, the vulgarisms of the past have been repealed, and the historically progressive potential and impact of the artistic "avant-gardes" recognized more and more vis-à-vis their internal contradictions. The breadth of tolerance for progressive music has grown considerably larger. A realistic and socialistic orientation now tends to be viewed programmatically as a specific mark of progressive music. Even prior to the fundamental shift in foreign, domestic, and cultural policy initiated by Gorbachev in the Soviet Union, and in spite of the dominance of old ways of thinking, for several years there had already been relatively great leeway for progressive music of both national and international origin—in a few major cultural centers and special programming forums. However: that was and is by no means identical with a conscious orientation on the part of progressive musicians toward the current political situation or toward political engagement in the socialist sense. Nevertheless, there have been and still are a few progressive musicians who have held fast to both the ideal of socialism and a concept of progressive music that is politically progressive as well. But in light of historical and contemporary experience (respectively) during the period of stagnation, the majority maintained a skeptical if not increasingly disinterested attitude with respect to the political avant-gardes, especially since this coincides with a general value crisis in the historically new situation of humanity, a skeptical attitude if not growing disinterest in politics altogether. A policy of laissez-faire by no means guarantees a productive reciprocal relationship between the political avant-garde and musical progressives (who for their part can by no means be lumped together and defined as apolitical, functionless, asemantic, or esoteric). And after all, even under such conditions, the individualistic, not explicitly political but nevertheless progressive music that was allowed has time and again had a disruptive impact with regard to both the politically active and inactive, the musically sensitive and insensitive, in like manner, as an (of course) isolated moment of uneasiness, of some vague protest against the representative affirmation of the status quo with its harmonizing prolongation into the future managed by the conservatives as well as the moderate modernist and epigonal musicians.

Unfortunately, as of today, with respect to the current situation of musical politics in the socialist countries as well as the communist and workers' parties in the capitalist countries and Third World, it cannot be said that the musical revolution of the twentieth century, the electrification of music, has found a degree of consideration corresponding to both its dimensions and progressive political possibilities. Such a moment of inertia with regard to general perception and the practical implementation of the new, and not only in music, is quite "normal" for any organization aimed at the masses—also for politically progressive, socialistically oriented ones.

With a view toward the generally needed revolutionary transformation of all aspects of life in both of the currently prevailing social systems, now forced at the price of survival to coexist and coevolve, the following can be concluded concerning the relationship between political avant-gardes and progressive music: the political avant-gardes must—above and beyond their traditional, revolutionary orientation toward socialism—be conceived of more broadly, such that a great "united front" of quite different and oppositely thinking people can be empowered with regard to the basic matters of securing life and peace—with all of its consequences for a new quality of tolerance in intellectual and philosophical-ideological debates. And the progressiveness of music on quite different levels—above and beyond the traditional conception of a relatively self-governing, developmental logic in music—might well be measured in the first place against the overall context of sounding forms and contents with regard to variously accentuated, constructive efforts for the future of humankind in the sense of potential and real mass emancipation: in the sense of a liberation from the consequences of the noncontrolled processes of social transformation. It may be obvious that the (in this sense) politically engaged musicians in the capitalistic countries, the socialist countries, and the countries of the Third World (including the as-yet-progressive or once-again progressive or aesthetically most advanced) have decisive things to contribute to this effort on the basis of their tradition and history in our century (including the bitter experiences). It may be just as obvious that building a musical coalition of reason between progressive musicians of various types (both the politically engaged or "unpolitical") and all other musicians requires no less effort, patience, and endurance than in the general realm of politics.

That may be viewed as utopian—but it is absolutely necessary.

The more people there are who act in a dismissive, indifferent, or wait-and-see manner with regard to this exigent need for a comprehensive politically and musically progressive attitude and the difficulty of its formation, the more certain final destruction or barbarism becomes.

Translated by Michael Gilbert

Jost Hermand

Avant-garde, Modern, Postmodern:
The Music (Almost) Nobody Wants to Hear
(1991)

I.

Anyone who invokes any sort of concept of progress in ongoing discussions of art is immediately castigated by the overwhelming majority of disillusioned, cynical, or so-called realistic critics as being hopelessly naive. This viewpoint, allegedly naive in the face of today's atmosphere of economic, ecological, and nuclear crisis—is regarded at best as a vestige of that simpler past before anyone had heard of Theodor W. Adorno's often-cited *Dialektik der Aufklärung* (Dialectic of the Enlightenment). If any notion of the new, progressive, or even revolutionary does crop up nowadays, it is solely on the level of the cheapest marketing slogans, coined by advertising executives who constantly strive to boost consumption by pushing the "brand-new." Thus we all enjoy the blessings of a revolutionary toothpaste, but not of revolutionary art, a total reconception of certain bathroom fixtures, but no longer any subversive dramas or poetry that appeal to the masses.

Yet we know that this was not always the case. There once were times when such concepts as new, rebellious, or even revolutionary still had an undeniable aura, and the best among the artists were proud to be distinguished with these adjectives—when even art, so often belittled as ineffectual, was granted the function of bringing about change. And the key concept connected to this was usually the term *avant-garde*. What this phenomenon meant beginning in the early nineteenth century was an art that attempted to base itself on the most progressive social ideas of its own time and strove to develop into progressive conceptions of art corresponding by parallel, analogy, or homology to those social principles; in other words, concepts of art that evinced an inner correlation of aesthetic and social progress. That—and just that—is what was once meant by *avant-garde*, whereas purely formal innovations, regardless of whether they were of a technical or aesthetic nature, were viewed as mere *modernism*. Thus the status of the avant-gardistic could be claimed by a work of art whose progressive quality was realized both in content as well as in form. By comparison, modernistic art was that in which the emphatically progressive became hypostatized on a formal or formalistic plane.

If we proceed from this definition of *avant-garde*, then there have been only three great avant-garde movements in Europe that have attempted to synchronize sociopolitical and artistic-formal progress, whereas modernism has been an integral component of many bourgeois trends in art over the past 150 years. These are the three time periods in which avant-garde movements came to the fore: (1) the years between 1830 and 1848–49, when the progressive bourgeois artists were oriented toward the revolutionary models of thought such as Left-Hegelianism, Saint-Simonianism, anarchism, socialism, or democratic parliamentarianism, and also tried to convey these basic ideological convictions in their works, which expressed the urge toward a new "realism" and an intense social and political involvement, (2) the years between 1870 and 1889, i.e., between the Paris Commune and the centennial of the French Revolution, when progressive artists for the most part turned to a Naturalism based on Darwinist or social-democratic ideas, and (3) the years between 1905 and 1925 when, set against the most varied revolutions—such as the Russian revolutions of 1905 and 1917 and the German November revolution of 1919—such movements as cubism, futurism, expressionism, dadaism, constructivism, and surrealism developed. In their aversion to bourgeois taste as manifested in Victorian, Bonapartist, and Wilhelminian cultures, these isms radically rejected *all* bourgeois concepts of art and proclaimed instead a politically enriched way of living. In the most general terms, these were the three great periods of the European avant-garde. Everything that occurred along with, in-between, and after-wards in the area of so-called innovative art can only be termed modernism.

The number of writers and painters who joined in these three avant-garde movements is legion. The number of composers who could be considered avant-garde is, on the other hand, hardly consequential (and later we shall hear the reasons for that). In the years between 1830 and 1848–49, Richard Wagner approached the status of a prototype among avant-garde composers. During those years, Wagner read Ludwig Feuerbach, became well-versed in the ideas of the Young Germans and Saint-Simonists, established contact with Heine in Paris in 1840, was interested in the works of Pierre-Joseph Proudhon, counted Georg Herwegh and Mikhail Bakunin among his friends, wrote—as did the young Engels—a *Cola di Rienzi,* in which a Roman tribune incites the populace to revolt against the ruling families, temporarily professed communism in his writing *Das Künstlertum der Zukunft* (Artistry in the Future), battled at the barricades in Dresden in 1849, finally had to flee to Switzerland and there wrote such essays as *Die Kunst und die Revolution* (Art and Revolution) in 1849 and *Das Kunstwerk der Zukunft* (Artwork in the Future) in 1850, in both of which he turned against the commodification of music and professed a belief in art for all, dedicated to the highest social ideals. Although Wagner later betrayed nearly all these ideas and embraced an obscurantism based on racial theories and an aristocraticism, his earlier ideas long remained the only model for a true avant-garde in music. August Bebel hailed them as "entirely socialistic" in 1879 in his book *Die Frau und der Sozialismus* (Woman and Socialism). Even Clara Zetkin and Anatoli Lunacharski praised the young Wagner as late as the 1920s as the illuminating model for a noncommercial, spriritualized art relevant to all of society.

Yet the real development in bourgeois musical life after 1848–49 took a completely different course, as we well know. The so-called high music, in today's parlance *serious music,* remained a privilege of the upper ten thousand of the population during the Victorian, Bonapartist, and Wilhelminian era. Thus the opera houses and concert halls became the sacred temples of "inwardness secured by force" as Thomas Mann later wrote. Their doors were open only to those who had at their disposal both a large wallet and a soul susceptible to emotional transports. Here they surrendered willingly to feelings and left their brains at the coat-check. Here was the place for zealous idolatry of Tchaikovsky, Grieg, Lalo, Gounod, Bruch, Dvorak, Saint-Saens, Massenet, Fauré, Scriabin; i.e., one wallowed in those overblown works spanning all the way from the *Symphonie pathétique* to the *Poème de l'extase.*

The avant-garde of the Naturalists between 1870 and 1890, oriented toward the natural sciences and social democracy, thought very little of the music of its own era. It perceived the current tone poems and musical dramas to be emotional pomposity without redeeming social value, even to be vain noise and rapture. Thus Heinrich Hart, for example, wrote in 1891 in the *Freie Bühne* (Free Stage), the leading journal of the Naturalist avant-garde in Germany, that one should give up music, "for the sake of truth." Music is, he explained apodictically, a "luxury like women and wine." It "intoxicates," "lulls to sleep," "causes chaos and confusion and the soul's decay." Hart continued, it is the lowest form of degradation, pulling down to the "sensual" depths: in short: it is ridiculous, without purpose, and thereby retards further "intellectual growth." "Anyone who has figured out," he stated with avant-garde emphasis, "what it is to be human ought to begin without delay a course in 'music nonappreciation.'"

The message of the small group of Naturalists necessarily fell on deaf ears, at least for most bourgeois music connoisseurs around 1900. For ultimately it was not Naturalism that gained acceptance as the leading art movement in the 1890s, but rather an aestheticism tinged with impressionism and symbolism, showing a special affinity for precisely that sort of purely emotional, sensual, even culinary music decried by the Social Democrats. Yet in spite of this striking continuity, there were also a few new developments in the bourgeois music milieu around 1900. One group of bourgeois composers—including Sibelius, Puccini, Rachmaninoff, and to some extent Richard Strauss—continued to adhere to the emotional pathos of upper-class Victorians, Bonapartists, and Wilhelminians, thus contributing to their enormous popularity with that upper class and even creating an appeal that persists to the present day. On the other hand, during this time of growing aestheticism a smaller group of very serious composers branched off into the esoteric by professing a modernist-oriented secessionism whose chief criteria included aesthetic deviation and the status of social outsider. All those composers between Debussy and the young Schönberg who belonged to this group refused, starting in about 1900, to write any more *Capriccios, Turandots, Valses tristes,* or any of those spirited and sentimental piano concertos that would have ingratiated them with the standard concert and opera audiences drawn from the upper 3 to 4 percent of the population. Rather, this second group consciously limited its impact to the "elite," the upper 0.1 to 0.2 percent, or what was termed the connoisseurs. As a young man, for example, Schönberg performed his music only in private recitals, where neither applause nor any signs of disapproval were permitted, musical events that were eerily reminiscent of private poetry readings within the Stefan George Circle.

This, then, in broad terms, was the situation of serious music between 1900 and 1914, at the start of the third and final great avant-garde movement, to which we owe so many aesthetically committed and also aesthetically significant works of literature and painting. Little of the sort is to be found in the serious music produced during those years. The operas and concert halls of that era continued to be the refuges of the culture-conscious bourgeois, who still felt most at home in these "hallowed halls" at a time when, in the realms of literature and painting, one bastion of tradition after the other was falling victim to some avant-garde or modernist trend.

There was no real possibility of turning serious music into a medium for the avant-garde until the numerous technical innovations of the 1920s. Not until the era of radio and the phonograph record, the significance of whose invention nearly matches that of the printing press for literature, did it become possible to lend a broader social character to serious music, in other words to make the music of the upper ten thousand accessible to hundreds of thousands or even millions. Unfortunately scarcely anything of the sort occurred in the 1920s. The reasons for this are obvious: (1) the masses of clerks and factory workers lacked the cultural conditioning to feel any need for such music at all and (2) all these technical innovations were immediately deployed by the political and commercial power elites in the mass media that primarily sought to manipulate listeners rather than fulfill the program of aesthetic education envisaged by German classicism. Thus between 1923 and 1930, during the period of so-called relative stabilization, when the arts reflected new objectivity and the cult of technology numerous technical achievements fraught with possibilities for broad-based cultural education resulted only in formalistic or phoney and manipulative innovations.

Even the modernistic, elitist music was swept along by this trend toward technologization. This is proven by Schönberg's turn, in approximately 1924, away from the gestural expressiveness of his early works toward a rigidly executed twelve-tone technique that amounts to thoroughgoing mathematicization of the musical material. Other modernist composers or "objectivists," as H. H. Stuckenschmidt labeled them at the time, dreamed as early as 1925 of a "colossal orchestrion," that is, a type of supersynthesizer, which someday would supersede the symphony orchestra. Indeed, several serious composers even attempted to design such instruments and put them to the test. Electric pianos come to mind, such as the Neo-Bechstein grand piano or the Welte-Mignon piano, which enjoyed some popularity in the 1920s and for which even Stravinsky scored some of his works. Along with the mechanical piano and the mechanical organ, instruments such as the trautonium, hellertion, vibraphone, and sphere-o-phone caused a great stir at the time. But none of these instruments had a very wide effect. Even the formal innovation of Stravinsky, Bartók, Hindemith, Milhaud, Krenek, and others who attempted to incorporate jazz, folk, exotic, or classical elements, remained a brief episode of high culture and continued to be ignored by the mass of music listeners interested only in popular music from the phonograph, radio, or dance bands. This type of mechanical music was not even appreciated by the conventional concertgoers, who continued to expect music to provide solace, emotional depth, or at least melodiousness, and as a result, this new music had no audience whatsoever.

Of course the situation was even worse for those few composers who supported an ideology that called for change in the system and who wanted to create a truly avant-garde music that would serve both social and aesthetic progress. For their failure the reasons are quite obvious: (1) these composers had access neither to the concert hall nor to the opera, nor even to the mass media, which were largely controlled by the political right or by adherents of the status quo, (2) the masses, whom these composers wanted to address, were not at all prepared for their music, and (3) Marxist aesthetics in the period from Mehring to Lukács centered largely on literature, i.e., the printed word was assumed to be the best means of effective popular education. Thus, during all these years, music remained a secondary concern for the political left. What this camp did have was the applied form of the marches and songs, a vocal music for the class struggle in which the words clearly counted more than the music.

In this category of music on the left, the only exception was Hanns Eisler, who as a student of Schönberg—after joining the Communist party of Germany—tried to develop from a modernist to a consistent avant-gardist. He thus wrote not only marches or songs for Ernst Busch, but also attempted to compose antibourgeois music of high quality that utilized the bourgeois musical heritage in its most technically advanced form, in the deromanticized, nonbombastic, coldly objective form of Schönberg's twelve-tone technique. Eisler thus belongs to what Werner Mittenzwei has called the "leftist material aesthetics," which emerged around 1930 and endeavored to appropriate the highest technical standard of bourgeois-capitalistic modes of production, yet simultaneously sought to reshape this standard for the left—as did Brecht, Benjamin, Eisenstein, Piscator, and Heartfield. These practitioners of leftist material aesthetics thus viewed bourgeois modernism above all as an "arsenal of form," as Brecht later put it. Yet even this group failed, due to the Nazis' accession to power in 1933. It was solely in the Popular Front movement between 1935 and 1939 that this group had a final chance to make itself heard. Hanns Eisler, for example, wrote several exile cantatas during these years as well as a *Deutsche Symphonie* (German symphony), in which he attempted to combine Brechtian texts with Schönbergian twelve-tone technique. But this stylistic mixture was rejected not just by Eisler's Soviet friends (and enemies), but even by Brecht himself. Thus the few avant-garde experiments in music of the thirties faded away unheard. But these were times when even bourgeois modernism was able to prolong its existence only on the fringes. In the United States where they lived, Schönberg and Bartók went virtually unnoticed; in the USSR such composers as Prokofiev and Shostakovich were submitted to repeated rebukes on account of their modernist "pranksterism," as it was called.

II.

In the years after 1945, there were scarcely any signs whatsoever of a new musical avant-garde. In the Soviet-bloc countries, a moderate semimodernism à la Prokofiev, Shostakovich, and Kachaturian dominated in a music scene that attempted to cling to so-called late-bourgeois forms such as opera, symphony, concert, and chamber music. Eisler's theories concerning a truly "socialist musical culture" indeed continued to be discussed—especially in East Germany—but they remained an unfulfilled postulate in the actual musical practice.

In the West, on the other hand, these years witnessed a modernism à la Schönberg, which since 1925 had been of secondary importance within this part of the world, not only in the fascist countries, but also in democracies such as the United States, where in the thirties and early forties such traditional composers as Gershwin and Copland had been more likely to set the tone. As in the pictorial arts of that era, when realist elements were superseded after 1948 by a wave of nonobjectivist painting, the restoration of modernism in serious music also had a Cold War aspect. Nonrepresentationalism in painting corresponded to atonalism in music, and both of these isms were held up as proof of a feeling for freedom and used against any threatening, "totalitarian" restriction. In West Germany, the serious music scene was dominated between 1945 and 1949 by a semimodernist trend à la Stravinsky, Hindemith, and Bartók. After 1950, virtually everyone demanded a restoration of the Vienna School, a movement that centered principally around the Darmstadt summer workshops, the music festivals in Donaueschingen, the Musica Viva concerts in Munich, and various late evening music programs broadcast by the radio networks. Adorno provided the theory for this restoration in his *Philosophie der neuen Musik* (Philosophy of New Music) of 1949, where he ruthlessly consigned Stravinsky and Bartók to the ash heap of history while describing Schönberg's music as the only possible "message in a bottle" worthy of being dispatched to uncharted shores.

A modernist trend long considered defunct, namely the twelve-tone theory of the early twenties, underwent an unexpected revival during the early 1950s among listeners interested in serious contemporary music, i.e., that legendary 0.1 to 0.2 percent of the population already mentioned. The revival of twelve-tone music had at least two causes: (1) this musical form, as mentioned earlier, could be played off extremely well against the "outmoded" tonality of music from the Soviet bloc, where the principle of "being led on a leash" supposedly prevailed, as Adorno put it; (2) professing one's long-held admiration for the modernist music of the "Jew" Schönberg provided the desired alibi for many former Nazis, who just a few years earlier had supported tonality in "German music." Thus for the majority of the officious to official fanatics of modernism, contemporary serious music after 1950 could not be Schönbergian enough, i.e., it could not be elitist, esoteric, formalistic, experimental, or hermetic enough. The motto of these circles seemed to be: the more unintelligible, the better. The adherents of this Schönberg revival held in low regard such concepts as the nation, the masses, or the collective, which they regarded as harbingers of totalitarianism. They no longer felt any concern—as had the avant-gardists—for the population in its entirety, but rather only for themselves. Thus the journals of modernist music during those years consistently praised that music whose atonality and complete lack of melody consciously resisted the popular taste of the masses.

Two directions taken by this music can be distinguished. On the one hand there was a snobby, elitist path taken by those who wanted only to be separate and who took great pride in their areas of specialization, favoring a *musica reservata* for the very few, as Hans Renner put it on the last page of his book *Geschichte der Musik* (The History of Music) in 1955. The German music journal *Melos* actually used English to describe this elite tendency as the "music of the happy few" who wanted nothing more than to serve music. H. H. Stuckenschmidt claimed in 1955 that all great music is necessarily "esoteric," even "useless," and thus belongs in an "ivory tower." His ideal at the time was a "music against everyone," completely without purpose, an art-for-art's-sake absolutism that paid homage to and would refuse to compromise with any audience, regardless of how small it may become. Yet aside from this group there were music theorists such as Adorno who claimed to see a dialectical element in their very separatism. They saw their marginal position not as a mark of distinction, but rather as a conscious refusal, i.e., a final potential for resistance against the ever more powerful culture industry.

The interplay of these two tendencies in West Germany during the 1950s and early 1960s led within the so-called Darmstadt School to a dictatorship of precisely that modernism, for which Schönberg offered the following theoretical basis in a letter to Willi Schlamm dated June 28, 1945: "If it is art, it is not for the masses. If it is for the masses, it is not art." The first wave in this movement, as mentioned earlier, was a thoroughgoing restoration of Schönberg's twelve-tone technique. Starting in 1953–54, a wave of pointillist or serial music derived from Anton Webern's music joined the movement. This serial music took the mathematicization of the musical material beyond the level of the strict twelve-tone technique by subjecting all remaining musical parameters such as pitch, timbre, intervals, rhythm, etc., to a consistent serialization. Beginning with the midfifties—as had happened during the period of "relative stabilization" of the twenties—several technical innovations also played a role, such as the reemergence of bruitism in the framework of Pierre Schaeffer's *musique concrète* as well as the development of electronic music at the Cologne recording studio led by Herbert Eimert and Karlheinz Stockhausen. Any composer at that time who permitted echoes of conventional harmonies, melodies, or tonalities to creep into his works was simply the laughingstock of the Darmstadt clique.

The tyrannical claim to hegemony put forth by the advocates of serial and electronic music was occasionally so extreme that even Adorno began to fear all these sorcerer's apprentices of musical modernism. Looking back on the "heroic years" of new music between 1910 and 1925 when personal innovation had been all-important, Adorno wrote bitterly in 1955 in his essay "Das Altern der neuen Musik" (The aging of new music), that contemporary so-called music-festival music is dominated by an "accommodation to the spirit of the times," "radicalism that comes at no cost," even by "sectarian academicism" that merely "manages the new." In place of the "disruptive" music and all that unbridled "subjectivity" found in the earlier representatives of the Vienna School, Adorno argued that serious music since 1950 has been overwhelmed by a terrible normality of the abnormal. Even the most experimental works, Adorno explained, are characterized by observance of a "serial law" or mere "technical trickery" amounting to a "cult of inhumanity." A "critical potential" once present within music is now twisted into something "falsely positive" and results in "false fulfillment" of still-unsatisfied desires. When "composing becomes a hobby," the essay continues apodictically, the "idea of progress" forfeits its validity.

Yet Adorno's way of thinking—like that of Hans Magnus Enzensberger in his essay "Aporien der Avantgarde" (Blind spots of the avant-garde)—was shared by very few people. Most liberal music critics in West Germany during the era of the "economic miracle" were firmly convinced (or at least persuaded themselves) that even an empty, upside-down modernism diluted into mere form was still a thousand times preferable to any compromise with concepts of music based on intelligibility, in which they—representing consciously or not the Cold-War mentality suited to the ideology of that economic miracle—saw only a regression to totalitarianism. Indeed, some of these critics were shameless enough to pass off their conscious elitism as "avant-gardistic" without realizing that this classification made a mockery of the revolutionary spirit of earlier avant-garde movements. The historical avant-garde movements had, after all, always been based on a protest against the hypocritical concepts of autonomy held forth by establishment art circles, whereas the self-styled avant-garde of the fifties saw its own specifically avant-garde element precisely in the institutional acceptance of its autonomy.

Thus between 1955 and 1985, despite the warnings of Adorno and Enzensberger, this modernism became established as the most important stylistic formation of the leading social in-group, i.e., as an affirmative art for the establishment that sprang ideologically from a nonconformist conformity. This was an avant-garde without true avant-gardism, which lacked any social relevance, any relation to concrete reality—and which therefore was played up as the ideal art of unrestricted freedom in a formal democracy actually structured on the principle of "repressive tolerance." During these years, the adherents of nonrepresentational painting and atonal, elitist music received the most financial allocations, were granted scholarships, and were constantly awarded prizes by public and private entities. Because of their conscious meaninglessness, these arts did not offend any ideology; indeed their lack of ideology posed as the only ideology still possible. These arts thus won favor with all parties and social organizations, whether the Social Democrats or the Christian Democrats, unions, or the trendy tycoons in the "Federal Association of (West) German Industry." For this was art that had relinquished any social function, that sought to be nothing but art—and thus did not step on any ideologue's toes. Christian or nationalistic motifs, for example, certainly would have been unable to find that kind of support. But meaningless art was advanced from on-high since it kept out of partisan politics, presented itself as pure, autonomous art, and dispensed with any propagandistic intent, any function, or any concrete telos at all. That is why this sort of music remained mere music-festival music or Documenta-Art-exhibit music addressing the upper 0.1 to 0.2 percent of the population and was not even noticed by the other 99.8 to 99.9 percent.

Thus a paradox evolved that is still with us today. This music was tremendously patronized and prized (especially in West Germany, where high music has enjoyed the benefits of a well-established policy of subsidy from time immemorial), but hardly anyone wanted to hear it. Quite frankly, this was not music at all, but rather only an ideological medium, an alibi for freedom that was to quell any growth of truly avant-garde music. Nothing proves this better than statistics on record store customers and radio music listeners during the years between 1955 and 1985. The number of prospective consumers of modernistic serious music continually ranked lowest behind the listeners interested in chamber music and other so-called opus music. This was thus a music whose existence was due solely to its snob appeal or to its function as an alibi.

Until 1967–68 this situation changed little if at all in the higher realms of contemporary music. Not until then, with the onset of the student unrest, were there impulses toward an avant-garde in music too. These few modernistic ruptures could not, however, do anything to alter the basic outsider position of modern serious music and were abandoned after only a few years. In terms of contents and ideology, the representatives of the avant-garde focused primarily on the situation of the West European working class or on the struggles of liberation in the Third World (especially Cuba and Vietnam). The most important advocate of a music oriented toward the working class was Luigi Nono, who in such works as *La fabbricca illuminata* (The transfigured factory) joined in the best avant-garde tradition, the newest technical capabilities (i.e., electronic sounds, bruitistically reproduced factory noises,

Schönbergian elements, etc.) with a text that strove to express the tribulations, hope, and rebelliousness of steelworkers who labored under inhumane conditions. Mention must also be made of works such as *Das Floß der Medusa* (The raft of the medusa), the *Sixth Symphony*, and *Voices* by Hans Werner Henze as examples for seizing the struggles for liberation in the Third World in the serious music of those years. Like the works of Luigi Nono, Henze's compositions profess international solidarity as part of a worldwide alliance against imperialism and colonialism. They simultaneously try to make discernible an internationalism in the melody line without in the process dispensing with the highest technical standard of Western, modernistic concert music. Other avant-garde composers such as Hartmut Fladt and Rolf Riehm, on the other hand, followed more closely in the musical style set by Hanns Eisler, whose compositions were rediscovered in West Germany during those years.

Such avant-garde tendencies were of course vehemently repudiated from the very beginning by the advocates of elite modernism. Just as earlier in Hanslick's battle against Wagner, so now, too, there arose a massive defense of autonomous aesthetics against any aesthetics of heteronomy, which would seek to employ so-called extramusical means in the creation of music. Thus Tibor Kneif wrote in 1971 that it was not only "naive" but also downright "cynical" to fill music "with political or ideological contents." Hans Vogt in 1972 excoriated the political *"engagement"* of Nono, which he termed hopelessly outmoded. In the same year, Helmut Lachenmann vented his spleen about the "dogma-spouting idiots savants of Marxism-Leninism," in music, whom he charged with a tendency to "petit bourgeoisness." Mauricio Kagel wrote in 1974 that the "new music" struck him as a highly unsuitable means to "change our social order" and so on and so forth, a message echoed all the way to the music criticism of H. H. Stuckenschmidt and Carl Dahlhaus. These composers and theorists of elitist modernism continued to worship at the altar of absolute music and immediately interpreted any musical turn to the real and nonabsolute as a challenge to their own status as would-be "shocking" modernists. As a result, they considered the music of Nono and Henze, with its genuinely avant-garde impulses, a near sacrilege.

Yet these circles actually had no reason to worry. Events unfolded just as they would have wanted. Whereas status-quo criticism between 1967 and 1973–74 at least took notice of the avant-garde the following years were completely dominated by the principle of autonomy. And for this there are the following three explanations: (1) the avant-gardists had nearly no chance of gaining access to any sizable orchestras, choirs, opera houses, recording studios, etc., and thus faced the immediate prospect of total exclusion from musical life; (2) in 1973–74 the political change of course in the Federal Republic of Germany known as the "Tendenzwende" became felt in cultural life; and (3) the student movement finally folded after two or three years of "alienated" political activity for workers and the Third World, i.e., students turned to their own egos and thus gave up their specifically avant-gardist notions.

III.

As a result since 1975 this widely recognized modernism has dominated contemporary serious music, which in turn is playing to ever smaller audiences. If we may speak in the terms of Walter Benjamin, who mockingly termed the underlying principle of this modernism a "constant return of the constantly new," then we must reluctantly point out that attention has been shifted since the mid-1970s from social change to change of styles, trends, and fashion. Just as in modernistic painting since the midseventies, abstraction and conceptualism have returned to take the place of a socially critical tendency that had made full use of "realistic" means, so the old formalism came into full force after 1975 in modernistic music as well. Many modernist composers simultaneously attempted to continue developing the stylistic devices worked out by the serial, electronic, aleatoric, or stochastic trends. They defended their incomprehensibility by arguing that musical material automatically undergoes an ineluctable, even inevitable development, which supposedly does not allow resorting back to any exhausted, traditional musical forms (whether harmonic, tonal, or melodic). In West Germany, these views are shared by such serious music composers as Josef Anton Riedl, Nicolaus A. Huber, and Mathias Spahlinger, who are still trying to improve on the technical achievements of the musical style of Webern or Cage. In doing so, they put the chief emphasis on structure, musical abstraction, and minimalistic reduction.

Yet in addition to such modernistic experiments that still draw on the spirit of the old Darmstadt movement by believing in a further logical development of the material revolution, two more modernist directions have developed quite recently. These are labeled postmodern by some critics who lack other definitions or concepts and because it's fashionable. The first of these postmodern trends makes use of archaic, black African, or oriental forms of music. These are then reshaped in the manner of serial techniques of the 1950s or the *ars povera* of the following decade, and are transformed into abstract, monotonous sound structures that, in their provocative uniformity, are intended first to irritate the listener and then to hypnotically absorb the listener. Whereas around 1900 Debussy utilized the whole-note intervals of Indonesian gamelan music as exotic daubs of color, simultaneously keeping it at a certain distance, the tendency in today's postmodern movement is instead to try to transport oneself by meditation into the center of the spirit of the exotic. The theoretical pronouncements of this group often describe this meditation as an intentional repudiation of Eurocentric cultural arrogance. Thus this music is reminiscent of Indian ragas, Japanese No music, African drum beats, or Nepalese bells. It is supposed to communicate either the state of religious interiorization or wantonly uncontrolled sensuality. In the United States the hippies were the first to adopt such sounds, which then found their high-culture expression in the music of Terry Riley, Philip Glass, and Steve Reich, whose works—in spite of their staggering length—often show only "minimal variation" and thus are considered by the critics as paradigms of "monotonal" or "gradual" music.

In the 1950s, West Germany's Karlheinz Stockhausen tended toward a religiously tinged music of the spheres. He later became one of the first to favor the exotic and at the same time very consciously to try to use it as a defense against any concrete political commitments. That is evident as early as 1958 in his work *Stimmung* (Tuning in for Six Vocalists), composed in "happy" hippy days in San Francisco. He wrote that this meditative music is supposed to illuminate the "interior of the harmonic spectrum" in order to bring to full and simultaneous expression the "beauty of eternity" in the "beauty of sensuality." In such works as *Sternklang* (Stellar Sound) of 1971 and *Der Jahreslauf* (The Course of the Year) of 1977, he endeavored to continue this "tuning." Something similar is at work in such compositions as Peter Michael Hamel's *Samma Samadhi* of 1973 and *Maitreya* of 1974, which like Stockhausen's works are rooted in oriental and occidental sound combinations. All of this is supposed to sound moving, meditative, perhaps even religious—but for the most part it remains a mere experiment in modernistic formalism. In contrast to Asian music, this music does not have any ritual function, it is neither cultic nor collective, but rather only showcases its creators' ambition for formal ingenuity.

The same holds true for the second current within so-called postmodern music, which borrows some of its sound material and structure from nineteenth-century classical and romantic music. Its borrowings are evident as outright quotations—as is also true for postmodern architectural facades. In this area the most convincing work is being done by those composers whose borrowings do not have the character of literal quotes but rather adopt fundamental, romantic, expressive gestures of a certain work. West German examples of this are the compositions by Wilhelm Killmayer and Wolfgang Rihm, in which such extremes as ecstasy, madness, or even death are conjured up in a neo-neoromanticist fashion. Prime examples are such works as *Schumann in Endenich* of 1972 by Killmayer or the chamber opera *Jakob Lenz* of 1980 and the *Wölfli-Lieder* of 1981 by Rihm, in which displacement into madness dominates, although these works too are haunted throughout by verbatim quotations from Schumann, Brahms, and Mahler. The quote element is absolutely fundamental to compositions such as *Tanzsuite mit Deutschlandlied* (Dance suite with the German national anthem) of 1980 by Helmut Lachenmann, the Schubert Fantasy of 1978 by Dieter Schnebel, which is based almost entirely on the first movement of Schubert's Piano Sonata in G Major, and the requiem *Prince Igor, Stravinsky* of 1982 by Mauricio Kagel, composed for Stravinsky's funeral and based on an aria from the opera *Prince Igor* by Borodin. The goal of this music is to create a highly serious impression, which has also been the intention of the exotic trend within postmodernism. Yet like the work of the exotic camp, neo-neoromantic music remains mere modernistic experiments in sound, because although the music of romanticism is indeed quoted, it does not capture the rich world of emotions expressed in romantic music.

Thus not even these two trends are the highly valued "avant-garde" so often claimed by their managers.* A musical avant-garde worthy of the name would, after all, seek to base itself on the progressive "intonations" of its own time. The intonations of non-European cultures or of art music of nineteenth-century romanticism may very well be just as interesting, "beautiful," or pleasantly soothing as most modernistic sound experiments of the fifties and sixties dominated by choppy, shrill, and dissonant forms—but still they are not avant-garde. For in order to be an avant-garde that keeps the improvement of all society in mind, composers must seize the progressive intonations of their own era, as Beethoven did in his *Eroica* and Berlioz in his *Symphonie funèbre et triomphale*.

But—critics of this concept will begin to object here (if they haven't already)—what exactly *are* the progressive intonations of our own time, similar to the sounds used by Hans Werner Henze in his *Voices* at the start of the 1970s? Are there such voices left at all? Or formulated more radically: where are the progressive movements of our day that could possibly yield such voices? Well, such movements do in fact exist: whether in feminism, the Greens, the remnants of the left, or the peace movement. But have these movements actually brought forth new, progressive voices and intonations—or haven't they instead relied musically on commercial pop in hand-me-down form that they do not even reshape, but merely adopt as is? Thus, in its final hour before being stormed by the police, West Germany's pirate-wavelength alternative radio station "Republic Free Wendland" could think of nothing better to broadcast than a few Walter Mossmann songs and Pink Floyd's "We Don't Need No Education." Aren't these movements capable of making any better music, some voices that would better express their defiance, their desperation, their hope? Do these movements not have any intonations capable of being transformed into "art"? Or is the stereotypical the predominant feature in the music praxis of these movements, as it is in most commercial music? If there truly are only stereotypes at work here, then serious music will never develop the tonal quality that could give it the status of avant-garde music, but will continue to be a cliquish affair of the upper 0.1 to 0.2 percent of the populace. For after all, the artistic

---

*It is interesting to note that Stockhausen's *Stimmung* album appeared in the "avant-garde" series.

avant-garde, an "aesthetics of resistance," does sustain itself on the spirit of the movement from which it springs, from a collective conscience, from a gesture of rebelliousness. But any revolutionary spirit in music can scarcely be discerned nowadays due to the ever-widening separation between extreme subjectivity and stereotype-ridden commercialism. There are people who remain unaware of this, there are those who welcome it; but there are also people who regret it, and not just because of the resultant lack of serious music, but also because of the corresponding lack of an ideological telos.

Translated by James Keller

The Authors

THEODOR (WIESENGRUND-) ADORNO, German social philosopher, musical sociologist, critic, and composer, born 1903 in Frankfurt am Main/died 1969 in Visp, Switzerland. As a member and director of Max Horkheimer's Institute for Social Research, Adorno was a leading leftist apologist for musical modernism and critic of popular culture.

BETTINA BRENTANO VON ARNIM, German poet, singer, composer, and sculptor, born 1785 in Frankfurt am Main/died 1859 in Berlin. Associated closely with the German Romantic movement through kinship and marriage (as sister of writer Clemens Brentano and wife of writer Achim von Arnim), Bettina Brentano von Arnim was an admirer and friend of Ludwig van Beethoven, an acquaintance of Johann Wolfgang von Goethe, and a key figure in early nineteenth-century German musical life.

ERNST BLOCH, German philosopher, born 1885 in Ludwigshafen am Rhein/died 1977 in Tübingen. Known for his post-Marxian utopian philosophy of "hope," Bloch taught in Leipzig and Tübingen. His collected writings on music were published in 1974 (*On the Philosophy of Music*).

BERTOLT BRECHT, German playwright, poet, singer-songwriter, and critic, born 1898 in Augsburg/died 1956 in Berlin. Closely involved with music throughout his life and career, Brecht is known for his theory and practice of "epic theater" and collaborated with numerous composers, including Kurt Weill, Hanns Eisler, and Paul Dessau.

HANS BREUER, German youth movement leader, contemporary of *Wandervogel* founder Karl Fischer (born 1881)/died on the Western front in World War I. Breuer was associated with the *Wandervogel* movement from its earliest days in Berlin-Steglitz and wrote the introduction to the *Zupfgeigenhansl*, the famous *Wandervogel* songbook, of which over half a million copies were in print by 1914.

CARL DAHLHAUS, German musicologist, born 1928 in Hannover/ died 1991 in Berlin. Appointed professor of music history at the Technical University of Berlin in 1967, Dahlhaus wrote on a broad spectrum of topics in the areas of musical aesthetics and nineteenth/ twentieth century musical culture. He was also active as chief editor of the critical edition of the works of composer Richard Wagner and as coeditor of several major academic music journals.

DIETRICH FISCHER-DIESKAU, German singer, conductor, and musical journalist, born 1925 in Berlin-Zehlendorf. An acclaimed master of the German art song, bass-baritone Fischer-Dieskau attended the *Musikhochschule* in Berlin and made his operatic debut in 1948. Since the mid-nineteen seventies he has been active as a guest conductor in Germany and abroad, and has written books on the songs of Franz Schubert and the relationship of Richard Wagner and Friedrich Nietzsche.

JOHANN NICOLAUS FORKEL, German music historian, keyboard performer, theorist, biographer, and bibliographer, born 1749 in Mieder, near Coburg/died 1818 in Göttingen. Regarded as one of the founders of modern musicology, Forkel projected the first complete edition of the works of J. S. Bach and helped initiate the Bach revival of the nineteenth century. His *General History of Music* (1788) and *General Literature of Music* (1792) are, respectively, prime examples of the emerging academic study of music and a milestone in musical bibliography.

WILHELM FURTWÄNGLER, German conductor, author, and composer, born 1886 in Berlin/died 1954 in Baden-Baden. Having established a reputation as one of Germany's foremost orchestra conductors by the early 1920s, Furtwängler led, among other ensembles, the Gewandhaus Orchestra of Leipzig, the Berlin Philharmonic, and the New York Philharmonic. Following the war, he continued conducting throughout Europe and abroad, although the latter part of his career was overshadowed by the controversy surrounding his role in German cultural life during the Third Reich.

AUGUST HALM, German music educator, critic, and composer, born 1869 in Grossaltdorf, Württemberg/died 1929 in Saalfeld. Educated in Tübingen and Munich, Halm had a distinguished career as a music teacher and school administrator. His writings betray the influence of theorist Heinrich Schenker.

EDUARD HANSLICK, Austrian music critic, aesthetician, and civil servant, born 1825 in Prague/died 1904 in Baden, near Vienna. A prominent, early example of professional musical journalism and pioneer of music appreciation, Hanslick settled permanently in Vienna in 1852 and was appointed professor of music history and aesthetics there in 1856. He was closely acquainted with composer Johannes Brahms and is perhaps best known for his contribution to the so-called Brahms-Wagner debate in later nineteenth-century musical aesthetics.

FRIEDRICH VON HAUSEGGER, Austrian musicologist, born 1837 in St. Andrae, Carinthia/died 1899 in Graz. Following studies in law and music, von Hausegger was active as a teacher of music theory and history at the University of Graz from 1872 until his death. His collected writings were edited and published by his son, Austrian conductor–composer Siegmund von Hausegger, in 1939.

GEORG FRIEDRICH WILHELM HEGEL, German philosopher and aesthetician, born 1770 in Stuttgart/died 1831 in Berlin. Among the most prominent and influential representatives of German idealism, Hegel taught in Nürnberg, Heidelberg, and Berlin. His systematic philosophy of the fine arts and aesthetics was reconstructed from student notes and published posthumously.

JOHANN GOTTFRIED HERDER, German writer, critic, philosopher, and theologian, born 1744 in Mohrungen, East Prussia/died 1803 in Weimar. Following studies in Königsberg, where he was acquainted with Immanuel Kant and Johann Georg Hamann, Herder was active as a pastor, collector of (Latvian) folk songs, and court poet, collaborating at Bückeburg with J. C. F. Bach. He settled in Weimar in 1776.

JOST HERMAND, Germanist and literary/cultural historian, born 1930 in Hamburg. Following studies in literature and art history in Marburg, Hermand emigrated to the United States where he teaches and writes as Vilas Professor of German Studies at the University of Wisconsin, Madison. During the past decade he has devoted considerable time to the study of German musical culture and is the author/editor of several books and articles on music, including *Konkretes Hören* (Berlin, 1981), *Writings of German Composers* (The German Library, volume 51, New York, 1984), and *Beredte Töne* (Frankfurt, 1991).

ERNST THEODOR AMADEUS HOFFMANN, German writer, composer, critic, and civil servant, born 1776 in Königsberg/died 1822 in Berlin. Following studies in law, painting, and music, Hoffmann first came to Berlin in 1798. His career as a civil servant and difficulties with various governmental authorities subsequently led him to Posen, Warsaw, Bamberg, and Dresden before he finally settled in Berlin in 1814. Throughout his life, Hoffmann attempted with a greater or lesser degree of success to balance his duties as a legal official with his desire to write, compose, and conduct. His opera *Undine* premiered in Berlin in 1816.

IMMANUEL KANT, German philosopher, born 1724 in Königsberg/ died 1804 in Königsberg. Regarded as the preeminent systematic philosopher of the German enlightenment, Kant was educated in Königsberg and remained there his entire life as a teacher and scholar of philosophy, metaphysics, logic, and aesthetics.

GEORG KNEPLER, Austrian/German musicologist, born 1906 in Vienna. Educated in Vienna, Knepler left Austria in 1934 for England, where he became involved in the English working-class music movement. In 1950 he went to Berlin where from 1959 to 1970 he served as professor of music history and director of the musicological institute at the Humboldt University. He has written extensively on eighteenth and nineteenth century music history and musical historiography.

CHRISTIAN GOTTLIEB LUDWIG, German music critic, born 1709/ died 1773. A student of enlightenment literary critic and notorious opera opponent Johann Christoph Gottsched (1700–1766), Ludwig is known chiefly for the essay excerpted in this anthology. In it, he shows himself to have assimilated thoroughly his mentor's rule-bound, rationalistic critique of operatic theater ("the most nonsensical work ever created by the human mind"), while nevertheless conceding that opera affords the listener/viewer considerable sensual pleasure.

THOMAS MANN, German writer and essayist, born 1875 in Lübeck/ died 1955 in Zurich. Regarded by some as the preeminent German writer of his generation, Thomas Mann was influenced strongly by what he called the "three-star constellation" of Arthur Schopenhauer, Richard Wagner, and Friedrich Nietzsche. A post-World War I convert to the ideals of liberal democracy, Mann went into exile in 1933 and settled in Zurich after the war. Both his fictional work and essays deal extensively with the legacy of nineteenth and twentieth century German music. In 1929 he was awarded the Nobel Prize for Literature.

GÜNTER MAYER, German musicologist, born 1930. Mayer taught at the Humboldt University in Berlin and has written extensively on music history, philosophy, and aesthetics from a Marxist/ sociological-historical perspective. He has also served as coeditor of the critical edition of the works of composer Hanns Eisler (1898–1962).

FRIEDRICH NIETZSCHE, German philosopher, philologist, writer, and amateur composer, born 1844 in Röchen, near Leipzig/went insane and died 1900 in Weimar. Initially an ardent admirer and passionate defender of the music dramas of Richard Wagner (cf. "Richard Wagner in Bayreuth"), he later became one of Wagner's most virulent critics (cf. "The Case of Wagner"). A cultural critic of wide-ranging and controversial influence, he is known for his theory of the *Übermensch,* critique of the German idealist tradition, and rejection of Christianity. In music, he left his mark on a generation of composers, including Richard Strauss, Gustav Mahler, and Arnold Schönberg.

KARL WILHELM RAMLER, German critic and theater director, born 1725 in Kolberg (now Kolobrzeg, Poland)/died 1798 in Berlin. Educated in Halle, Ramler served as director of the Royal Theatre in Berlin from 1787 until 1796. He was acquainted with several of the leading cultural figures of the day, including writer–critic Gotthold Ephraim Lessing. The essay excerpted in this anthology (1754) is one of his earliest published works.

HENRICH SCHENKER, Polish/Austrian music theorist, critic, performer, and editor was born 1868 in Wisniowczyki, Galicia/died 1935 in Vienna. Although he obtained his university degree in law, Schenker received thorough training in music, including lessons in composition from Anton Bruckner at the Vienna Conservatory. The founding editor of the music journals *Der Tonwille* (1912–14) and *Das Meisterwerk in der Musik* (1925–30), Schenker is known primarily—and above all in the United States—for his "organic" theory and analysis of traditional tonal music.

ARNOLD SCHERING, German musicologist, born 1877 in Breslau/died 1941 in Berlin. Having initially pursued a career as a concert violinist, Schering turned to teaching and musical journalism. He served for many years as chief editor of the *Bach-Jahrbuch* and held teaching posts in Halle and Berlin. He is regarded as one of the pioneers of the study of early (pre-baroque) music.

ARTHUR SCHOPENHAUER, German philosopher, born 1788 in Danzig/died 1860 in Frankfurt am Main. Schopenhauer is perhaps known best for the influence that his magnum opus *The World as Will and Idea* had on composer Richard Wagner, who described his encounter with Schopenhauer's ideas as the most important event of his life. Schopenhauer viewed his philosophy of the "world as will" in post-Kantian terms; his life's work is based on this one essential concept and its systematic elaboration.

CHRISTIAN FRIEDRICH DANIEL SCHUBERT, German poet, journalist, critic, performer, and composer, born 1739 in Obersontheim,

Swabia/died 1791in Stuttgart. Schubert's influential treatise on musical aesthetics *(Ideen zu einer Aesthetik der Tonkunst)*—known especially for its programmatic characterization of musical keys— was written during a ten-year period of confinement at fortress Hohenasperg resulting from his outspoken criticism of the nobility. Upon release, Schubert was appointed poet to the court in Stuttgart.

HANS HEINZ STUCKENSCHMIDT, German musical journalist, critic, and musicologist, born 1901 in Strasbourg. By the end of the Weimar Republic, Stuckenschmidt had established a reputation for his advocacy of contemporary music. Following the war he directed the new music division of RIAS (Berlin) and was associated with both the *Neue Züricher Zeitung* and *Frankfurter Allgemeine Zeitung* as a music critic. Stuckenschmidt has written extensively on the history of modern art music and in 1974 was elected to the (West-) Berlin Academy of the Arts.

PETER SUHRKAMP, German journalist and publisher, born 1891 in Kirchhaffen/died 1959 in Frankfurt am Main. Suhrkamp was associated with left-liberal cultural circles during the Weimar Republic, making the acquaintance of (among others) young writer Bertolt Brecht. He later founded one of Germany's most distinguished and influential literary publishing houses, Suhrkamp Verlag of Frankfurt.

JOHANN GEORG SULZER, Swiss aesthetician and lexicographer, born 1720 in Winterthur/died 1779 in Berlin. Sulzer had little if any formal training in music. He taught mathematics in Berlin, was elected to the Royal Academy of Sciences, and wrote broadly on philosophy and aesthetics. His *Allgemeine Theorie der schönen Künste* is an encyclopedia; he co-authored most of the entries on music with Johann Philipp Kirnberger, while one J. A. P. Schulz wrote several others. Nevertheless, Sulzer's work remains an important and revealing document of its time.

WILHELM HEINRICH WACKENRODER, German writer, born 1773 in Berlin/died 1798 in Berlin. Educated in art history and law at Erlangen and Tübingen, Wackenroder is known also for his collection *Herzensergießungen eines kunstliebenden Klosterbruders*

(Heartfelt Effusions of an Art-Loving Friar, 1797), considered an essential document of early Romantic aesthetics. Together with his close friend writer Ludwig Tieck, Wackenroder was part of a circle including composer–critic Johann Friedrich Reichardt and Carl Friedrich Zelter, both known for their contributions to the genre of art song. Wackenroder's *Phantasien* were expanded, edited, and published by Tieck following his friend's premature death.

BRUNO WALTER (actually Bruno Walter Schlesinger), German conductor, critic, pianist, and composer, born 1876 in Berlin/died 1962 in Beverly Hills, California. Walter began his distinguished career as an assistant to conductor Gustav Mahler in Hamburg and Vienna (it was Mahler who advised Walter to change his name). Walter subsequently conducted the premieres of Mahler's *Song of the Earth* and Ninth Symphony. Following the annexation of Austria in 1938, Walter came to America and became a United States citizen. Regarded as a "classicist" among twentieth century conductors, Walter is remembered particularly for his devotion to the legacy of Mozart and the first Vienna School.

MAX WEBER, German social economist and sociologist, born 1864 in Erfurt/died 1920 in Munich. Weber taught economics and sociology in Berlin, Freiburg, Heidelberg, and Munich. Known widely for his influential essay on "The Protestant Ethic and the Spirit of Capitalism" (1904), Weber's work was wide-ranging, encompassing such fields as the sociology of religion and various aspects of cultural history. The essay excerpted in this volume was originally appended to volume two of his study *Wirtschaft und Gesellschaft* (Economics and Society), which appeared in 1921.

ACKNOWLEDGMENTS

Every reasonable effort has been made to locate the owners of rights to previously published works and the translations printed here. We gratefully acknowledge permission to reprint the following material:

From *Music and Aesthetics in the 18th and Early 19th Centuries* by Peter Le Huray and James Day. Reprinted with the permission of Cambridge University Press.

From Wilhelm Heinrich Wackenroder, *Confessions and Fantasies*, translated by Mary Hurst Schubert, University Park, The Pennsylvania State University Press, pages 178–81. Reproduced by permission of The Pennsylvania State University Press.

Johann Gottfried Herder, "Music, an Art of Humanity," in *Musical Aesthetics: A Historical Reader, volume 2, the Nineteenth Century*, edited by Edward A. Lippman (Stuyvesant, New York: Pendragon Press, 1988), pages 33–43. August Halm, "On Fugal Form, Its Nature, and Its Relation to Sonata Form," in *Musical Aesthetics: A Historical Reader, volume 3, the Twentieth Century*, edited by Edward A. Lippman (Stuyvesant, New York: Pendragon Press, 1990), pages 53–61.

"Bach the Composer," chapter 5, by Johann Nikolaus Forkel, from *Johann Sebastian Bach* (1802), translated by Charles Sanford Terry, by permission of Constable Publishers.

Friedrich Nietzsche, "Richard Wagner in Bayreuth" (1876) from *Unzeitgemäße Betrachtungen*, in Nietzsche, *Sämtliche Werke*, by permission of Walter de Gruyter & Co.

Wilhelm Furtwängler, "Probleme des Dirigierens," (1929) in *Vermächtnis. Nachgelassene Schriften* (F. A. Brockhaus, Wiesbaden 1956), pages 83–87. By permission of F. A. Brockhaus GmbH.

From *The Birth of Tragedy and the Case of Wagner* by Friedrich Nietzsche, Walter Kaufmann. Copyright © 1967 by Random House, Inc. Reprinted by permission of Random House, Inc.

From *Gedanken eines Schauenden* by Friedrich von Hausegger, published by Siegmund von Hausegger © 1903 F. Bruckmann KG, München.

From Eduard Hanslick, *On the Musically Beautiful*, translated with commentary by Geoffery Payzant, Hackett Publishing Company, Inc., 1986. Indianapolis, IN and Cambridge, MA.

"On the Use of Music in an Epic Theatre" from *Brecht on Theatre: The Development of an Aesthetic* by Bertolt Brecht, translated by John Willett. Reprinted by permission of Methuen London.

From *Essays on the Philosophy of Music* by Ernst Bloch. Reprinted by permission of Cambridge University Press.

Thomas Mann in Blunden, editor, *Thomas Mann Pro and Contra Wagner*, pages 45–48, and Carl Dahlhaus in Lustig, editor, *The Idea of Absolute Music*, pages 1–17. By permission of The University of Chicago Press.

From *The Rational and Social Foundations of Music* by Max Weber. Translated and edited by Don Martindale, Johannes Riedel, and Gertrude Neuwirth. Copyright © 1958 by Southern Illinois University Press. Reprinted with permission of the publisher.

Arnold Schering, "Musik und Gesellschaft" (1931), in A. Schering, *Vom Wesen der Musik. Ausgewählte Aufsätze*, edited by Karl Michael Komma (Stuttgart: Koehler Verlag, GmbH, 1974), pages 21–34.

Heinrich Schenker Introduction to *Der Freie Satz*, translated and edited by Ernst Oster. Reprinted with permission of Schirmer Books, a Division of Macmillan, Inc., from *Free Composition* by Heinrich Schenker, translated and edited by Ernst Oster. Copyright © 1979.

"Music Historiography in Eastern Europe" by Georg Knepler, is reprinted from *Perspectives in Musicology*, Edited by Barry S. Brook, Edward O. D. Downes, and Sherman Van Solkema, with the permission of W. W. Norton & Company, Inc. Copyright © 1972 by W. W. Norton & Company, Inc.

From *Schubert's Songs* by Dietrich Fischer-Dieskau, trans., K. S. Whitton. Translation Copyright © 1976 by Dietrich Fischer-Dieskau and Kenneth S. Whitton. Reprinted by permission of Alfred A. Knopf, Inc.

From Günter Mayer, edited by Albrecht Riethmüller, *Revolution in der Musik. Avantgarde von 1200 bis 2000*, Bärenreiter-Verlag, 1989.

Jost Hermand, "Avant-garde, Modern, Postmodern: The Music (Almost) Nobody Wants to Hear" (1991), translated by James Keller, in *Zeitgeist in Babel: The Postmodernist Controversy*, edited by Ingeborg Hoesterey (Bloomington: Indiana University Press), pages 192–206.

THE GERMAN LIBRARY
in 100 Volumes

Arthur Schnitzler
Plays and Stories
Edited by Egon Schwarz
Foreword by Stanley Elkin

Rainer Maria Rilke
Prose and Poetry
Edited by Egon Schwarz
Foreword by Howard Nemerov

Robert Musil
Selected Writings
Edited by Burton Pike
Foreword by Joel Agee

Essays on German Theater
Edited by Margaret Herzfeld-Sander
Foreword by Martin Esslin

German Essays on Art History
Edited by Gert Schiff

German Novellas of Realism I
Edited by Jeffrey L. Sammons

German Novellas of Realism II
Edited by Jeffrey L. Sammons

Hermann Hesse
*Siddhartha, Demian,
    and other Writings*
Edited by Egon Schwarz
    in collaboration with Ingrid Fry

Friedrich Dürrenmatt
Plays and Essays
Edited by Volkmar Sander
Foreword by Martin Esslin

German Radio Plays
Edited by Everett Frost and
    Margaret Herzfeld-Sander

Max Frisch
Novels, Plays, Essays
Edited by Rolf Kieser
Foreword by Peter Demetz

Gottfried Benn
Prose, Essays, Poems
Edited by Volkmar Sander
Foreword by E. B. Ashton
Introduction by Reinhard
    Paul Becker

Hans Magnus Enzensberger
Critical Essays
Edited by Reinhold Grimm and
    Bruce Armstrong
Foreword by John Simon

All volumes available in hardcover and paperback editions at your bookstore or from the publisher. For more information on The German Library write to: The Continuum Publishing Company, 370 Lexington Avenue, New York, NY 10017.